Work and Family—
Allies or Enemies?

Work and Family— Allies or Enemies?

———

What Happens When Business Professionals Confront Life Choices

Stewart D. Friedman
Jeffrey H. Greenhaus

OXFORD
UNIVERSITY PRESS

2000

OXFORD
UNIVERSITY PRESS

Oxford   New York
Athens   Auckland   Bangkok   Bogotá   Buenos Aires
Calcutta   Cape Town   Chennai   Dar es Salaam   Delhi
Florence   Hong Kong   Istanbul   Karachi   Kuala Lumpur
Madrid   Melbourne   Mexico City   Mumbai   Nairobi
Paris   São Paulo   Singapore   Taipei   Tokyo   Toronto   Warsaw

and associated companies in
Berlin   Ibadan

Copyright © 2000 by Oxford University Press, Inc.

Published by Oxford University Press, Inc.
198 Madison Avenue, New York, New York 10016

Oxford is a registered trademark of Oxford University Press

Library of Congress Cataloging-in-Publication Data

Friedman, Stewart D.
Work and family—allies or enemies? : what happens when business professionals
confront life choices / Stewart D. Friedman, Jeffrey H. Greenhaus.
p.   cm.
Includes bibliographical references and index.
ISBN 0-19-511275-X
1. Work and family—United States. 2. Industries—Social aspects—United States.
I. Greenhaus, Jeffrey H. II. Title.
HD4904.25.F754 2000   306.3'6'0973—dc21   00-020663

1 3 5 7 9 8 6 4 2

Printed in the United States of America
on acid-free paper

To Audrey Bernstein Kessner,
a cherished friend, who in her too brief time on
this earth, showed how to live a full life. —SDF

To my family, who have always been
my allies in work and life. —JHG

Contents

Preface

Our book provides new evidence and ideas that help us understand the choices we make as individuals and employers, about life's two central domains, work and family. We must understand the consequences of those choices, and what we can do to make allies of work and family.

The research evidence comes from our study of the values, work lives, and family lives of business professionals, graduates of two business schools in Philadelphia. We've taken this evidence, interpreted it, and written about its practical implications for action in a way that we hope will be useful to anyone seeking insights about the increasingly difficult challenge of balancing work and family.

We've got some good news, and we've got some not so good news. Some of what we show will confirm what many readers already suspect about how work and family affect each other. Other findings will be surprising—and provocative. We've taken a fresh look at an enduring dilemma by examining in considerable depth both the work *and* the personal sides of the work–family story.

In recent years there has been a spate of management books on the work–family connection. Many of them focus on women and how they cope with the obstacles they face as they try—often with great difficulty—to combine productive careers with satisfying personal relationships and family lives. Researchers in a variety of other disciplines have also addressed work–family issues. But in each case, the focus is on only a small slice of this complex subject. Some treat family dynamics as a function of a narrow range of career and work factors. Others concentrate on the impact of work and careers on limited aspects of family life. We've found something lacking: research into the details that are crucial to understanding the tensions experienced at the nexus of work and other life roles.

Work and Family—Allies or Enemies? addresses this gap. Our hope is to make a lasting contribution to the literature in the work–family field—not just on the business or organizational side, and not just on the family side, but for both domains. We're convinced that if society is to achieve greater integration of work and family, and make it possible for people to lead more ful-filling personal lives while contributing more effectively to organizations, work like ours—which shows how these two central life domains affect each other—is critical.

Why do we call it *Work and Family—Allies or Enemies?* People face tensions in their lives: tensions between career and family, and tensions that flow from the very different experiences of men and women. We also find opportunities to enhance integration between the work and family domains, to turn seem-ing enemies into allies. If our book broadens the understanding of these ten-sions and how intelligent choices might better resolve them for individuals, the business organizations to which they contribute, their families, and our society, we will have succeeded.

In her seminal work of 1977, *Work and Family in the United States*, the noted sociologist and organizational theorist Rosabeth Moss Kanter issued a call to action for a generation of researchers to take a *cross-domain* approach that examines how work and family affect each other. She also challenged researchers to study the particular combination of work and family circum-stances that either promote or stifle well-being. More than twenty years later, it seems the rate of research progress has failed to match Kanter's sense of urgency. We hope our work gets closer to fulfilling at least part of her mandate.

This book differs in its purpose and scope from other recent books on work–family linkages in some important ways. The first has to do with the book's research underpinnings. We wanted to make sure there was a strong foundation for our conclusions, and we have built upon and sought to inte-grate prior conceptual and empirical studies on career–family dynamics, stress, social support, and strategic human resource management conducted by ourselves and others.

The second has to do with our survey. Our book is based on original data gathered through a large-scale survey of approximately 860 employed alumni of business schools in two Philadelphia universities, Drexel University and the University of Pennsylvania. With all this information we can show how demographics, values, attitudes, and experiences influence women's and men's career and lifestyle choices and attainments.

We have given equal emphasis to work and family for men and for women, seeking to redress the lack of balance or symmetry that has characterized most previous literature on work–family linkages. Past studies with a domi-nant interest in the careers of men have focused on examining the influence of men's career experiences on their family roles. On the other hand, studies dealing with women's careers have tended to focus on the role of family vari-ables in limiting their career choices, expectations, and career success.

We have included both men and women precisely so we could examine reciprocal relationships—how work affects family *and* how family affects work—for both genders. Our survey data are as much about career and work as they are about family and personal life. Further, we focus on both the organization and the individual. By integrating these multiple levels of analysis, we hope you will agree that we've charted new and worthwhile territory.

Acknowledgments

_____

As we conclude later in this book, support from people who care about our work and our family is a necessary ingredient for successful integration of both. There are many people we take the pleasure of now thanking for the support they've given us along the way.

We want to begin by expressing our deep gratitude to the alumni of Drexel and Wharton who gave substantially of their time in sharing information with us about their lives and careers. Our universities provided very supportive environments within which to both work and pursue our lives beyond work. In particular, Stew would like to thank Wharton colleagues Tom Gerrity and Janice Bellace for their leadership and support for the Wharton Work/Life Integration Project. He is also grateful to Joel DeLuca, Mike Useem, Peter Cappelli, Harbir Singh, John Kimberly, Jitendra Singh, John Paul MacDuffie, David Thomas, Monica McGrath, Ross Webber, Hans Pennings and Howard Kunreuther. Jeff thanks his OB colleagues at Drexel— Frank Linnehan, Saroj Parasuraman, Jason Shaw, Sid Siegel, and Joan Weiner—for their stimulation, support, and friendship.

Students participated in many ways in this project. At Drexel, doctoral student Barrie Litzky conducted interviews of Drexel alumni, and doctoral students Yasmin Purohit and Romila Singh provided valuable assistance in data preparation and analysis. At Wharton, Miki Toliver, Sara Sterman, Norm Wright, Brian Borowsky, Phyllis Siegel, and Kathy Cosmas made very useful contributions to this research. At both schools, through informal dialogue and classroom conversation, hundreds of our students and alumni have given us great insights into the challenges of integrating work and personal life.

We would also like to thank our colleagues in the work/life field who have provided inspiration, wisdom, mentoring, and friendship. In particular, we would like to acknowledge Bob Kahn, who blazed the trail, Perry Christensen, Jessica DeGroot, Sharon Lobel, Faith Wohl, David Thomas, Mary Dean Lee, Sue Shellenbarger, Dana Friedman, Ellen Galinsky, Ellen Kossek, Brad Googins, Lotte Bailyn, Joan Kofodimos, Fran Rodgers, Roger Brown, Linda Mason, Debbie Hufnagel, Susan Seitel, Marilyn Kraut, and Elliot Lehman.

A very special thanks and debt of gratitude go to Saroj Parasuraman, Distinguished University Professor of Management at Drexel University, for her substantial contributions to the research that forms the basis of this book. Saroj was an equal contributor to the team at the inception of this study, when she participated extensively in the conceptualization of the initial research model, the development of the surveys, and the collection and preliminary analysis of the data. Although a redirection of her writing interests have precluded Saroj's continued participation in the preparation of this book, her expertise, wisdom, and insights have contributed enormously to our final product.

We are grateful for the encouragement and enthusiasm provided by Herb Addison, of Oxford University Press. Herb has been a constant source of inspiration, guidance, and support throughout the preparation of *Work and Family—Allies or Enemies?* Early on in the project, he encouraged us to expand our vision of the book, to prepare one that would be read and appreciated by the broadest possible audience. While urging us to write a widely "accessible" book—and providing many helpful suggestions along the way— Herb always understood and reinforced our desire to reach work/life researchers and practitioners as well as a general business reader audience. Herb's experience, wisdom, and compassion have enabled him to push at times and to ease off at other times—always done in a totally supportive and professional manner. Herb, thanks for challenging us.

We want to thank Scott Cooper, writer-editor *extraordinaire*, for leading us through a set of revisions that took our original manuscript and enriched it in many different ways. His insights and wisdom about language and ideas, and how to present them in meaningful and useful ways, were invaluable to us. And we benefited greatly from Scott's constructively critical point of view, drawn from his own experience, about the things we were trying to explain.

We both deeply appreciate the assistance of Michele Levine, who read the entire manuscript with the keen eyes of a young woman seeking work–family balance, and who provided very helpful suggestions that improved the book substantially.

Jeff thanks his wife, Adele, for her love, support, and fresh perspectives; his daughters, Joanne and Michele, for being such loving, caring, and interesting people, and his parents, Sam and Marjorie, who instilled in him—very early in life—a love for family and hard work.

Stew would like to thank Hallie, his life partner, for her courage to act in a way that's consistent with her values and for a wellspring of support that has sustained and enhanced his life beyond what he imagined possible. Stew thanks Gabriel, Harry, and Lody—the true sources of inspiration and motivation for this work. Every day they delight and teach new lessons about what's really important. Finally, Stew thanks his dear parents, Victor and Leah, for modeling how to blend the many wonderful things that life offers.

Stew and Jeff also thank each other for sharing in this adventure. Our working relationship developed into a new level of friendship and respect that permitted us to capitalize on each other's unique strengths and perspectives. We listed the authors alphabetically to symbolize this partnership that produced equal contributions to this book.

S.D.F.
Merion, Pennsylvania
May 1999

J.H.G.
Philadelphia, Pennsylvania
May 1999

Work and Family—
Allies or Enemies?

1

The Changing Dynamics of Work and Family

Work and family, the dominant life roles for most employed women and men in contemporary society, can either help or hurt each other. They may be allies, or they may be enemies.

People are finding it increasingly difficult to cultivate pursuits outside of work that enhance their quality of life. Parents find themselves working more and more hours[1]—with significant implications for the nurturing of the next generation. But time is certainly not the only problem. Indeed, it may not even be the main problem. We've observed something that runs much deeper: the *psychological* impact and interference of work on home and of home on work.

The conflict between work and family has real consequences. It affects the career attainments and quality of family life of both men and women. For women, these consequences include serious constraints on career choices, limited opportunities for career advancement and success in the work role, and the need to choose between two seeming opposites: an active and satisfying career, or marriage and children.[2] Many men face having to trade off career and personal values while they search for ways to make dual-earner families work. Often this requires embracing family roles far different, and more egalitarian, than those they learned as children.

Men and women today are asking how they can find the time and energy to fulfill their various commitments to work, family, and other people and groups, and how to achieve satisfaction and success in all the different facets of their lives. They need to ask as well about how to find the psychological wherewithal. We think we've found some of the answers, by examining the tensions that come from living in what are, essentially, two worlds: work and family. We've explored how business professionals of different ages juggle the often incompatible demands that come from work and from family. We've asked whether integration between the two worlds is even possible and, if so, what can be done to create greater opportunities for that integration to occur, and to make allies of work and family.

As we sought the answers from our in-depth examination of 861 business professionals, several themes emerged that make up the core of our book. We introduce them here, along with some of the findings that gave rise to each theme. These themes have significant implications for future efforts to achieve greater integration between—and hence make allies of—the two worlds of work and family. They play a vital role in Chapter 9, where our agenda for action is organized specifically around each of the six themes.

After we have reviewed these themes, we introduce a model we developed to help understand how work and family affect each other. We then discuss what we call the "great divide" between men and women—the differences in gender identity that exercise such a powerful influence over how work and family may be allies. We then draw a picture of the future, where we forecast how our careers will change and what these changes mean for understanding work and family.

Six Major Themes

1. We can have (much of) it all, but it's especially tough for working mothers.

There is some good news coming out of what we have found in our research. It *is* possible to have both a fulfilling career and a satisfying family life, but it requires *balanced* involvement in both these spheres of our lives.

What are the challenges to having it all? One obstacle is that traditional values continue to shape the division of labor at home, which means it is easier for men than women to invest time and energy in both work and family. As a result, working mothers are the most vulnerable to suffering career penalties and work–family stress. They are generally less satisfied with their personal growth and with their careers. They earn less income than women without children, a penalty they suffer in part because they work fewer hours. It's a vicious circle: their career satisfaction is lower because they work fewer hours, are relatively uninvolved psychologically in their careers, receive fewer opportunities for career development, and spend more time on their household activities. Motherhood turns out to be a career liability as things exist today.

For men, however, fatherhood is a career asset. By choice or by favored treatment, fathers have more authority on the job than men without children have. This greater authority is the main reason why fathers are more satisfied with their careers and why they achieve more.

Tradeoffs between the conflicting demands of work and family are inevitable and are another major obstacle to being highly involved in both. Unfortunately, it is still the case that women make—indeed, feel forced to make—more of these tradeoffs than do men. Women spend more time on household activities and far more time on children, and they make more adjustments to their work schedules.

Conflicting demands present a challenge. In general, the more time we spend on household activities and children, the less our income, advancement up the hierarchical ladder at work, and career satisfaction. People who are highly involved in their careers tend to limit their involvement in their families, just as family-oriented people often restrict their career involvement.

How do we deal with these conflicting demands? It requires choice. Choices depend at least in part on values and life stage. Unfortunately, the range of choices is limited by the discriminatory constraints we've just described, to which dual-earner mothers are the most vulnerable. To create options that help make allies of work and family, so that more of us can have (much of) it all, we need to change the traditional gender roles. Mainly, men must take up more of the childcare and household responsibilities. This, of course, might well benefit men by increasing their satisfaction with their family lives.

2. Work and family can be allies.

Other good news: certain aspects of work and family life help affect integration between the two domains and make them mutually enriching. These assets include resources, involvement, and emotional gratification, which are major elements of the model we use to explain how work and family affect each other and how they can be made allies.

There are many ways that work and family can help each other, although they play out differently for men and women. For instance, women build close ties and acquire useful information and support for managing family issues from their social networks at work, which are a resource that make work an ally of family. The enhancement of esteem that comes from work and career is another potential asset for life beyond work. Careers can provide emotional gratification and create opportunities for satisfaction with personal growth. As but one example for men, greater success on the job generally leads to a better feeling about family.

The support partners offer each other at home also helps make allies of work and family. Family-friendly employers provide additional assets. There is less of a career penalty on mothers in these organizations, and they are better able to enjoy the benefits that a satisfying job has on parental performance. Both men and women experience less conflict between work and family when they feel their employer supports their lives beyond work. Family-friendliness leads to feeling better in our personal life and about our job and employer. Those of us in family-friendly firms do spend less time on work and more on life outside work—but our job performance is no different from that of people in nonsupportive organizations, and we are more committed to our organizations.

Individuals and families need to seek out new and creative ways to make integration between work and family a reality. Employers must strive to create work environments that promote integration by respecting the whole person and allowing for flexibility. Society, too, has a stake in enhancing opportunities for work–family integration, and making allies of the two domains. As we describe in Chapter 9, we need to build an infrastructure for flexibility that supports options for individuals and organizations.

3. Time is not the major problem.

Everyone knows that work sometimes gets in the way of family, and vice versa. But is time the major problem? Yes, the "time bind" is real, but a more subtle and pervasive problem is the *psychological* interference of work with family and of family with work. Psychological interference reduces family satisfaction and satisfaction with personal growth. Although time interference is a problem, it does not affect these feelings about personal growth.

Psychological interference between work and family also diminishes the parental performance of both mothers and fathers. And while a parent might be physically present, kids rarely miss picking up on the psychological absence of a mom or dad who's with them but whose mind is elsewhere.

It is critical that we acquire the skills to manage the boundaries between these two spheres of life. That is the way to reduce psychological interference and help make allies of work and family.

4. Authority on the job is essential for work–family integration.

Managing boundaries is only one step toward an alliance between work and family. Authority over work—control over when, where, how, and with whom work gets done—has a major impact on both career outcomes and satisfaction with life beyond work.

In the new century, big changes in careers are coming (some which we describe below). It will be increasingly important that employers give employees autonomy. This is about more than flex time and telecommuting. Employees, as individuals and as groups, are best suited to figure out and implement new and creative approaches for getting the job done in a way that fits—and supports—their lives outside of work.

5. Women may be better adapted for the jobs of the future.

Success in the brave new world of twenty-first century careers will require the ability to handle ambiguity, manage multiple tasks simultaneously, and build networks of support at work and in the community. Each of us needs to be adept at juggling career, family, and other commitments. Women seem to be more skilled in these areas than men.[3]

Employers should be willing to invest in women as leaders for the future, and to create a work environment that values their particular skills. Men need to develop these skills as well, and organizations should find ways to aid this process.

6. Kids are the unseen stakeholders at work.

Parents' work experiences and career values influence children's health and welfare in significant ways. For instance, kids whose parents are more focused on career than on family have more behavior problems and do worse in school, because there is greater interference on these families from work. These parents are less psychologically available to focus on their children.

The issue is complex, however, and plays out differently for men and women. Children whose mothers are highly involved in their careers, for instance, experience relatively few behavior problems. Why? These mothers, with their greater self-esteem and greater competence, are providing a positive role model. A child's mental health is also affected positively by the self-esteem and sense of competence that comes with a father who is satisfied with his job. In contrast with mothers, however, it is *less* career involvement for a father that increases his psychological availability to his children, and results in kids with fewer behavior problems.

What is the bottom line? Corporate responsibility to kids and parents must go beyond providing childcare facilities and benefits. Work needs to be designed so parents can be available—both behaviorally and psychologically—so they can focus on their children.

How Work and Family Affect Each Other

How can work and family become allies? We are convinced from what we've found in our research that it is a matter of using the strengths from each domain to help create integration between the two. The model we derived from our research focuses on the mutual and reciprocal effects of work on family and of family on work. We are interested primarily in *cross-domain effects*—how experiences and choices in one domain affect outcomes in another.

We focus on cross-domain effects because we're looking for what causes conflict and what increases opportunities for integration. We want to find the implications, based on our original research, of the impact work has on families and vice versa. Of course, identifying cross-domain effects is only useful to a point. The key question is whether work and family are enemies or allies. Does each domain promote well-being in the other (which would make them allies) or create difficulties or conflict (which would make them enemies)? Our answer—that they do *both*—guides every recommendation, every bit of our analysis. Knowing this is the answer is central to figuring out what can be done to enhance the integration of work and family, and reduce conflict between them.

In Chapter 8, we go over in detail a model we developed for capturing and explaining the complex relationships between work and family lives. We'll introduce it here in overview.

To build our model, we took the answer to the allies–enemies question and then posed another: Is it more plausible that work influences family in a given situation, or vice versa? What we find is that the work–family linkages can act as bridges that help people travel successfully in and between the two worlds. What we call resources, involvement, and emotional gratification are derived from each role. While these three elements can be an asset in making allies of work and family, they serve this purpose only if employed intelligently.

Resources

A resource is a supply of support or aid that helps make us more capable of dealing with a situation or meeting a new difficulty. Some resources, such as time or money, are tangible. Others—information, acceptance, and self-esteem—are all examples of important but less tangible resources. We've found that the resources provided within one role enable us to be more available to people in the other role, to become more competent in the other role, and to experience greater satisfaction in the other role. That's why the availability of resources is so important: they foster work–family integration, and help make allies of the two domains. Conversely, their absence produces work–family conflict, because we don't have the time, flexibility, information, or self-esteem to participate in the other role fully, effectively, or happily. The result: the two domains are enemies.

Involvement

Our model also shows that work–family integration is more likely to occur when our involvement in both domains is balanced. When we are involved in both roles—when we care deeply about work *and* family—we are likely to apply the resources derived from one role to the other. But an intense involvement in one role to the exclusion of the other has the opposite effect, and produces conflict. Balance makes the difference between allies and enemies.

Emotional gratification

Positive emotions experienced in a role also promote work–family integration. We can transfer our good moods directly to the other role and thus participate without extensive stress or distraction. When negative emotions spill over from one role into the other, however, they interfere with satisfaction and success.

The bottom line, again, is this: when work and family provide these assets, there is a strong likelihood that they will be allies. But when work or family fails to supply resources or emotional gratification—or when involvement in work or family is so strong that it crowds out the other role—work and family are likely to be enemies in conflict.[4]

The Great Divide Between Men and Women

If there is one thread running through the six themes we introduced above, it is the great divide between how career and family affect men and women, and how the different genders view these two life domains. It is a divide as great as the divide between career and family themselves. Study after study in organizational behavior, sociology, family systems, and labor economics point to the same conclusion: men and women have very different career and family experiences. Few of these differences are benign; in fact, most put constraints not only on women but on men as well.[5]

Consider this, for instance: it used to be that men could give their individual attention, energy, and time to their careers because they had the full-time support of a stay-at-home wife who assumed almost total responsibility for keeping a home and tending children.[6] In the world of the business professional (the focus of our book) being married with children has long been a sign of personal stability and responsibility. Back in 1959, the classic book *The Organization Man* showed the manager's wife playing a vital and complementary role in promoting her husband's advancement on the job, in what was later called the "the two-person career."[7] It was the era of the male breadwinner and the stay-at-home wife. There was little variation in personal lifestyles, and problems related to the link between work and the family, if they did exist (and surely they did), were largely ignored. If they were ever raised, the focus was exclusively on how the managers' excessive time commitments to work affected family life.[8]

Things could hardly be more different today. Revolutionary changes have taken place in the composition of the workforce. There has been tremendous growth of nontraditional family structures, and societal values have shifted as far as striking a balance among roles is concerned. Consider these facts:

- Women now comprise about half of the American workforce. The number of women in the workforce has grown to levels greater than at any time since careful statistics have been kept.[9]
- 63 percent of married women with children under six years old are in the workforce.
- 40 percent of all workers are part of a dual-earner couple. There is less pressure on men to be the sole breadwinners.
- The percentage of workers with working spouses and children at home is 50 percent higher than it was just 20 years ago.
- 23 percent of employees are single parents.
- A third of all dual-earner couples in the United States work split shifts.
- A growing number of families have responsibility for the care of elders.

What hasn't changed is also noteworthy: despite these changes, most men have not increased their participation in the family domain to the point where it's equal to women. Nonetheless, gender roles *are* changing—but at different rates and in different ways for men and women. There is a new social contract emerging for men and women in business and in other sectors of our society.[10]

These changes in how gender roles are defined in our culture are also beginning to bring changes to the meanings of career and of family in the lives of men and women. This, in turn, raises far more questions than reassuring answers about central roles people play in life: husband, wife, worker, manager, friend, community member. For many in our society, the role behaviors learned through early socialization are no longer viable. Many readers surely find themselves in an uncomfortable place, somewhere between the old world of traditional gender roles and a future where new definitions of these roles seem to offer greater flexibility and opportunity for fulfillment. Unlike the typical member of earlier generations of employees, a large segment of today's workforce—particularly women—faces new and intense pressures to find ways of "getting a life" while satisfying the needs of demanding careers. It's a mantra heard everywhere.

When it comes to life choices about career and family, our available options are changing and increasingly diverse, with some growing and others shrinking. This makes lifestyle decisions more complicated than in the past. And the choices are made even more complex because we find ourselves in a period of transition, one that is forcing many of us to navigate our way, without the benefit of social and organizational road maps, through a thicket of emergent roles at work and at home. Clearly, individuals, organizations, and society are going to have to adopt a new kind of flexibility to make it possible for men and women to contribute meaningfully in a variety of roles. Society is just beginning, however, to grasp what it means to get to the point where that flexibility is the order of the day rather than the exception. Our goal is to broaden the understanding of how to get from here to there.

Throughout our book, the model we've introduced here applies differently to men and women because of the great divide between the two sexes. For example, work—having a "job"—is a means of building self-esteem. But as such, work functions differently for men and women. Men have traditionally found in their work the opportunity to enhance self-esteem by providing for their families. For women, however, work as an esteem-builder functions differently, because role expectations are different. Traditionally, women have found work to be an esteem-builder because it provides an opportunity for self-expression and development outside the home. These traditional role expectations, while still prevalent, are changing. There does appear to be a trend toward more egalitarian arrangements in which men and women take a greater share of responsibility in *both* work and family domains.

In *Working Fathers*, James A. Levine and Todd L. Pittinsky make this case, noting that while "fathers still do less housework and child care than mothers . . . over the last three decades, men's participation in these areas has increased substantially in both proportional and absolute terms."[11] Even so, there remains a significant gender gap. As Levine and Pittinsky point out, even with the changes ". . . it is still mothers, on average, who take the responsibility for worrying about what has to get done, when, and by whom. And it is mental energy, not just physical energy, that goes into caring for anybody or anything."[12] This relates directly to the question of whether time is really the problem or whether it is a matter of the psychological conflicts that come from thinking about one domain when trying to focus on the other.

Some try to make the point that the problem of work–family conflict transcends gender.[13] They are right in some respects, but in our view it's also still *about* gender. The fact remains that expectations for behavior and commitments in men's and women's roles are neither equal nor the same. Men and women are still expected to do things differently, to value things and relationships differently.[14] That is why the task of creating allies of work and family for both women and men requires taking gender roles and gender inequity into account. And it is precisely why one of our major conclusions is the need to change the values, norms, and expectations for gender roles, both at home and at work.[15] It's about getting to the point where what matters isn't really gender but *roles*—where the choice to invest either in work or family is available in equal form and measure for both men and women. One motivation for this change stems from the differences in wage and career success that result from societal stereotypes about women and their capacity to commit to work outside the home.

Some readers may remain unconvinced. Our findings throughout the book reinforce the centrality of differences in gender roles, so much so that it is worth setting the stage for our exploration of the differences and similarities between the men and women in our study by posing two key questions: In the context of work and family, what is a man? And in the same context, what is a woman?

Of course, the answers will be different, depending on whom you ask and when you ask. Let's review in brief some of the important elements that go into figuring out the answers, beginning with the work side of the equation. Here are some interesting findings from the American Graduate Survey 1998, part of an annual survey of students in business schools around the world conducted by Swedish researchers.[16]

- A greater percentage of female respondents than male report that "working with increasingly stimulating tasks" and "professional development" are career goals, whereas men are more often concerned with attaining a sound financial base. Likewise, more men than women show interest in becoming affluent quickly.
- Men expect to make long-term commitments to their first employers more often than women do.
- Men are more likely to be amenable to working over 80 hours per week.

- Some astonishing—and dismaying—discrepancies between men and women appear in regard to their expected income after achieving their MBAs. Five years after graduation, women expect to earn an average of $67,000 per year less than their male peers anticipate, and after ten years women expect incomes that are, on average, $200,000 less than what the men believe they will earn.
- Men are more likely than women to choose opportunities for reaching managerial levels as an attractive characteristic of potential employers. Women, on the other hand, appear more intent on connecting with and relating to people.
- Higher percentages of women than men are attracted to companies whose work benefits people and society.

Another study of men's and women's attitudes toward career and family issues found important differences on such issues as employer and government support for childcare, parental responsibility, and traditionally defined gender roles.[17] So, "although there has been considerable change in attitudes toward the role of women in society," this study concludes, "research suggests that general stereotypes about women are deeply held and resistant to change."[18]

What is a man?

These studies provide us some insight into more external measures of the differences between the genders. But what is a man's self-identity? What has it been traditionally? And what changes are taking place?

In *The Male Ego*, Willard Gaylin makes the case that American manhood is eroding in three long-held, traditional roles: as protector, procreator, and provider. "Nothing," he writes, "is more important to a man's pride, self-respect, status, and manhood than work. Nothing. . . . Pride is built on work and achievement, and the success that accrues from that work. Yet today men often seem confused and contradictory about work."[19] It is in that confusion that we find the seeds of change.

Michael S. Kimmel, a leading researcher in the area of men and masculinity, provides us with a fascinating overview of the changes in how men's roles are defined from the 1950s up to the present.[20] He explains that men have to redefine themselves because women are changing themselves and their roles. Men are now "searching for ways to control their lives outside of work." Women want both work and family, and so men have to as well. But even as men say they want both, Kimmel reports, "the desire to change is often more rhetorical than real; few men would actually switch places with their non-working wives if given the opportunity. In reality, taking on an increasing share of domestic responsibilities usually represents a trade-off."[21]

Men who call themselves "involved" fathers often report that their lives are more meaningful.[22] Still, writes Kimmel, the "definition of masculinity has proved remarkably inelastic—or, depending on your perspective, amazingly resilient—under its current siege. Except for a few involved fathers, it binds men as tightly as ever to success in the public sphere, in the world of other men, as the markers of manhood and success."[23]

Of course, the traditional male role comes with costs. There is the lost opportunity to contribute to the development of our children, and to gain satisfaction from this aspect of life. There are health costs, too. It turns out that being involved as a father is good for our health, and good relationships with kids provide a buffer against work stress for fathers.[24]

What, then, is a man? Are they breadwinners? Nurturers? It looks as if the answer is becoming, more and more, a combination of the two.[25]

What is a woman?

Childcare is still largely viewed as the primary responsibility of women, while men are supposed to provide for the family.[26] This forms the backdrop for a brief exploration of women's changing role definitions and gender identity.

Elizabeth Perle McKenna calls women "the half of the human race that still takes the dog to the vet."[27] But a woman in the workplace, with ever-increasing responsibility, is also a phenomenon of our times. And while progress has been slow, the number of women in the professional and managerial ranks is greater than ever—and "in almost every dimension, the numbers are moving in the right direction." That's from a 1997 report on women in top management positions by Catalyst, an organization dedicated to advancing women in business leadership. But Sheila Wellington, Catalyst's president, was quick to make this point: "It is clear that women have a long way to go in order to achieve parity in these influential positions or in earning power."[28]

The Catalyst report contains some telling statistics. The highest percentage of women officers are found in diversified financial companies (31 percent) and apparel companies (28 percent). They find none in the textile industry, and none in mining and crude oil production companies. Just over one out of every ten corporate officer positions overall are held by women, and only half of these positions have responsibility for profit and loss. Even fewer of these female officers (3 percent) hold titles in the very highest ranks of the company (executive vice president and above).

The percentages for women are even smaller when one looks at earnings data. Of the 2,458 most highly compensated people in Fortune 500 firms, only 61 were women. That's a mere 2.5 percent—a percentage which, nonetheless, has doubled since 1994.

Unfortunately, there is plenty of evidence that involvement in family hurts the career achievements of women managers. It produces time conflicts that tend to be resolved by women reducing their level of career involvement. It produces symptoms of strain that intrude into the job domain. It reinforces stereotypes that limit opportunities for development. And it provokes husbands' feelings of competition and jealousy, to which women may respond by curtailing their career involvement—and thus their career success.[29]

All this is quite unfortunate, because there's plenty of research in addition to ours to show that women are likely to have higher self-esteem and emotional well-being if they are employed, especially if they work by choice and in jobs that stimulate and challenge them.[30] And it is not only the women who lose out; there is evidence to suggest that parent–child relationships depend more on the satisfaction a working mother finds in her job than the number of hours she spends with her children.[31]

Wives are much more likely to restructure work around family needs than are husbands. Mothers feel the pressure children put on marriages more strongly: in most families, mothers take primary responsibility for childcare and housework. Again, it's the traditional gender role. And even when childcare responsibilities are shared, mothers are more likely than fathers to worry about their children and are usually more willing to express those feelings.[32]

These differences between men and women have a lot to do with whether work and family will be allies or enemies—especially in a dynamic world of changing careers. It makes sense that traditional gender roles go together with the traditional model of a career. At its base, that traditional model has several implicit assumptions: that the professional is a male breadwinner who is employed full-time; that his spouse or partner is not employed (or, if employed, is a secondary wage earner); and that she bears primary responsibility for housework and childcare. Within this concept, career success for a man is defined narrowly—in terms of the job level he has attained, the salary he earns, how he has advanced in the hierarchy of increasing levels of responsibility, and how long that has taken. The observable, external indicators of success are what matter.

Such a model of careers, though, is simply irrelevant to the work experiences of many women. Their careers have likely included periods of part-time employment or nonemployment for childbirth and child-rearing.

What does the future hold? And what are the differences between men and women that will matter in the future?

The Changing Face of Careers

Despite large numbers of married women with children in the workforce, organizational career systems—the implicit and explicit means by which organizations manage the flow of people through their careers—continue to be based, by and large, on traditional concepts. And those concepts, with their narrow view of career progress and success, apply primarily to men.

The traditional concepts, with career progress and success defined so narrowly, do not respond to the fact that there is an increasingly diverse workforce, with different needs, values, and aspirations than in the past. And it does not respond to the transformation of careers themselves that has already begun, and which in the new century promise even to challenge what we mean by a "job." The traditional concept of career is being shaken to its very core, and the differences between men and women—as well as whether work and family are allies or enemies—will play a big role in the successes and failures of the future.

Tim Hall calls what is coming the "protean careers of the 21st century," recalling the sea god in Greek mythology who could change his shape at will. Hall predicts a new world of careers that are adaptable, that are continually revised by the individual.[33]

- The new careers will represent a move away from traditional emphases on externally defined indicators of progress and success, where the firm controlled the career. Instead, the career will be in the hands of the individual, whose employment security will come from continual learning and adaptation.
- The emphasis on learning will really be on learning *how* to learn. That is how individuals will continually develop and extend their career identities. The self-directed, protean career will have learning to learn as its basic currency.
- The old competencies will give way to the *meta*-competencies of adaptability and self-management.

Some contend that hierarchies will disappear. Individuals will have to manage themselves, which means they'll need self-management skills. Outside the old corporate structure, getting ahead will require foresight—the worker will have to plan the next useful career step as a managerial career becomes, increasingly, a do-it-yourself project.[34] The ability to self-analyze, to figure out what kind of job is available and how that job will evolve, will become crucial.[35] The key to tomorrow's success will be resumes reflecting not simply the positions that people have held, but rather the life experiences they have had.[36]

The firm itself will have a new role. No longer providing established career tracks, the "place of employment" will need to provide opportunities for individuals to develop their skills and contribute on projects to add value to the business. Plus, these organizations will need to be more family-friendly—a prerequisite if they are to manage the self-directedness that will be required of employees. The connection between employer and employee, once seen as a life-long relationship built on blind faith, will transform to be a continually negotiated exchange of value.

Could it be the "end of the job," as William Bridges suggests? He contends that the job is a "social artifact" and that we are entering a brave new world—a "de-jobbed" society where everyone will be a freelancer. We'll do projects and work on things, but we won't have jobs in the traditional sense of rungs on an organizational career ladder. To survive, we'll need what he calls the "DATA approach" to managing our own careers—knowing our own Desires, Abilities, Temperament, and Assets.[37] His is another call for the self-managed career, with employability, not employment, as the goal.

Careers in the future also imply a changing balance between work and family.[38] More and more of us will be working free of bosses, rules, and offices. We'll be able to make choices about where and when to do our work. Some have suggested that the old dilemma managers have faced—"How can I spend more time with my family?"—may become a new dilemma tomorrow: "When will I be able to do my work?" Individuals, not the company and the boss, will determine schedules, and so individuals will be more responsible for managing their time, including the time they spend with their families.[39]

This transformation of careers alone, however, will not be sufficient to make it possible for men *and* women to "have it all." While these changes at the nexus of work and family hold out real promise, they will not be realized unless they are accompanied by substantial changes in how gender roles are defined—which suggests a future requiring some radical alterations in the fabric of what is typical in employers and society today. We've already noted as one of our themes that women may be better adapted to this brave new world than are men.

We have a lot more to say about the transformation of gender roles and of how work is organized throughout the book, especially in the last chapter where we tie the implications of our research to the specific recommendations that constitute our action agenda. For now, here's an encapsulation of what we think needs to be done to build the much-needed infrastructure for flexibility.

- Employers should value what people bring to their business roles from their other roles. Doing this would mean recognizing and supporting the *whole* person. At the same time, we must maintain healthy boundaries between work and family.
- Firms need to redefine how work is structured to allow for greater flexibility, not only on a day-to-day basis but also over the long term. For example, we should embrace ways to make parents more available for their kids.
- Let us recognize as well that dual-earner families are becoming the norm—which has implications for individuals, employers, and society. We must build a future that recognizes the need for commitments from each parent at different times.
- Society as a whole needs to embrace a redefinition of gender roles, one that allows both mothers *and* fathers to take on more of each other's traditional roles. It is time for gender equity in the workplace *and* at home.
- We also need to redefine what it means to commit to work. And we need to rethink the traditional timing of career and family life stages.[40] People's career interests may change, and life stages affect career stages.

The chapters of our book reflect, to a greater or lesser degree, these overall ideas. Chapter 2 is the first of six in which we describe different aspects of our findings. Figures and tables appear in most chapters, and there are more detailed data in "Additional Tables" at the end of the book. These tables are identified in the Notes. In Chapters 2 through 7 we highlight in boxes some of the critical choice points—for individuals, employers, and society—that are implied by our findings. We focus in Chapter 2 on the choices people make about the time and energy they devote to work and family roles, and introduce four types of people in terms of how they prioritize life roles.

As a starting point, we look at the personal values that underlie decisions about investments in different roles. We examine these choices in light of the social and cultural forces that influence these decisions, particularly those relating to differing expectations for and by women and men. It is in Chapter 2 that we begin to develop our sense of the challenges both women and men face in seeking to manage dual involvement in both work and family, particularly given the traditional roles.

In Chapter 3 we address family life and career success. Our central question in this chapter is whether it is possible to be highly involved in our families and still be successful in our careers, given that the time and energy required to be successful at home intrude on career pursuits. Here we explore in some detail the ways in which the quest to "have it all" is similar or different for men and women. And this chapter is where we test how persistent gender role stereotypes affect careers, and show that marriage and children are resources for many men's careers but hindrances for the careers of many women.

Our focus in Chapter 4 is on how work and career affect satisfaction with family and with personal growth and development—in other words, having a life. Here we develop our contention that having a life is not so much an issue of time as it is a matter of managing the psychological interweaving of work and family and of capitalizing on the assets careers generate. We also explore how the issues of time, inter-role dynamics, and the impact of values are different for men and women, and take a close look at time allocations and the experience of role conflicts at different life stages.

Chapter 5 is about kids. How do work and career affect the children of working parents? And is it different for mothers and fathers? As we show in this chapter, children are stakeholders in the workplace, even if unseen and with no voice in decisions about parental work experiences. We examine the impact of work and career on parents' perceptions of their performance as mothers or fathers, their feelings about childcare, and three indicators of child development: behavior problems, physical health, and school performance.

In this chapter, we develop a theory about the causes and consequences of parents providing support to their children, which we use to explain our observations about how parents' careers affect their children. We also look at how role conflicts affect parents and children. And we explain how both work and career can generate resources that help parents *and* create obstacles. As in Chapter 4, we conclude that it is psychological experiences, more than the amount of time, which have the greatest impact on children—pointing once again to the importance of managing the boundary between work and family.

In Chapter 6 we look at the impact of support provided by one's life partner or spouse. Two essential questions motivate our discussion: Why do partners provide support? How does it help? We show how support, provided at the right time, can prevent work–family conflict. We draw the distinctions between the impact of emotional support and behavioral support, showing who benefits and how. And we illustrate the cross-domain nature of support: for example, how a partner's support at home affects one's career experiences and success.

Chapter 7 is our examination of the forces at play in family-friendly employers, which we view as an essential element in the web of resources and support needed for people to effectively integrate their work and family lives. There is good and important news here on the economic and social benefits of family-friendliness. This chapter also includes our look at how the combination of employer and partner support affect each other in the impact they have on work and family life. We're looking for the answer to an important question: Does support from one domain enhance or compensate for lack of support in the other domain, or are they independent?

Having explored the family-to-work and work-to-family relationships in the previous chapters, in Chapter 8 we look closely at the *reciprocal* nature of the relationships between work and personal life. This is where we flesh out the model that shows how resources, involvement, and emotional gratification in one role affect the other. We also summarize our major findings on the effects of family on work and of work on family, as well as on differences between men and women.

Our final chapter is about building the bridges that will get us from a world where work and family are most likely to be enemies to one where being allies is the norm. We present our agenda for action implied by our findings, and we look to the future, reviewing the key work–family integration issues that need to be addressed over time as well as what must be done today.

2

Choosing Work or Family . . . or Both?

How involved should I be in my career? In my family? Can I "have it all"—a fulfilling career and a satisfying family life? Why is it so hard to balance work and my family life? In today's busy world, it seems people are increasingly concerned with the answers to these questions.

The good news from our study is that as tough as it can seem, it is possible to be highly involved in both career and family. Some people, though, choose not to be highly involved in these two domains. And women endure far more constraints than do men when it comes to making choices about involvement—indeed, to many working mothers the option of being highly involved in career isn't really available.

Choices and priorities are key.[1] In this chapter, we begin our exploration of how the choices we make and the priorities we set govern to a large degree whether career and family will be allies or enemies. We introduce a classification system for understanding life priorities, and explore some of what distinguishes people who fall into different groups based on those priorities. Our understanding of these groups forms the basis for a good portion of the analysis in the remaining chapters, where we show how our personal values determine how work affects family and family affects work. Readers even have the opportunity to apply our measures to their own lives.

Most business professionals we surveyed do pursue demanding careers *and* active family and personal lives, but they do not necessarily value the two domains equally. Record numbers of women have entered professional and managerial careers in recent years, and many remain in the workforce after having children. This dual-earner lifestyle—with both part-ners pursuing careers—translates into a difficult and often painful effort, especially for women,[2] to combine extensive career and family responsibili-ties. And there are greater demands on men to be more engaged with their families, because of their wives' increasing career commitments.[3]

The upside to this trend is that involvement in *both* career and family can enhance the quality of our lives by expanding our capacity for self-fulfill-ment.[4] In this respect, the two domains become allies. At the same time, how-ever, the extensive demands from career and family force us to make choices, and these choices involve tradeoffs, sometimes conscious and other times not. When we make those choices, we may feel the two domains are enemies.

How much time do I want to devote to my work and family roles? How emotionally involved do I want to be—can I be—in each role? As each of us realizes that we'll probably have to make some tradeoffs between career and family, our involvement in one sphere of life likely diminishes the level of investment we are willing or able to make in the other part. For most people, career and family are life's most demanding roles. Each requires time and emotional involvement.[5]

As we show in this chapter, people who are deeply involved in their careers tend to restrict their engagement with family life. The converse is true as well: people who are heavily involved in their families limit their career com-mitments. In fact, the higher the involvement in one domain, the lower the involvement in the other.[6]

Why are we likely to have low involvement in one role when we're highly engaged with the other? It takes substantial time and energy to be highly involved in *any* role. Extensive involvement in both work and family roles can bring us fulfillment and satisfaction, especially if we have high-quality experi-ences within the roles, but it can also increase the likelihood that the roles will conflict.[7] There's only so much time in a day or week, and the demands of work and family often pull us in different directions.

Inevitably, a weekend meeting with work colleagues or a lengthy business trip conflicts with some family-related activity, perhaps a daughter's soccer match or a son's music recital. Many people anticipate that extensive involve-ment in both work and family roles will produce high levels of conflict and stress, and decide, perhaps even unconsciously, to lower their involvement in one of the two roles to reduce the conflict. And beyond the issue of time alone, our focus of attention to one role might make us less available psycho-logically for our other commitments.

Allies or enemies? Undoubtedly, each of us must make sacrifices. And of course, no one can truly have it *all*—but each of us can have more of it all than we may think.

Not everyone responds in the same way to the need to make tradeoffs between life roles. Why do some of us and not others reduce our career com-mitments in favor of family responsibilities, or vice versa? Why do others seem not to favor one domain over the other? We believe it has to do with the relative importance each of us attaches to the different roles we play. Figure

FIGURE 2.1

We may take steps to limit our involvement in one or the other role

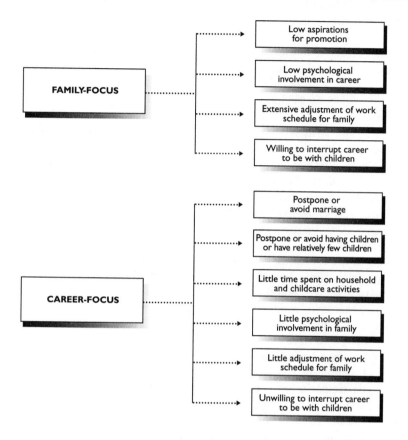

2.1 shows some of the ways people who focus primarily on family limit career commitments so they can devote time and energy to family, and how people who focus mainly on career limit their involvement in the family role to meet career needs.

There appears to be an important distinction between a focus on career and one on family. This leads us to one of our key findings: that people fall into distinct groups based on the value they place on different life roles.

Life Role Priorities

We asked a series of questions about the importance of different roles in life and found that people we surveyed fall into one of four different groups. We call these *life role priorities*. People in each group have a somewhat different life orientation, having made the choice to spend their time and invest their emotions in particular ways. Life role priorities are shaped by family structure, personal values, work experiences, and other factors. The groups are

- Career
- Family
- Career + Family
- Self/Society

With Figure 2.1 in mind, let's discuss each one.[8] Readers will likely recognize themselves in the descriptions of the groups.

What Is My Life Role Priority?

Life role priority is a measure of the relative priority or focus attached to work, family , and other roles. Readers can determine which life role priority group they fall into by responding to the survey questions we used with our business professionals. Knowing your life role priority group can make a difference in efforts to create allies of career and family. Here's how to calculate it:

Step 1
From the following list, please select the two things or activities in your life that give you the most satisfaction. Place a "1" next to the activity that gives you the *most* satisfaction and place a "2" next to the activity that gives you the second-most satisfaction, respectively. Please choose only two in total.
__ Career or occupation
__ Family relationships
__ Religious beliefs or activities
__ Participation in activities directed at national or international betterment
__ Leisure and recreational activities
__ Participation in community affairs

Step 2
Please rate the importance of each factor in judging your success in life by checking the appropriate number from 1 to 5.

	Not important		Moderately important		Very important
Career	1	2	3	4	5
A long-term relationship	1	2	3	4	5

Step 3
Calculate your life role priority as follows:
Career = If the ranking of "career" is higher than the ranking of "family" in Step 1 and the rated importance of "career" is higher than the rated importance of "a long-term relationship" in Step 2.

Family = If the ranking of "family" is higher than the ranking of "career" in Step 1 and the rated importance of "a long-term relationship" is higher than the rated importance of "career" in Step 2.

Career + Family = If the ranking of "career" is higher than the ranking of "family" in Step 1 but the rated importance of "a long-term relationship" is as high or higher than the rated importance of "career" in Step 2.

Career + Family = If the ranking of "family" is higher than the ranking of "career" in Step 1 but the rated importance of "career" is as high or higher than the rated importance of "a long-term relationship" in Step 2.

Self/Society = If neither "career" nor "family" is ranked highest in Step 1.

The career group

Some 13 percent of the business professionals we surveyed fall into the *career*-focused life role priority group, making it the smallest of the four. It includes people whose careers are clearly the center of their lives. Men are more likely than women are to be in this group.

What characterizes people who prioritize their careers, relative to the other groups?

- They work longer hours.
- They are more psychologically involved in their careers, and less in their families.
- They are more likely to aspire to senior management positions.
- They are less likely to be married (especially true for women).
- They anticipate having fewer, if any, children.
- They spend less time on household activities.
- If they do have kids, they spend less time on childcare responsibilities (especially true for women).
- They take little or no time off from work following the birth or adoption of a child.
- They tend not to adjust their work schedules to accommodate family or other personal needs.
- Career-focused people are less likely to relocate for family reasons.

In short, people in this group are more oriented to work than to any other part of their lives. And it has little to do with being young, just starting out in a career, and looking to get ahead early: this group is among the oldest in our sample.

The family group

At the other end of the spectrum, the *family*-focused group is the largest among our business professionals. For 42.4 percent of our sample, family is the most important life domain. Not surprisingly, women are more likely than men are to have family as their life role priority.

Here are some characteristics of people whose life role priority focuses on the family, again relative to other groups.

- They are most likely to be married and have children.
- They expect to have a relatively larger number of children.
- They spend more time on household activities.
- They spend more time on childcare responsibilities (especially true for women).
- They are more psychologically involved in their families, and less in their careers.
- Family-focused people take more time off from work following the birth or adoption of a child, and are more likely to return to work part-time.
- They are more likely to adjust their work schedules to accommodate family or other personal needs.
- They are less likely to aspire to senior management positions.
- They are less likely to believe their careers have a higher priority than do those of their partners.
- Family-focused people are more likely to relocate for family reasons.

The two lists we just presented are the "what" piece of the equation—in other words, what characterizes the career and the family life role priority groups. Why, though, do people in these groups restrict their involvement in either family or career? One reason is the *anticipation* that intense involvement in both family and career will produce conflict between the two roles (see Figure 2.2).

For many of us, it may be true that working long hours means not being able to spend much time with the family. What about the reverse? Some of us probably think about how spending a great deal of time with our family will make it difficult to travel extensively or work evenings and weekends. Those conflicts make enemies of our two main life roles.

If we fall into either the family-focused or the career-focused life role priority group, it stands to reason that we resolve the dilemma—the role con-

FIGURE 2.2

The anticipation factor

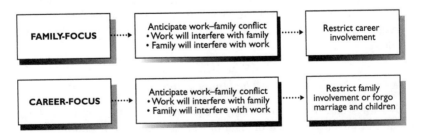

flict—by devoting substantial time to the role we hold to be most important and by reducing involvement in the other role. Family-focused people focus on family and restrict their career commitments, and career-focused people do just the opposite.

Of course, nothing in life is quite so uncomplicated. A person's life does not easily fit some simple description of how much he or she focuses on this or that life domain. But we can see from this overview of these two groups among our business professionals that life role priority determines, at least in part, what gets emphasized in life and what does not.

Let's now look at the two other groups.

The career + family group

Some 29.6 percent of the business professionals we studied fall into the life role priority group we call *career + family*. These people place about equal emphasis on the two life domains as they juggle their work and family commitments.

In some respects, members of this group—more likely to be men than women—are similar to those in the career-focused group. For instance, their career commitments are at least as high. Career + family people

- Work long hours.
- Are psychologically involved in their careers.
- Are likely to aspire to senior management positions.

They are also likely to relocate for career reasons, as do people in the career-focused group. But in other respects, people with the career + family life role priority are more like those in the family-focused group:

- They are likely to be married and have children.
- They expect to have a larger number of kids.
- They spend a moderate amount of time on household and childcare activities.
- They are psychologically involved with their families.

These characteristics reveal that career + family people make a choice *not* to limit their engagement with one role to accommodate the other role. Because career *and* family are both sufficiently important to the self-identity of people in this group, they focus on pursuing both roles with high intensity. So, while it's true in general that high involvement in one role restricts involvement in the other, this doesn't have to be the case.

The career + family group generally fares quite well as they juggle work and family. They seem to handle tradeoffs differently from people in the other groups. And, as we'll see in the next several chapters, the career + family-focused people are generally satisfied with various aspects of their lives. The important lesson here is that while many others may choose to focus their lives on *either* career or family, members of this group demonstrate that it is possible to focus on both roles—with success.[9]

The self/society group

The last of our four life role priority groups comprises the people for whom life role priority is neither career nor family, but instead is either themselves or our society. We call this group *self/society*, and it includes 15 percent of business professionals. Self/society-focused people have several distinguishing characteristics, relative to other groups:

- They work fewer hours.
- They are less psychologically involved in their careers, and in their families.
- They are less likely to aspire to senior management positions.
- They are less likely to be married or have kids.
- They spend a moderate amount of time on household and childcare activities.
- They spend more time on leisure activities.

In most instances, leisure or religious activities play the dominant role in the lives of people in this group, although for some community or political interests are central. A slightly higher percentage of women than men are represented in the self/society group. Compared with others, members of this group are relatively dissatisfied with their lives (as we show in Chapter 4).

Shaping Life Role Priorities

Since our life role priority influences our decisions—our *choices*—about how we spend our time and where we invest our emotions, it is important to understand how these priorities develop. We compared the four life role priority groups on a range of demographic background factors, personal values, and work experiences. Several trends emerge.

Demographics

First, we find that when it comes to shaping the life role priority of a business professional, his or her educational aspirations don't seem to matter much, nor do country of citizenship, race, religion, or political orientation. Parents' education and work experiences also have no noticeable influence. In other words, most of the background factors we considered do *not* distinguish people holding different life role priorities.

We do find gender and age differences in life role priorities, however. For example, men are more likely to be in the career or career + family groups. Women are more likely to be in the family and self/society groups. People in their forties are more likely to be found in the two career-oriented groups, whereas those in their twenties and thirties are more likely to be self/society-focused.

We shouldn't view life role priorities as permanent characteristics of people that remain constant over time.[10] For instance, nearly 38 percent of our family-focused group have a preschool child in the home, compared with only 5 percent of the career-focused group—suggesting that a focus on family may emerge as kids enter the picture. Moreover, the fact that people in their forties are more likely than people in their twenties and thirties to be in either the career or career + family group suggests that a heightened interest in career may appear as children get older and are less dependent on their parents.[11] Changes in life circumstances may produce shifts in the levels of involvement in career and family roles over the span of a lifetime.[12]

On the other hand, some people retain or even strengthen their life role priority as they get older. For example, family-focused individuals who limit their career commitments may place even more importance on family activities in the future to justify their earlier decision.[13] Moreover, because low levels of career involvement among family-focused types may reduce the rewards they derive from work, they are more likely to invest additional time and emotion in the family role, where the satisfactions may be greater. Conversely, through a cycle of reinforcement, career-focused types may become increasingly engaged in work since it provides substantial rewards and accomplishment, thereby making the family role seem less attractive by comparison.[14]

Definitions of success

What most strongly distinguishes each of us as members of a life role priority group is how we define, and ultimately value, success in our careers and in our lives. Our analysis focuses on two sets of values.[15] The first set relates to *career success*.[16] We asked: How important is each of the following in defining success in your career?

- *Status*—having social status, prestige, and power in one's career; earning a great deal of money; advancing rapidly.
- *Time for self*—having flexibility in determining work hours; having time for self and family.
- *Challenge*—having a career that is challenging, creative, and enjoyable.
- *Security*—having a career that provides for steady employment and a secure retirement; living in a preferred geographical area.
- *Social*—helping other people and being respected by others at work.

The second set relates to how people judge their own *life success*.

- *Growth*—having a life that provides for creativity, personal growth and development, helping others, friendships, and political involvement.
- *Wealth*—having a life of material wealth, a high standard of living, and career success.
- *Family*—having a life that includes children and a long-term relationship.

The values associated with the four life role priorities vary from group to group. The career-focused group places substantial importance on status and career challenge as well as on material wealth. This same group places relatively little importance on time for self in their careers, or on opportunities for personal growth, or on developing a family. In contrast, the family-focused group is most concerned with having sufficient time for themselves and their families, and places a great deal of importance on family relationships in their lives. This group is relatively unconcerned with career status, personal growth opportunities, and material wealth.

Not surprisingly, the career + family group places a high value on status, career challenge, and material wealth as well as on family relationships. The self/society group is most clearly distinguished by its low concern for career status and material wealth, and by its substantial concern for time and personal growth opportunities.

Experiences at work

The experiences we have at work are also related to our life role priority group.[17] Business professionals who have a great deal of authority in their jobs, receive developmental assignments, feel accepted by their coworkers, and successfully establish networking relationships are most likely to be career-focused or career + family-focused. In other words, there is a connection between the kinds of work experiences we have and the importance our careers play in our lives.

Positive work experiences may influence the extent to which a career becomes the focal point in our lives. Growth experiences at work can encourage us to attach substantial importance to our work role.[18] Of course, it's impossible to determine precisely whether positive work experiences encourage people to hold careers in high priority, or whether career-oriented people actively seek these experiences from work. Most likely, both explanations fit.

How Gender and Family Structure Affect Our Involvement in Career and Family

Life role priority is only one indicator of involvement in different life roles. There are other factors that illustrate the different levels of involvement men and women have both in their careers and in their families. Here we explore in depth how gender and family structure—whether we are married, and if so whether our partner is employed, and whether we have children—help us understand the work and family commitments of our business professionals.

Gauging involvement in career

How highly involved are we in our careers? The life role priority measure gives us a summary indication. Here we look at several specific aspects of career involvement: the amount of time we spend on work-related activities, psychological involvement in career, aspirations to climb the corporate ladder, and the priority given to our own careers compared to those of our spouses or partners.[19]

In a number of ways, and just as we observed with life role priority groups, we see that men are more highly involved in their careers than are women, as Figure 2.3 shows. Men work about three hours more a week than women, on average.[20] And men's career aspirations are substantially higher than are those of women. Nearly twice as many men as women aspire to senior management positions and more than twice as many men as women hope to become a CEO. In addition, men are much more likely to believe their own career takes precedence over that of their spouse or partner.

Our career commitments are also influenced by our family structure—our marital status, our spouse's employment status, and whether we have children.[21] For example, dual-earner men and women are about equal when it comes to psychological involvement in their work, as are single women and men. While dual-earner fathers work substantially more hours a week than do dual-earner mothers, dual-earners without children—both men and women—work about the same number of hours a week. So do single men and single women. In fact, single women and dual-earner women without chil-

FIGURE 2.3

How involved are we in our careers?

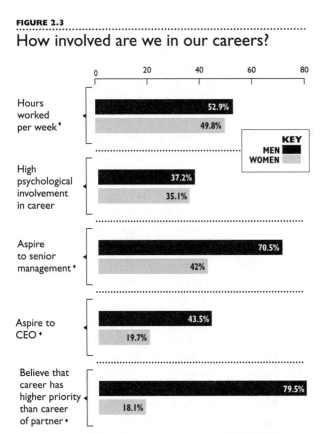

◆ Difference between men and women is statistically significant.

dren work as many hours a week as dual-earner fathers. It is the dual-earner mothers among our business professionals who most limit their time commitment to work.[22]

The gender difference in career aspirations takes on a new light when we view it in the context of family structure. Among dual-earner fathers and mothers, there is no difference in aspirations for senior management or CEO positions. Take children out of the picture, however, and a gender difference emerges: dual-earner men without children have substantially higher aspirations than do their female counterparts. The most ambitious career aspirations are held by men in the traditional family structure; stay-at-home wives rearing the children make it possible for single-earner fathers to strive for advancement up the corporate ladder.

Gender and family structure work in tandem in other ways to influence our involvement in career. This is illustrated by the fact that single women are the most psychologically involved in their careers—even more so than dual-earner fathers and dual-earner mothers. The joint effects of gender and family structure are important. Let's explore more deeply the causes of these effects, which can be explained, in part, by cultural norms.

It is true that men and women who share the same family structure are equally involved psychologically in their careers. And women are just as likely as men to view work as a major source of meaning and gratification in their lives—although in very different ways. But one aspect of career involvement where gender plays the dominant role is career priority relative to one's partner. It doesn't matter whether there are children in the family: dual-earner men place a higher priority on their own career relative to their partners' career than do dual-earner women. And, despite the fact that dual-earner fathers and mothers have essentially equal aspirations for advancement in the corporate hierarchy, aspirations are higher for men in general.

Traditionally, our culture has emphasized career success for men and the maintenance of interpersonal relationships for women.[23] Indeed, many men still equate making money and achieving status and power with their masculinity. But we don't think this is the entire explanation. It's likely that many more women would aspire to top management positions were it not for two additional factors: the "glass ceiling" effect and the demands of family life, disproportionately borne by women.[24]

The glass ceiling, while invisible, is a very real barrier that prevents women (and minorities) from reaching the seats of organizational power, often stalling their careers at lower- and middle-management levels.[25] Institutional sexism, gender-role stereotypes, and biased management practices—all elements of the glass ceiling—can serve to discourage even the most ambitious women from striving for top management positions. For most of us, reality has a way of dampening our aspirations.

Of course, many women have concluded the path to the executive suite is simply not worth pursuing, glass ceiling or no. Every accomplishment comes with a price, and a senior management position may simply demand more time and greater single-minded devotion to career than many women (and men, for that matter) are willing to devote, especially if status and power are not important personal values.

Women face a lot more competing demands for their time than do men, because child-rearing remains women's responsibility. We mentioned that dual-earner mothers substantially reduce their work hours compared to all other groups of business professionals. Many of these women, realizing that long work hours get in the way of family responsibilities, make a choice to limit career involvement, at least temporarily, to meet family needs. Less than 10 percent of these dual-earner women believe their careers have a higher priority than do their husband's careers.

These findings would seem to imply that women are generally less involved in their careers than are men because they are more highly engaged in their family lives. To explore this possibility further, let's look at the family involvement of both women and men.

Demonstrating involvement in family

Many circumstances attest to our involvement with family life. We get married, or perhaps establish some other long-term relationship. We become parents. We devote a substantial amount of our time to home and family activities. We adjust our work schedules to accommodate family needs. We become psychologically involved in the daily lives of family members.

If being married and having children defines "family involvement," it would appear from our business professionals that men are more involved in family life than women. But a closer look at other aspects of family involvement reveals a different picture (see Table 2.1). For example, women spend about two hours more each week on household activities than do men. When we factor in family structure, we see an interesting contrast in dual-earner families with children: the difference in time spent on household activities by women and men is nearly four hours a week. Granted, these differences in time spent are not that great. But when it comes to childcare activities, the differences are dramatic. In general, women average *more than three times* the number of hours per week than men. This disparity in time spent on the kids is even greater between dual-earner mothers and dual-earner fathers. Indeed, there is a substantial difference in the *total* number of hours spent each week on work, home, and children by dual-earner mothers (96 hours) compared to dual-earner fathers (76.3 hours).[26] It is plain to see that dual-earner mothers take on a "second shift" of family responsibilities when they get home from work.[27]

Women are more focused on family than men are in other respects, too. For example, women are more psychologically involved than men are with their families of origin (their own parents and siblings). The same holds true for their families of creation (their own spouses and children). Moreover, women are much more likely than men are to take an extended amount of time off from work after childbirth and to return to work part-time.

Why this greater involvement? In large part, the answer lies in the way

TABLE 2.1
....

How involved are we in our family lives?

	MEN	WOMEN
▸ **MARRIED**	◂ 80.5%	63.7%
▸ **PARENTHOOD**		
Currently parent*	◂ 68.4%	34.9%
Expect to become parent*	◂ 69.1%	72.1%
Number of children now *	◂ 2.2	1.6
Number of children anticipated	◂ 2.4	2.3
▸ **HOURS PER WEEK SPENT ON**		
Household activities*	◂ 9.4	11.5
Childcare activities *	◂ 13.2	40.5
▸ **HIGH PSYCHOLOGICAL INVOLVEMENT**		
In family of origin*	◂ 30.5%	44.6%
In family of creation*	◂ 77.8%	92.5%
▸ **ADJUST WORK SCHEDULE FOR FAMILY**		
	◂ 21.3%	22.3%
▸ **CAREER INTERRUPTIONS**		
Took time off after first child *	◂ 47.3%	77.7%
Amount of time taken off (median)*	◂ 1 day-1 wk	6 wk-3 mo
Returned to work part-time*	◂ 1.7%	34.9%

♦ Difference between men and women is statistically significant.

females are socialized, beginning in childhood. Generally, the process of establishing intimate relationships with other people is a central part of a woman's self-identity.[28] Since the family is a natural arena in which to establish intimate relationships, it is no surprise that women commit more time to their families than do men.[29] It could even be that for women—having traditionally had responsibility for the family domain—involvement in the intimacies of family life becomes second nature.

Socialization affects males as well, of course. Men are taught to expect their wives to assume responsibility for the family's emotional well-being. These expectations are reinforced in the media, at work, and in other social institutions. Even with the changes we've seen in recent years in the division of household labor,[30] women are still expected to restrict their careers to accommodate family needs.[31]

This is where our finding that women in managerial and professional circles are less likely than men to be married and have children comes into play. It's something observed in other research and undoubtedly reflects the tension many women anticipate between career and family.[32] Sensing that marriage or parenthood will interfere with a demanding career, some of these women make the choice to focus on work and postpone or even avoid marriage or motherhood altogether.

Gender differences emerge perhaps most strongly when it comes to the issue of tradeoffs between life domains. While it may appear to some people that everyone has equal access to a variety of options, there are in fact some striking inequities in how tradeoffs unfold.

Inequities in Our "Available" Choices

How we spend our time, where we invest our emotions, and where we're willing to forego involvement is often a choice. But is it as much a choice for women as it is for men?

Who has more choice?

How often have we heard that men can have it all—a successful career and a satisfying home life—whereas women have to make tradeoffs between commitment to a career and commitment as wife and mother? Here are some examples that speak to the issue of how, for many women, work and family are competing priorities in a zero-sum game.

> ### The Choices We Face
> *As a society, we must choose to correct the problem of unequal access to success in both work and family roles. This will require creating the options that allow more of us—especially women, but men too—to match our values with our actions.*

- Women who are highly focused on their careers are less likely to get married than women not focused on their careers. For men, the likelihood of marriage is the same whether or not they are highly focused on their careers.
- Women who are highly focused on their careers are less likely to have children than women not focused on their careers. Yet men who are highly focused on their careers are just as likely to have children as men who are not focused on their careers.
- Women who are highly focused in their careers have fewer children than women not focused on their careers. For men, it makes no difference: those highly focused on their careers have just as many children as men not focused on their careers.

These examples could mean that women who are highly focused on their careers are discouraged from starting or expanding a family, and thus make a choice not to get married, not to have children, or to have a small number of children (see Figure 2.2). But they could also mean that a high level of involvement in family—being married, having children—deters a woman from becoming highly involved in her career. Most likely, both scenarios apply. And both are consistent with the idea that women, compared with men, are more likely to experience constraints; to have to make tradeoffs between career and family.

The dynamics of tradeoffs

We asked our business professionals directly about being forced to make tradeoffs, and whether they believe family interferes with career. The results are shown in Table 2.2.

What exactly do we mean by tradeoffs? The dictionary definition is "the exchange of one thing for another."[33] In the work–family arena, a tradeoff involves foregoing success and fulfillment in one area of life to gain success and fulfillment in another. As with other compromises, these imply achieving less in either the work or family domain.

The vast majority of us are making tradeoffs all the time as we juggle career and family responsibilities. What drives all of us to make these trade-offs? First, there is the sense that we can't have it all in life. Then there is the realization that the conflicting demands of work and family *require* that we

TABLE 2.2

Does family interfere with career?
Are tradeoffs necessary?

Percentage of men and women who believe their family interferes with their career[♦]

	MEN	WOMEN
▸ MARRIED	◂ 15.6[a]	27.5[a]
▸ NOT MARRIED	◂ 5.2[a]	15.9[b]
▸ PARENT	◂ 15.6[a]	46.0[a]
▸ NOT PARENT	◂ 9.1[a]	9.3[b]
▸ HAVE PRESCHOOL CHILD(REN)	◂ 17.9[a]	53.6[a]
▸ NO PRESCHOOL CHILDREN	◂ 13.3[b]	11.9[b]

Percentage of men and women who believe tradeoffs between career and family are necessary[★]

	MEN	WOMEN
▸ PARENT	◂ 16.4[a]	34.3[a]
▸ NOT PARENT	◂ 9.0[a]	21.4[b]
▸ HAVE PRESCHOOL CHILD(REN)	◂ 17.3[a]	40.0[a]
▸ NO PRESCHOOL CHILDREN	◂ 13.7[b]	21.4[b]
▸ HIGHLY INVOLVED IN FAMILY	◂ 13.0[a]	30.6[a]
▸ NOT HIGHLY INVOLVED IN FAMILY	◂ 16.4[b]	18.2[b]

NOTE. For each comparison, groups in the same column with the same superscripts are not significantly different from each other.

♦ Percentage of people who agree with the following statement: "The demands of family life interfere with achieving success in my career."

★ Based on averaged responses to the following two statements: "I can have it all: a rewarding career, satisfying family relationships, and a fulfilling personal life" (reverse scored); "The conflicting demands of career and family require that I decide which is more important."

decide which area of our life is most important, forcing us to adjust our commitments. Many people we surveyed—nearly 43 percent—believe they had to decide which was more important to them, their career or their family.[34]

One thing on which nearly everyone agrees is that making tradeoffs is not particularly satisfying. The more people believe they are making a tradeoff, the *less* satisfied they are with their careers, their families, and their lives. Although many people who make family–career tradeoffs do so with conviction, believing it's the right thing to do, those tradeoffs are still compromises—and few if any compromises come without some dissatisfaction, or at least ambivalence.

Are tradeoffs between career and family inevitable? Yes, at least somewhat, since the demands of these two roles often conflict with one another. They are also inequitable. They fall disproportionately on one group within society.

More dual-earner mothers report that family interferes with their career than all the other groups—an indication of what happens as a result of these women having to bear the brunt of home and child responsibilities. Women with children (especially preschool children) and those who are highly involved in their family lives are most likely to feel they must make tradeoffs between career and family. Dual-earner mothers are more likely to make these tradeoffs than dual-earner fathers, dual-earner men in general, and women without children.

When we ask people more specifically about how work interferes with family and the tradeoffs they make, the conventional wisdom—that women, compared with men, are more likely to experience constraints or have to make tradeoffs between career and family—prevails again (see Figure 2.4). And when we narrow things down and compare dual-earner mothers with dual-earner fathers, the differences between the sexes become even more pronounced.

One of our particular interests is the decision to forego career success (or a higher level of career success) for family commitments. People in this situation deliberately restrict their pursuit of career success to accommodate the needs of their family. More dual-earner mothers than fathers believe that family demands—especially the demands of being a parent—limit their career success, and that they must make sacrifices in family and personal life to achieve career success. Mothers, more preoccupied with family concerns while on the job, experience greater stress and pressure at work. Because of their extensive family responsibilities, they tend to turn down career development opportunities. Clearly, gender is a major factor when it comes to tradeoffs.

Some of us make more tradeoffs than do others. One reason is the strong desire (or need) to devote a great deal of time to one particular life domain. For many women, that usually means family—and undoubtedly, the allocation of time to family cuts into the time available to devote to career. This is why dual-earner mothers we surveyed report making tradeoffs more than all other groups. Nearly 70 percent of the dual-earner mothers feel they must decide whether work or family is more important—and in their case, it gen-

FIGURE 2.4
....
What interferes with career and family?
Percent who agree

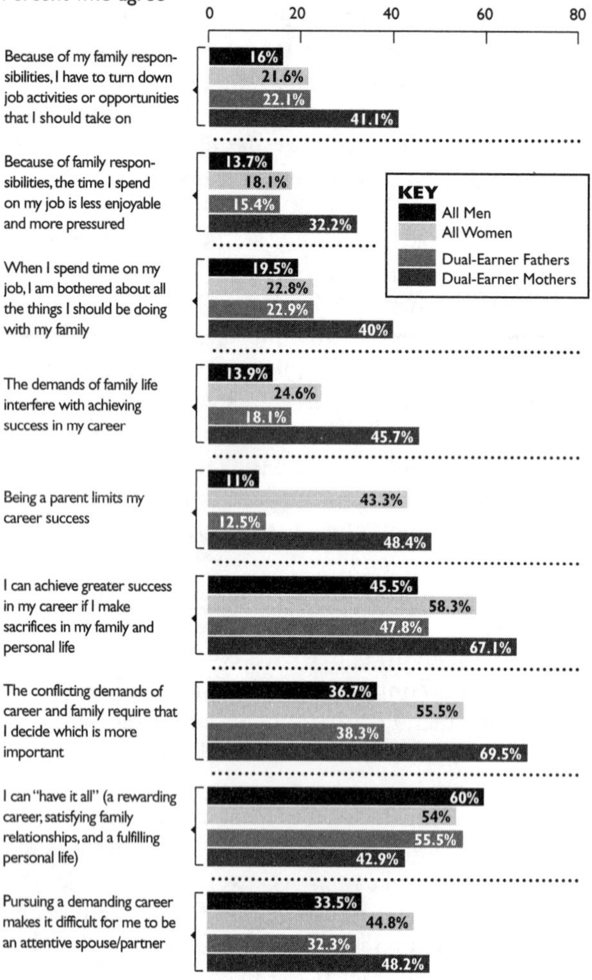

NOTE. All differences between men and women and between dual-earner fathers and dual-earner mothers are statistically significant.

erally means making sacrifices in career so that they can participate more fully in home and family life.

We believe a woman's conception of what it means to be a good parent drives these sacrifices. If being a successful mother means having a rich emotional relationship with children, being a consistent source of tangible and emotional support, and being physically and emotionally accessible to children when needed, then it is virtually impossible to succeed without taking considerable time and attention away from the career. These values, developed through early gender role socialization and reinforced by the unwillingness of many husbands to participate more in home life, cause these women to restrict their career involvement and trade off career success for family fulfillment and well-being.

This conception women have of their family role helps explain our earlier suggestion that some career-oriented women may avoid extensive family commitments by remaining single or choosing not to have children. Why? They are more likely than men to perceive that career commitments and career success are, or will be, jeopardized by the responsibilities that come with those choices. This isn't surprising, since women overall tend to be more highly involved in their families than do men. These conflicting pressures from career and family require women, more so than they require men, to decide which role is more important in their lives. The unmarried women who have not directly experienced these conflicts may learn about potential conflicts from family, friends, and the media, and hence anticipate extensive career–family conflict.[35]

Another problem women face is the perception of their employers that those among them who want to balance career and family are not committed to their work.[36] These women, stereotyped as lesser contributors and with bosses who may choose not to invest in them, lose out on training, coaching, and other career development opportunities.[37] Then there is the issue of flexibility in work arrangements—because employers often provide little, women are often left with two alternatives: work long hours or quit. In this way employers actually discourage career-oriented women from establishing strong family commitments—in other words, forcing a tradeoff.

The Choices We Face

Employers that choose not to support life beyond work create an imperative for their employees: choose between career advancement and devotion to family.

Among our business professionals (women and men alike) who work in organizations they feel are not supportive of their personal life interests, more than half believe they must choose whether work or family is more important. Contrast this with those who work in supportive organizations, where one-third feel they must decide between the two. If employees are required to choose between advancing their careers and devoting time to their families, if the employer is unsympathetic to employees who are juggling work and family responsibilities, and if the employer fails to provide flexibility, family-involved employees find it difficult to meet family commitments and still succeed at work. Chapter 7 explores the context and consequences of employer support for life beyond work; there we show how an employer's family-friendliness can, among other benefits, increase the chances of career success for working mothers.

Society encourages men to succeed in their careers, spurring a high level of career involvement among many dual-earner fathers. Women, however, invest more time and emotional energy in their families than do men, and many believe it is virtually impossible to be fully engaged in their careers and still live up to society's (and their own) expectations about their roles as wives and mothers. It is small wonder then that substantially more dual-earner mothers than dual-earner fathers believe a demanding career makes it difficult to be an attentive spouse or partner. And it should come as no surprise that many family-involved women avoid making extensive commitments to their careers, at least while their children are very young. In fact, dual-earner mothers with preschool children work nine fewer hours each week (39) than dual-earner mothers with older children (48).

Are tradeoffs constant? Each of us may find that our criteria for what we consider a successful career shift over the course of our lifetime. Some women, and perhaps some men, may willingly restrict their career involvement when their children are very young without feeling devastated by the tradeoff. The importance of being physically and emotionally available to their children outweighs the importance of attaining career growth and success. Several years later, however, these same people may reevaluate their family responsibilities and their career aspirations and decide to increase their level of involvement in work.

Tradeoffs are inevitable. After all, most people want to experience some level of fulfillment in a variety of life activities—family, career, community, and self-development—and it's unlikely to happen without some compromises. We think it is important to prioritize life goals, to decide which activities and accomplishments provide the most meaning to our lives at any given time. Facing tradeoffs might not be so bad, therefore, because it forces us to define our priorities. But tradeoffs become problematic when they are too severe and when they detract substantially from our quality of life—as in when being a loving spouse or parent cuts too deeply into a satisfying work life.

The Choices We Face

Tradeoffs between work and family are inevitable. The downside of these tradeoffs can be mitigated, at least in part, by seeing them as opportunities to make conscious choices among life priorities; to become clearer about our values.

Of course, not all men and women respond to the inevitable tradeoffs by favoring one domain over the other. Some people have figured out how to ease some of the pressures that come with tradeoffs by, for example, successfully managing the boundaries between their different life domains and taking advantage of the resources available to them at work and at home. More on this in later chapters.

Four Conclusions about Choice and Involvement

From what we have presented so far, we reach four major conclusions about involvement in different spheres of life.

*It is difficult to be highly involved in both career
and family at the same time.*

Career-focused people are less psychologically involved in their families, are less likely to adjust their work schedules to accommodate family or personal needs, spend fewer hours per week on household activities, and take less time off from work following childbirth compared to people who are less engaged in their careers. At the same time, individuals with family as their life role priority are less involved in their careers and are less likely to aspire to senior management positions.

We believe the *expectation* or *anticipation* of work–family conflict leads many people to focus their lives on either career *or* family. This is not to say that people in the career group ignore their families or that family-focused individuals disregard their careers. Rather, people in each group give primary emphasis to one role or the other, which guides the way they divide their time and distribute their emotional energy. The fact that more than 70 percent of our sample are focused primarily on one part of their lives (the career group, the family group, and the self/society group) lends further credence to this view.

*Nonetheless, it is possible to be highly involved
in both career and family.*

Remember that nearly 30 percent of the people we studied are in the career + family group. These people are generally satisfied with their lives, and they demonstrate that people *can* reap the benefits and cope effectively with the demands of being highly engaged in both career and family, often with the support of other people in their lives.[38] Social support can help us juggle our work and family lives, as we show in Chapters 6 and 7. The information, understanding, and direct help we receive from partners and employers can help reduce role conflict and increase both our sense of personal well-being and our career success.

*Women experience more constraints than do men
and must make more tradeoffs.*

Career-focused women are less likely to get married and have children than are other women (and, for that matter, career-focused men). Moreover, those women who do combine marriage and children with a career—the dual-earner mothers—substantially reduce the time they spend at work and experience more interference between family and career than do dual-earner fathers. Working mothers are the most vulnerable to pressures to curtail their career commitments.

Of course, we could attribute these differences to the fact that women are more likely to have family as their life role priority, whereas men are more likely to be in the career group. But this doesn't tell the entire story. Even *within* the family-focused group, women work fewer hours and hold lower career aspirations than men. And even within the career-focused group, women are less likely to get married and have children than men. Thus, the constraints women face are due to more than their life role priorities. No surprise: it is the unfortunate reality that women face more obstacles than men do in juggling career and family.[39]

> *There is a great deal of diversity in the priorities people attach to different parts of their lives.*

From what we found among our business professionals, we conclude that life role priorities depend very little on our background characteristics. Mostly, they develop from how we define success in our careers and in our lives. Career-focused people value status, challenge, and money; family-focused individuals value family relationships; and people in the self/society group value personal growth and development. Giving priority to specific roles in life enables us to live in ways that in turn reinforce our basic values.

We return to the life role priorities—choices about where we devote our time and energy—in subsequent chapters as we examine the ways in which career and family affect each other over the course of life. To begin, we'll explore how family life affects career success. Do extensive family responsibilities limit the success we achieve in our careers? If so, why? What role do our work experiences play in this process? Are women, in fact, more constrained by family responsibilities when it comes not just to their career involvement, but also when it comes to their capacity to achieve actual career success?

The next chapter presents answers to these questions, as we extend our exploration of how our values and the specific choices we make influence whether work and family will be allies or enemies. We focus on the effect of family on career, follow that with a chapter on the effect of career on family, and then explore more specifically how parents' careers affect their children.

3

How Family Affects Career Success

Despite the variations in life role priorities that we've just observed, it is still the case that for many (if not most) business professionals, having a successful career means a great deal. It does more than pay the bills and provide a nice lifestyle—a successful career carries social status and creates a feeling of self-fulfillment. It is no surprise, then, that the majority of the business professionals we studied—more than 80 percent—told us that when they judge the success of their own lives, their careers are a very important part of the equation.[1]

Most business professionals eventually get married and have children, which creates the challenge of achieving a meaningful integration of family life and career. We've seen that it can be difficult to maintain a high level of involvement in *both* career and family—although it is possible. But can we really achieve success in one domain if we are highly involved in the other? Our focus in this chapter is on whether it's possible to achieve career success if we are deeply involved with family—which has implications for employers and employees alike.

Here we explore how family responsibilities affect our business professionals in the career domain. Not surprisingly, we discover that marriage and children can limit career success, but not always. Women pay a hefty price, while men can actually benefit. How this works may come as a surprise.

One may justifiably conclude that the story of how family affects career is a story about enemies. When it comes to career, we see that there *are* detrimental consequences that accompany commitments to marriage and children, particularly for women. Traditional sex role stereotypes exact a considerable toll—there is even a bias against men who do not fit the traditional mold. We believe (and recent research affirms) there is a bias in many organizations against dual-earner fathers and in favor of men whose wives stay at home.[2] Generally speaking, we see that having a family is a career asset for men: Compared to single men and those without children, married men and fathers have greater authority on the job, which improves their chances of career success.

The challenge of transforming social roles for men and women, and of transforming organizational cultures, is daunting—but necessary if we are to make family an ally of work not just for some, but for all. Transformation is the subject of our concluding chapter, where we offer some practical recommendations for change. Before that we'll show how aspects of one's life outside of work—for instance, social support from our spouses and partners—can actually create value for one's career and thus make family work's ally.

Here we want to explore what is behind the bias faced by women and by certain men with families—how family works as a bonus or penalty—and gain an understanding of the choices and tasks facing each of us as individuals. Men and women need to see how involvement in their families affects their career accomplishments. Such insight can be invaluable as each of us makes our individual choices about what really matters to us in our lives, and as we look for ways to cope effectively with the pressures and stresses of our different life roles. Ultimately, we believe it can help us achieve success and satisfaction in our lives, and will strongly affect whether the adverse effects discussed here can be reversed and family can become more of an ally of work.

Two Questions

We are able to answer two important questions, thanks to what we learn from the business professionals we studied. Knowing the answers, we believe, helps clarify the choices men and women face.

- Do family responsibilities restrict career success or do they enhance career success?
- Do family responsibilities have the same effects on the careers of men and women?

A sizable group of our business professionals believe the demands of family life interfere with achieving career success. And even more are convinced they could achieve more success in their careers if they were willing to make sacrifices in their family and personal lives. But are these beliefs well-founded?

The idea that family commitments can limit career success is not new. The reason for the limit is straightforward enough: family commitments intrude into the time and energy we could otherwise devote to a career. That is surely why married women and women with children work more sporadically than women without these family responsibilities, and why they are more likely to hold part-time positions than all other groups of adults in the workforce.[3] We also know that men and women who are highly involved in their families often adjust their work schedules to accommodate the needs of their families.[4]

Are the effects the same for men and women? Some researchers argue that women incur a "family penalty" in their careers because women shoulder most of the family and home responsibilities. A man, conversely, gains a resource or "bonus" from having a family, one that actually boosts his career success—his wife's involvement in the home enables him to pursue career interests relatively free of family distractions.[5]

We want to understand whether and how such bonuses and penalties apply to our business professionals. How persistent and pervasive are they? What role do bonuses and penalties play in whether family and work are or can become allies or enemies? To answer these questions, we first need a definition of career success.

What Is Career Success?

Success, whether in career or family, means different things to different people. Each of us has our own set of values and our own feelings about what success looks like. It is possible, however, to go beyond subjectivity and apply some extrinsic indicators of whether people have, in fact, achieved career success.

We measure career success from two perspectives. One is the *objective* perspective—career success viewed from the outside. Two of the most common and recognizable objective yardsticks of career success are the income we earn and the level we reach in a corporate hierarchy. These translate into familiar terms: *money* and *power*, two of the most widely shared values among people pursuing managerial and professional careers in business.[6] The world typically views wealthy and powerful people as successful in their careers.

The business professionals we studied are successful, at least by the world's objective money and power measures. A third of them earn $100,000 or more annually, and a fifth earn more than $140,000 each year.[7] The vast majority are in middle- or upper-level positions. Moreover, about a quarter indicate that their current level is as high as they wish to go in their organization. Of the rest, a full two-thirds are moderately or highly optimistic that they will reach their desired level in the organizational hierarchy.

The other perspective is *psychological*. In this sense, career success is in the eye of the beholder. Who better than ourselves to judge the success of our own careers? We know what's important to us, and we know how we feel about the direction our careers have taken. Any reasonable definition of career success, we believe, must account for the individual's satisfaction with his or her career accomplishments. Taking into account the psychological perspective, relatively few of our business professionals are dissatisfied with their careers. By the subjective career success measure, then, they are doing well. Figure 3.1 provides an overview.

FIGURE 3.1

Different measures of career success

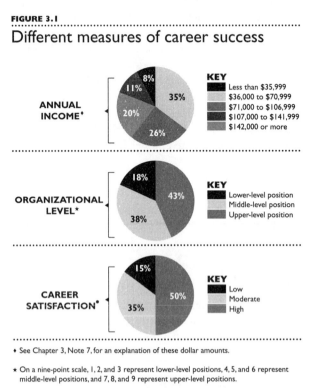

♦ See Chapter 3, Note 7, for an explanation of these dollar amounts.

★ On a nine-point scale, 1, 2, and 3 represent lower-level positions, 4, 5, and 6 represent middle-level positions, and 7, 8, and 9 represent upper-level positions.

● On a five-point scale, 1 and 2 represent low satisfaction, 3 represents moderate satisfaction, and 4 and 5 represent high satisfaction.

What Leads to Career Success?

Are there particular characteristics that lead to career success? Some people seem to be more or less likely to attain success than others, as we learn from the business professionals we surveyed.

Gender, age, and background

Not surprisingly, we find that a person's age makes a considerable difference: older business professionals are more likely than their younger counterparts to earn higher annual salaries, be in upper-level positions, and be highly satisfied with their careers. The greatest differences in career success are found between those above forty and those in their twenties and thirties.

There are also striking gender differences in income and achieved hierarchical level, although not in career satisfaction. Nearly two-thirds of men—compared to only 38 percent of women—earn annual salaries of $71,000 or more. In addition, more than twice as many men as women occupy upper-level positions.[8]

A person's race is unrelated to income but is related to achieved hierarchical level and career satisfaction.[9] About twice as many whites as nonwhites are in upper-level positions, and whites in general are much more likely to be satisfied with their careers as well.[10]

Self-employment and industry are also related to career success. Self-employed individuals are more likely to be in upper-level positions and to be highly satisfied with their careers than are salaried employees in organizations. In addition, people in the financial or banking field earn more money and are more satisfied with their careers than those in other fields.[11]

Life role priorities and other values

We also explored the effect of people's values on their career success outcomes. Those who place substantial importance on status in their careers and those who value material wealth in their lives are most likely to earn high incomes, occupy upper-level positions, and experience high levels of career satisfaction.

Life role priorities consistently relate to career success. People whose life role priority is career + family are more likely to have reached an upper-level position than are those in any of the other three groups. These same people are also more satisfied with their careers. At the other extreme, those in the self/society group earn the lowest incomes, are least likely to be in upper-level positions, and have the lowest career satisfaction.

Work experiences

By the measures we've just presented, the most successful business professionals are likely to be white men in the career + family life role priority group, over forty, self-employed, working in finance or banking, and placing a strong value on status and material wealth. Most readers will probably not fit this description. What else, then, matters?

The experiences we have at work matter a great deal. Not surprisingly, the most important determinants of career success occur in the work environment. The people who are most successful in their careers

- are psychologically involved in their careers
- put in long hours at work
- have a great deal of authority in their jobs
- receive developmental job assignments that build their skills
- network extensively with others, both inside and outside their employer organization

It's not difficult to grasp why career involvement promotes career success.[12] Employers tend to have the highest regard for employees who devote the most time to work, who appear to demonstrate that they are highly motivated, and who are most involved psychologically in their careers. This view reinforces itself: not only do highly involved employees often perform more effectively on the job (as we find with our business professionals), they also may be given more attention and more opportunities to achieve success. We observe, for example, that individuals highly involved in their careers receive more coaching and more developmental job assignments than do those who are relatively uninvolved in their careers. It has been well documented that these factors—job authority, developmental assignments, coaching, and networking—play an important role in promoting career success.[13] Each factor can help an employee develop skills and contacts that in turn contribute substantially to a successful career.

It makes sense that employers in general are most willing to invest in the people who appear to be the most committed to their work. As we will see below, however, this preference has a negative effect when it comes to the career success of women.

Family: Bonus or Penalty?

It is often claimed that when it comes to careers, certain elements of family are a help to men and a hindrance to women.[14] Presumably, employers view married men as motivated, responsible, and stable, and are therefore more willing to invest in the careers of married men than unmarried men. There seems to be a bias in favor of married men in the traditional family structure. Moreover, married men often have the active support of wives, who can bolster their husbands' careers.[15] Hence the bonus.

The flipside—the penalty—is that marriage detracts from a woman's career success. Married women, goes the conventional wisdom, are less likely to be committed to their own careers and are less likely to relocate for their jobs because of the constraints of their husbands' careers. In addition, organizations may view married women as a risky investment—after all, they're likely to have children and become even less committed to their careers in the future.

We've dubbed this hypothesis "BOP"—for family "bonus or penalty." It is rooted in old stereotypes, flowing from the view that married men are so focused on generating income for their families that their work demands will inevitably take precedence over other family responsibilities. Further, the hypothesis is based on the belief that married women—especially mothers—are so committed to their families that their family responsibilities will inevitably take precedence over their careers.

As with most stereotypes, there is an element of truth here, although gender differences in career and family orientation have diminished in recent years and will likely diminish even more in the years ahead. We're glad to see these stereotypes starting to fade. We later discuss some concrete suggestions for how individuals, employers, and society in general can make advances toward changing these stereotypes.

The question before us here is whether the BOP hypothesis answers the questions we posed earlier about the effect of family life on career success. Specifically, what are the effects of marriage, the influence of children, and whether a spouse works outside the home? The answer, put bluntly, is that gender rules. Let's look more closely at the ways in which women—particularly working mothers—are the most vulnerable to suffering career penalties and work–family stress.

Marriage: help or hindrance?

Does marriage affect the careers of men and women in the same way? Our findings on marriage support half of the BOP hypothesis. Marriage *does* provide a bonus for men, but it does not exact a penalty on women.[16] As we see in Figure 3.2, married men reach a higher-level position in the organization than do unmarried men. In fact, 58 percent of the married men we surveyed occupy upper-level positions in their organizations, compared to only 34 percent of the unmarried men. And these higher-level positions translate into more money for the married men, who in turn are more satisfied with their careers.[17]

Why are married men more successful in their careers than unmarried men? We looked at a wide range of factors in search of the answer: how involved they are in their careers, how likely they are to relocate for their careers, and how much coaching they receive from others at work (to mention just a few). It turns out that only one factor explains the greater success of married men: these men have more *authority* in their jobs than unmarried men. Authority has a positive impact on their income, the organizational level they attain, and their career satisfaction.[18] Authority over work—control

FIGURE 3.2

Does being married help a career?

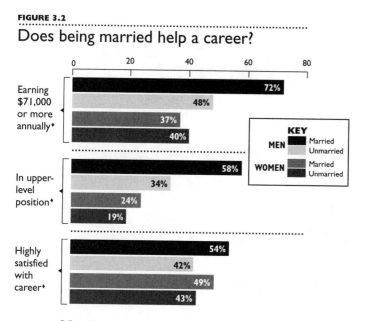

* Difference between married men and unmarried men is statistically significant.

NOTE: In determining significant relationships between marriage and career success for men and women, the measures of income, level, and career satisfaction were adjusted for age and other relevant background factors.

over when, where, how, and with whom work gets done—does indeed create greater career success.

How do these men come by greater authority on the job? As the BOP hypothesis suggests, married men may be given more authority or encouraged to take on additional authority simply because they are perceived as mature and responsible. Alternatively, it might be that married men, because of their own needs and their feelings about themselves, actively seek more authority in their jobs.[19] Perhaps they *are* more mature or more self-confident *because* of their family responsibilities. We do know from our research that married men are actually *less* interested in pursuing challenging work and material wealth than unmarried men, so it seems unlikely that they are seizing opportunities to grab more authority on the job. It is more probable (although we can't prove it directly) that organizations treat married men differently from the way they treat other men, at least with regard to the authority they give to people on their jobs. Such a conclusion would certainly fit well with prevailing stereotypes.

As for women, marriage certainly doesn't help career success, but it doesn't detract from it either. In this respect, the BOP hypothesis is off— there is no marriage penalty for women. Add children to the equation, however, and the picture becomes quite different.

FIGURE 3.3

Does having children help a career?

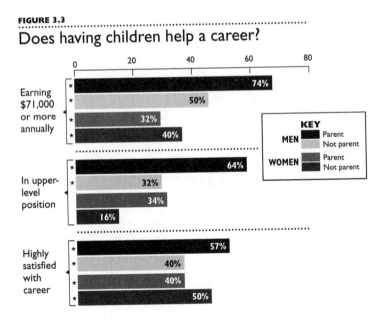

★Difference between parents and non-parents is statistically significant.

NOTE: In determining significant relationships between marriage and career success for men and women, the measures of income, level, and career satisfaction were adjusted for age and other relevant background factors.

Does having children interfere?

Like marriage, fatherhood has a positive effect on a man's career (see Figure 3.3). Fathers make more money and are more satisfied with their careers than men without children. More than two-thirds of the fathers earn $71,000 or more a year compared to one-half of the men with no children. Twice as many fathers are in upper-level positions. Some 57 percent of the fathers, compared to only 40 percent of the men without children, are highly satisfied with their careers. Again, the one factor that explains these differences in career success is the greater authority fathers report they have on the job.

Unlike marriage, motherhood does indeed work against the career success of women on both objective and psychological dimensions. At the objective level, mothers incur an income penalty (they earn less). So, in this respect, our findings support the BOP hypothesis.

Delve deeper into the many factors that might explain this income penalty, and one stands out above all others: the number of hours worked in a week. Income increases the more hours we are willing to work, even if we are on salary—and mothers work about thirteen fewer hours a week than do women without children. Many mothers make a choice to limit the time they devote to work so they can meet their family responsibilities, and this decision has an obvious negative career consequence: if we choose to work fewer hours, we restrict our financial success.

The Choices We Face

With the way things are now, unfortunately, choosing motherhood can mean not only decreased financial success for women, but a career satisfaction penalty as well.

It should come as no surprise that women who put in fewer hours at work are penalized. Most people believe, quite reasonably, that the more time spent at work, the more we can produce. Add to this that employers typically use presence in the workplace—so-called "face time"—as an indicator of career commitment and work contributions.

Fathers in general are not as restrictive of the time they devote to work. In fact, the fathers we surveyed work about the same number of hours a week as do men without children. No wonder so many more mothers than fathers— 47.4 percent compared with 11.9 percent—believe that being a parent has limited their career success!

In addition to the income penalty, there is a second penalty at work here. We call it the *satisfaction penalty*. Being a mother detracts from a woman's degree of career satisfaction. Why? A number of factors explain this phenomenon. Compared to women without children, mothers

- spend more time on household activities
- spend less time at work

- are less involved psychologically in their careers
- receive less coaching at work

As we've already noted, career satisfaction is enhanced if we work long hours, are psychologically involved in our work, and receive opportunities for career development. Conversely, spending a lot of time on household activities detracts from our career satisfaction. No wonder mothers are less likely to experience high levels of satisfaction with their careers.[20]

When we look closely at an array of factors that represent a woman's involvement in home and family—being a mom, having young children, being psychologically involved in family life, devoting many hours to household chores—a pattern emerges: a woman's family commitments diminish her career activities and outcomes. Figure 3.4 provides an overview of how attention to the world of family can result in career penalties for women.

There are several differences between women who have a great deal of family commitments and women who do not. Women in the former group[21]

- spend less time at work
- are less involved psychologically in their careers
- make more adjustments to their work schedules to accommodate family and personal needs
- receive fewer developmental assignments
- receive less coaching at work

A woman and her family have some control over the first three. Women with heavy family responsibilities may choose to limit the time they devote to work to meet their family's needs. In a similar vein, some women may decide to limit their psychological involvement in work or adjust their work schedules, at least for some time during their careers. Work may simply be a less central part of their lives compared to their family commitments.

FIGURE 3.4
A woman's commitment to family has a detrimental effect on her career

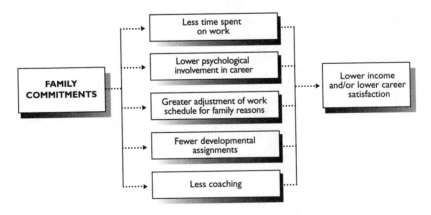

Why women with extensive family commitments—in particular, women with young children—receive fewer developmental job assignments is more complicated. Part of the answer is that many of these women decide to limit their career involvement to some extent. We find that nearly twice as many dual-earner mothers as dual-earner fathers turn down job activities or opportunities they feel they should take on. Clearly, this is a concession that allows some women to attend to home and family matters. In that sense, the decision is voluntary—although there may be considerable ambivalence involved.

It is also possible that employers simply do not offer as many developmental assignments to these women. Perhaps employers assume in advance that the opportunities will be turned down. Or employers may believe these mothers won't be able to handle the assignments satisfactorily because they involve extra hours, evening or weekend work, perhaps travel. Or employers may simply believe it's not worth investing in the careers of these mothers, who may quit their jobs because of work–family conflicts.[22] Most likely, several factors are working in tandem here, some based on the woman's own decisions (which may in part reflect the *anticipation* of conflict) and others on the discriminatory treatment they experience at their employer's hands.

We have already shown that certain work experiences—time, psychological involvement, authority, and opportunities for career development—promote career success. We've also seen that women with families suffer a penalty that constrains career success—a penalty that men do not generally experience. Now we can see an important reason: women's family responsibilities interfere with some of the very work experiences that would have improved their chances for career success.[23]

These family responsibilities limit the career involvement of women more than they do men. And, as we've said, having young children reduces a woman's exposure to developmental job assignments. Then there is the issue of work schedules: having children is more likely to lead women than men to adjust their work schedules to accommodate family or personal needs.

In short, family responsibilities penalize women; they inhibit career involvement and opportunities for career-building assignments. The result is diminished career success.

A working spouse: advantage or disadvantage?

If there is any sort of family-related penalty for men, it has to do with whether their spouses work outside the home. If husband and wife both work, they are likely to share home and childcare activities more than men or women whose partners stay at home. But are individuals in the latter group more successful in their careers? It is plausible to expect they would be; after all, as the BOP hypothesis suggests, stay-at-home spouses may make it possible for sole breadwinners to devote more time and energy to the workplace.

To find the answer, we compared the career success of two groups of men: dual-earner fathers (whose wives are employed outside the home) and single-earner fathers (whose wives stay at home). We would have liked to contrast the career success of dual-earner mothers and single-earner mothers (with stay-at-home dads) as well, but the small number of single-earner mothers among those we surveyed precluded such an analysis.

What do we find? There are no differences in organizational level or career satisfaction between the two groups of men. However, single-earner fathers do earn higher incomes.[24] Why? We know it's not a matter of age or type of employment, because we adjusted our measure of income for these factors.[25] We did find that single-earner fathers are more psychologically involved in their careers and spend less time on household activities than dual-earner fathers, and that the wives of single-earner fathers spend more time on household and childcare activities than the wives of dual-earner fathers. Even these factors, however, do not explain the salary difference between the two groups.[26]

We wondered if the discrepancy was related to the number of hours worked, or factors on the job. But single-earner fathers do not work longer hours. They don't relocate any more frequently, nor do they receive more coaching, authority, or developmental assignments than do dual-earner fathers. Educational achievements, career/life values, or job performance—all of which are essentially the same for both groups—cannot explain the greater income of single-earner fathers. Why, then, do single-earner fathers earn higher incomes?

Ours is not the first study to demonstrate that there's an income penalty for dual-earner fathers.[27] And the specific reasons behind this penalty remain a matter of conjecture. The disturbing conclusion we come to is that the family bonus appears to be available mainly to men in "traditional" marriages—those with children and a stay-at-home wife.

It seems that employers, consciously or unconsciously, favor single-earner fathers when it comes to distributing financial rewards. There are several possible explanations.[28] One is that employers may believe single-earner fathers require more money than single men (whose expenses are less) or dual-earner men (whose wives contribute to the family income). The result, though, is that employers are allocating financial rewards based not on merit but on *perceived need*.[29] Maybe employers prefer the traditional male-headed household structure. Today, most senior managers are themselves single-earner men. Perhaps those in power personally prefer others who have family structures similar to their own. Managers may be more likely to develop relationships with their own kind, and in turn reward those with whom they have these close relationships—establishing, in effect, a sort of cycle where they perpetuate their stereotype of the single-earner father.[30]

Whatever the answer, when it comes to the family income bonus, not all married men are created equal. Of the four groups of married men we studied, the single-earner fathers earn the most money. Dual-earner fathers, then, don't do as well as single-earner fathers. How do they stack up against their female counterparts, dual-earner mothers, when it comes to career success? We might expect to find greater career success among dual-earner fathers because they are highly involved in their careers. Dual-earner mothers, remember, are more highly involved in their families. If there are differences in career success between these men and women, perhaps we can attribute it to these patterns of career and family involvement.

What we do find is that although dual-earner fathers and mothers reach similar organizational levels and are equally satisfied with their careers, dual-earner fathers earned substantially more money than dual-earner mothers. In fact, 70 percent of the dual-earner fathers earn at least $71,000 a year, compared to 33 percent of the dual-earner mothers. And 23 percent of the fathers earn in excess of $142,000, compared to only 8 percent of the mothers.

Why such a pronounced difference in salaries? It relates to something we demonstrated earlier: dual-earner fathers spend less time on household and childcare activities than dual-earner mothers. They seem to believe their working wives will pick up any slack at home. Presumably, dual-earner mothers spending a great deal of time on household and childcare activities are freeing their husbands to devote more time to their careers.[31] Consequently, these men can spend more hours at work, and hence they are rewarded with greater income. Put simply, if you are a dual-earner father or mother, your financial success is due primarily to how you allocate your time. The old gender role expectations are in full force here: men devoting more time to work, women taking primary responsibility for the household and children.

What Conclusions Can We Draw?

At the outset of this chapter we posed two questions: Do family responsibilities restrict career success or do they enhance career success? And, do family responsibilities have the same effects on the careers of men and women? We've shown that family life can and does indeed influence career success, but in different ways for men and women, and we can draw two major conclusions.

Work-related experiences are crucial and powerful determinants of career success.

The most successful individuals work long hours, are psychologically involved in work, have a great deal of authority on the job, receive many developmental job assignments, and network extensively inside and outside the company. In fact, these work-related experience are much more important than family factors (such as marriage and parenthood) in determining income, hierarchical level achieved, and career satisfaction. From the business professionals we surveyed, we can actually quantify how much: work-related experiences are roughly three times more important than family factors in determining income, five times more important in determining organizational level, and *fifteen* times more important in determining career satisfaction.

Women, however, find their involvement in work—and consequently their exposure to career development opportunities—determined in large part by their family responsibilities. It's a vicious circle: these women cannot (or do not choose to) be as involved in work as their male counterparts, and as a consequence do not get the same opportunities as men—opportunities that are crucial to career success. In a sense, this very connection between family responsibilities and work experiences produces the family bonus or the family penalty.

There is a family bonus for men and
a family penalty for women.

Married men and men with children are advantaged in their careers. And only one factor explains this family bonus: the amount of authority on the job, which married men and fathers possess to a disproportionate degree.[32] But why should this be? As we mentioned earlier, the "B" or "bonus" part of the BOP hypothesis is that marriage and children enhance the aura of a man's maturity, responsibility, and stability. Family men, employers may reason, are more committed to their work and to their employer than men without such family ties.[33] It is ironic, then, that we find married men are no more involved in work and no more committed to their employers than single men or men without kids. Stereotypes run deep and die hard.

There are exceptions, however. Fathers as a group fare well in their careers compared to men with no children, although dual-earner fathers suffer some penalty. And some fathers are penalized for their family involvement. For example, fathers who spend a great deal of time on household activities earn less money, reach lower organizational levels, and experience lower career satisfaction than fathers who spend only a modest amount of time on home chores. Clearly, whoever cares for hearth and home experiences diminished career attainments.

Again, gender is the key factor. Whereas marriage and children can promote the careers of men, marriage has neither a positive nor a negative effect on women's career success. The presence of children, though, has a detrimental effect on women's income and career satisfaction.

These conclusions about how family affects work seem to be largely negative. They are the unfortunate reality of having to make the tradeoffs we discussed in Chapter 2. Except for the traditional male head of household whose wife stays at home, family does appear to be the enemy of career success. For this traditional father, however, career success comes at a significant price at home, as we learn in the next chapter.

Career and family can be allies—if choices are made and priorities are set to achieve that outcome. In Chapter 9, we offer some ideas about how to get there for people in a variety of family structures. First, though, we will explore the ways in which our careers can affect our family and personal lives, and then move on to look specifically at the positive and negative impacts of our careers on children—where the picture becomes more complex.

4

Having a Life

"Get a life!" How often have we heard someone urge us to develop interests beyond our job? All around us, we're being exhorted to do things that will enrich and round out our life experiences and make us better human beings. And if we take the advice, we're supposed to end up healthier, more productive, more whole.

For most of us, this means spending time with our loved ones or doing things that we value—recreationally, spiritually, or in some other way that's important to us. It also means making the conscious decision to spend time or energy on those activities even if that choice may have negative consequences for our economic status or career advancement. It means finding a way to make work the ally of "getting a life"—of finding a way to overcome the inevitable conflict between two different life domains.

How do we get to the point where we *can* get a life? And how do we know if we've succeeded in getting one? The answer, in part, is to find a way to be satisfied with work *and* family. As we've been doing throughout, we're emphasizing what we call cross-domain effects. Our last chapter addressed how family affects work and career. This chapter is about how work and career affect family and personal life.

Some of what we report will come as little or no surprise to most readers. We get confirmation that what each of us values—what we care about—influences our satisfaction with the different domains of our lives. We also see that choices we make about our involvement in our careers have a lot to do with our family and personal life satisfaction, and hence with whether work is the enemy or ally of life beyond career.

It will come as little surprise that persistent gender role stereotypes have a lot to do with the life satisfaction of people in our survey, and probably that of most readers. Most men are busy being breadwinners. They experience greater satisfaction in their family roles to the degree they spend *more* time at work—which is consistent with the traditional notion that a man's identity is shaped largely by his work role, and that a good breadwinner is a happy family man.[1] Women, however, derive family satisfaction when they play their nurturing roles at home, and when they take advantage of the emotional support that comes from social networks at work. This fits well with the traditional view of women.

Is there anything surprising, then, in our findings about how work affects life? Most surprising is what we learn about time. It appears that the problem of overwork[2]—too many hours spent at and on the job—may be getting more attention than is warranted. To be sure, this time problem cannot be ignored. And, yes, many business professionals really do feel overwhelmed by work. But that feeling comes not so much from time spent as from the psychological and behavioral impact of work on other life roles. The mental struggle each of us goes through to interweave and strike a balance among our different life roles affects whether we can get a life to a greater degree than how we allocate time.

Another seeming contradiction is that many women feel better about their families when they spend more time on themselves, as opposed to spending time on nurturing others. Perhaps they have a greater need than do men to refresh and rejuvenate, given that they face not only the pressures of work but also childcare and household demands—their "second shift."[3]

Let's take a closer look at these and other findings that tell us what it means to have a life, and how our experiences at work, our values, and our family structure affect the effort to make allies of work and family. Among other things, we'll explore the attributes of our experiences at work, beyond the mental struggle of interweaving, that we find can help make work the ally of the family. We discuss the critical importance of establishing boundaries. And we also show evidence that supports the theme we introduced in Chapter 1: It is possible to have a fulfilling career and a satisfying family life, but it requires balanced involvement in both these spheres of our lives.

Where Our Career and Life Values Lead

What we experience in our work and our careers influences not only our satisfaction in the work domain, but also our satisfaction with both our families of creation (spouses and children) and our sense of personal growth. If satisfaction is a step toward making allies of the two domains, it certainly helps to learn what creates it. In this book, we're most interested in those aspects of our lives where there is *choice*—where each of us can act as our values suggest.

But first, let's ask whether our business professionals are indeed satisfied with their lives. It turns out that most feel very satisfied with their personal growth and development. Even more are very satisfied with their families. (See Table 4.1.)

Satisfaction with different aspects of life for men and women does seem to depend, at least in part, on age and family structure (Table 4.2). For instance, men whose wives stay at home—traditional male breadwinners—rank lowest when it comes to satisfaction with family. Being a parent appears to have pos-

TABLE 4.1

Satisfaction with family (of creation) and personal growth

Percent highly satisfied with[♦]

▸ SEX*	FAMILY	PERSONAL GROWTH
Men	◂ 69[a]	52
Women	◂ 77[b]	54
▸ FAMILY STRUCTURE[●]		
Dual-earner women with no children	◂ 84[a]	57
Dual-earner mothers	◂ 76[a,b]	48
Dual-earner fathers	◂ 73[a,b,c]	57
Dual-earner men with no children	◂ 71[b,c]	44
Single-earner fathers	◂ 66[c]	50
Single women	◂ —	58
Single men	◂ —	48

♦ Respondents were asked to rate how satisfied they were with different aspects of their lives using a scale of 1 = not satisfied, 3 = moderately satisfied, and 5 = very satisfied, with 2 and 4 between 1 and 3 and 3 and 5, respectively. The measure for family satisfaction combined 3 items, as described in Appendix One. Those with scores of 4.0 or higher on the combined measure are considered highly satisfied.

★ Those with any of the same letters in superscript are not significantly different from each other.

● Based on a test of the mean differences among the seven groups, those with the same letters in superscript are not statistically significant in their difference from each other.

TABLE 4.2

Does age make a difference?

Percent highly satisfied with[♦]

	FAMILY		PERSONAL GROWTH	
▸ AGE GROUPS*	MEN	WOMEN	MEN	WOMEN
20s	◂ 87[a]	92[a]	55	57
30s	◂ 69[b]	78[b]	43	54
40s+	◂ 66[b]	58[b]	58	52

♦ Respondents were asked to rate how satisfied they were with different aspects of their lives using a scale of 1 = not satisfied, 3 = moderately satisfied, and 5 = very satisfied, with 2 and 4 between 1 and 3 and 3 and 5, respectively. The measure for family satisfaction combined 3 items, as described in Appendix One. Those with scores of 4.0 or higher on the combined measure are considered highly satisfied.

★ Within each column, those with any of the same letters in superscript are not statistically significantly different from each other.

itive effects on whether men (but not women) feel satisfied with their personal growth and development.[4] Compared to mothers, women *without* children feel somewhat better about family. The parental role imposes far fewer constraints on men than on women, and men derive greater societal status from being a parent. Our findings also suggest that traditional family roles for men, which limit the father's role in child-rearing, actually diminish the capacity of these men to appreciate the satisfaction of fatherhood to its fullest. Meanwhile, women are busy working their second shift, bearing the brunt of responsibility for raising the kids. As a result, they're less able to invest in their own personal growth and development.[5]

In general, people in their twenties are more satisfied with their families than are people thirty or older. It may be the case that families are perceived as less demanding when we're younger, because of simpler demands from children and fewer demands from aging parents.

Beyond our age and our family structure, there are of course many other factors that determine how satisfied we are with our lives. One key is how we *value* the different domains of our lives. The life role priorities we introduced in Chapter 2 have a strong influence, as shown in Tables 4.3 and 4.4.

When it comes to satisfaction with family, it's not surprising that people in the family-focused group come out on top. Nor is it that surprising that peo-

TABLE 4.3

Do life role priorities affect satisfaction with family?

Percent highly satisfied with family

► LIFE ROLE PRIORITY [*]	MEN	WOMEN	TOTAL
Career + Family	◄ 73	78	74[a]
Family	◄ 77	81	78[a]
Career	◄ 45	38	44[c]
Self/Society	◄ 53	67	57[b]

[*] Those with any of the same letters in superscript are not significantly different from each other.

TABLE 4.4

Do life role priorities affect satisfaction with personal growth?

Percent highly satisfied with personal growth

► LIFE ROLE PRIORITY [*]	MEN	WOMEN	TOTAL
Career + Family	◄ 57	59	57[a]
Family	◄ 55	52	54[a,b]
Career	◄ 41	67	48[a,b]
Self/Society	◄ 41	50	44[b]

[*] Those with any of the same letters in superscript are not significantly different from each other. The main effect of life role priority and the interaction between sex and life role priority is significant.

ple in the career-focused group are less satisfied with family than are people in all the other groups. Those in the career + family group are more satisfied with personal growth than the other three types.[6] Why? They balance their commitment to the work and personal life domains, and end up with more of a "life" in the process.

In addition to life role priorities, we looked at a related set of personal and career values that matter in how much satisfaction we feel with our families and personal growth.[7] For instance, the more one values family as a success factor in life, the more likely one feels satisfied with family and with personal growth.[8] Conversely, the more one values the material wealth and standard of living that derive from career achievements, the *less* likely one is to feel satisfied with family. And the more highly one values personal growth, the greater the satisfaction with that aspect of life. These findings confirm in general the findings related to life role priority.

The message here? Making the strongest allies of work and family may require that we adopt certain values. As an example, choosing to value material wealth at the expense of family satisfaction may be counterproductive. If indeed building satisfaction with our lives in both domains is important to us, we must find ways to ensure that our choices lead toward that goal.

Where does time come in? Many employers, public policymakers, and analysts are seeking ways to provide time so that people in the workforce can achieve greater satisfaction with their lives beyond work. How people allocate time has become a national concern. Vice President Al Gore went so far as to convene a conference in Nashville, Tennessee, in June 1996, to focus attention on the need to make time available for family. Both President Clinton and Hillary Rodham Clinton addressed the gathering. But is more time the remedy to what has been called the "time famine?"[9]

How Time Matters

What we've found shows that to craft solutions to the problem of getting a life we must look beyond time alone. How we spend our time is only one factor in determining how we feel about family and personal growth. Our experiences at work are more important. Attention must be paid not only to the impact of worktime on our lives beyond the job, but also to the psychological and behavioral impact of work on our lives outside of work.

Still, it would be wrong to diminish altogether the degree to which time *does* matter. After all, how we allocate our time in a typical week can speak volumes about our priorities—or the priorities imposed on us. And whether and how much time is available has an impact on the choices we make.

Two aspects of time in particular carry some weight when it comes to satisfaction with our families and our personal lives, depending on our age and whether we're men or women. First, there are the *hours we work*. Second is *relaxation time*. How these times are allocated affects whether work and family are enemies or allies.

For our sample, hours spent at work generally have no impact on satisfaction with family or personal growth. But this masks what we find when we look more closely by gender and age. For men, working more hours increases satisfaction with family. This may seem paradoxical, but it certainly supports traditional notions about the male role.[10] Similarly, young men starting out in their careers feel better about their personal growth when they spend more time at work.[11]

It is the opposite case for women over thirty. More time working means less family satisfaction—again, an affirmation of traditional gender role differences. For younger women, however, the length of the workweek doesn't make much of a difference when it comes to family satisfaction. It may be that these women don't experience the family problems caused by long work weeks because many don't yet have children.

Relaxation time appears to be crucial. Overall, ten hours spent relaxing each week goes a long way toward creating satisfaction with family for most people. This is particularly true for women when we look across all age groups: they feel better about their families the more time they take for themselves.

The Choices We Face

Experiment with how time is allocated between work and relaxation, seeking a balance that supports a sense of satisfaction with family and personal growth.

Allocating more time for relaxation, however, will only affect our satisfaction up to a point. Similarly, addressing the number of hours spent working will only take us so far toward getting a life. There are many other work and career factors that affect how men and women feel about their families and their personal growth. These factors help illustrate how time, while important, is not the primary issue. And they play a crucial role in our discussion in the next chapter, where we seek to understand the impact of parents' values and career experiences on their children's health, behavior, and performance in school.

Looking Beyond Time

We need to look beyond time, to factors that make up our work-related experiences in order to understand how work affects our personal lives. These factors, many of which are about the way we *feel* about various aspects of work and career, play a critical role in determining the degree of satisfaction we feel with our lives.[12]

Psychological involvement in and satisfaction with career

The first of these factors is the degree to which we are involved psychologically in our careers. Too much involvement can have a detrimental effect at home—if we think a lot, and worry a lot, about work, we're likely to be less satisfied with our family. Conversely, the deeper our career involvement, the *greater* our satisfaction with personal growth. Psychological involvement in career, then, works in opposite directions when it comes to satisfaction with family and with personal growth. This is a key point.

A second factor is career satisfaction. It may appear paradoxical that satisfaction with career signals a high level of satisfaction with family life *and* that people feel worse about their families the more psychologically involved they are in their careers. However, it's not an enduring paradox: feeling good about our families *is* greater to the extent we enjoy our careers, but not when we become *too* immersed in work. That can lead to detachment from our families.

People become overinvolved psychologically in their work for all sorts of reasons. One may be that work serves as some sort of refuge from a dissatisfying family life—a place where people can have the gratification that comes with being rewarded for labor, and where emotional intimacy is simply not required.[13] But this can become a vicious circle: when work consumes too much of our attention, we're left with little room for developing satisfying family relationships, which in turn can lead us to pour every drop of emotional energy into work.

Authority

As we mentioned earlier, another issue that has little to do with time is the importance to our personal lives of having authority in our work roles. Authority translates into autonomy—discretion in choosing what work to do, how to do it, and even where and when to do it. Having decision-making authority enhances personal growth because it can make it easier for us to arrange our work life to allow for the pursuit of personal life interests beyond work. It also fits in with where the world of work is headed—careers and the design of work increasingly in the hands of the individual, with self-management the norm. This need for authority and control plays an important part in our recommendations in the final chapter.

Future career prospects

Beyond authority on the job, several other work factors affect our levels of satisfaction, particularly with personal growth. These factors are connected to the sense we may have of future career prospects. For instance, people are more satisfied with their personal growth to the extent that they have had recent developmental assignments at work, which suggests they're being prepared for future career challenges. Similarly, people are more satisfied with their personal growth when they feel they're likely to be promoted within the next two years, and when they feel that achievement of their ultimate aspirations for advancement is likely.

Yet another work factor beyond time is the commitment we feel toward our work organizations. For instance, employees (both men and women) feel greater satisfaction with their personal growth when they have a sense of commitment to their employers. And people are more committed employees to the extent that they perceive their employer as supportive of family and other non-work pursuits.

When it comes to our careers, a positive orientation toward the future is associated with feeling good about personal growth and development, and that positive outlook reduces the psychological pressures of work. Hope for a bright future is a matter more of psychology than of time. Along with authority and psychological involvement, it plays an important role in determining how work affects family life and personal growth.

How Gender Matters

Thus far, in discussing factors other than time, we have not referred to any differences between men and women. But such differences are ever-present, and a powerful determinant in the struggle to make allies of work and family. Where, then, do they come into play in looking at how work and career affect personal life?

A different meaning of work

In our opening chapter, we introduced an idea that is central here: that work itself means something different for women and men. The traditional gender roles society assigns to men and women become part of the complex psychology each of us internalizes, conditioning us to experience work in particular ways and, by doing so, reinforcing these differences. [14]

Several findings support our conclusion. Men are more likely than women to measure their personal growth according to how well they perform in their jobs. Men also highly value that their careers provide a venue for achievement in the world, and help establish their place in society as breadwinners. Our study's men confirm the power of this stereotype: work and career in today's world mean for them providing for family and performing well, above all else. For women, work and career mean first and foremost being able to grow personally while simultaneously caring for others outside of work. [15]

Gender roles are undergoing change—at least somewhat—and the traditional differentiation may also change as choices for men and women expand. We're making progress toward the goal of a more egalitarian society in which the range of choices available to men and women must be more than what we have today. Still, the differences persist.

The social world of work

A key difference is the dissimilar way in which men and women view the social world of work and career—that is, the value they place on the social attachments that derive from work and career, and how they see their personal lives affected by the social value of their careers.

For example, the more men value the social aspects of career, the *less* satisfied they are with their families. It's the opposite for women: the more they value these aspects, the more satisfied they are with their families. And the more women feel accepted at work by others, the more likely they feel satisfied with family.[16]

Men today may have only so much capacity for social relationships, and investing in social relationships at work leaves too little for building relationships at home, and vice versa. Or it may be that men who are relatively dissatisfied with their families fill an emotional void with their social relationships at work. In effect, they compensate for the absence of, or the failure to establish, gratifying family relationships—just as with psychological overinvolvement with career. Both explanations are plausible, but we think the former is more likely. Gender role socialization and cultural conditioning make many men less skilled than women in establishing close social ties.[17]

Men and women get different *resources* from their social networks at work, and they use those networks differently.[18] We believe that networking for women has a greater impact on enhancing self-esteem, generating a feeling of acceptance, and creating a pool of useful information and advice. In turn, those resources help make women more emotionally available and more competent in their family roles.

A man may also find that networking activities contribute positively to his self-identity and to how he sees his role in society. When networking increases a man's sense of his own value in his career, it also enhances his self-esteem, which leads him to feel better about himself in other important social relationships, such as family.[19] So, for a man, success in the networking part of his career serves mostly to raise his self-esteem as breadwinner.

Both women and men advance their careers through networks. But why does the greater value women place on social relationships at work increase their family satisfaction? It may be that women are better able to draw upon connections with others as sources of support in coping with conflicts between work and family. That social support, in turn, reduces conflict and enhances their family lives.[20]

The social value of career may be more accessible to women, because society sanctions this in ways it may not for men. Is it simply more acceptable for women to say that helping others and being respected by others are important to them in assessing the success of their careers, whereas men are less likely to feel comfortable including this as part of their definition of career success? It may be that men in our society are not trained to derive the same kinds of resources from social relationships as women—who in doing so make work an ally of family life.

Women may rely more on the support of others at work to understand—even to accommodate and help meet—the needs they have as working family members who still carry primary responsibility for the social and emotional health of their families. Women can get important resources from their work relationships—information, advice, and understanding—that help them manage the dilemmas they face as mothers. This would certainly explain why the women in our study who most value the social aspects of their careers also feel most satisfied with their families.

Role conflicts

The interweaving between our work and personal lives (beyond the issue of time) is a psychological phenomenon, one with profound impact. Our experiences in our different life roles, both psychological and behavioral, can make allies of work and family—or they may breed enemies. When mental pressures from work interfere at home and with personal life, work can become family's enemy.[21] This impact of work interference, which can cause us to experience conflicts between our roles at home and work, is often quite different for men and women at different ages.

To understand how perceived role conflicts affect us requires drawing an important distinction between real-time allocations to work and personal life and the *psychological* attention we pay to these different roles.[22] With that understanding, we can make sense of several seemingly incongruous observations, particularly about women and their relaxation.

We find that mothers over thirty experience *greater* family satisfaction the more they experience work psychologically interfering with their leisure. The converse, of course, would be that their family satisfaction is lower when psychological interference with their relaxation is lessened. Yet earlier we observed that women in general feel better the more time they take to relax—in other words, when they spend *more* time on themselves. What does this mean?

Without understanding the difference between real-time allocations and psychological attention, these findings would appear to be completely contradictory. Could it be that these mothers, even as they benefit from taking time for themselves, feel better about their families so long as they believe that their own leisure suffers because of their mental preoccupation with work demands?

The "guilt" argument—that women feel more guilty if they spend time on their own leisure, because they feel more responsible than men for the welfare of their families—finds further support among young married women without children. They also experience greater family satisfaction to the degree work interferes psychologically with their relaxation. Conditioned as they are by society to play caregiving roles, it may be that these women feel better about their marriages when they attend not to themselves but to their husbands—who represent the family members to be cared for, a kind of equivalent to the children of the older women.

Clearly, working women—especially mothers—are the most vulnerable to suffering work–family stress.[23] The results for satisfaction with personal growth show a fairly clear difference between how women in their thirties and women in other age groups are affected by role conflicts. Specifically, satisfaction with personal growth for thirty-something women is reduced when work interferes with both family and leisure. It seems these women run the greatest risk of suffering diminished satisfaction with personal growth from psychological conflicts caused by work demands.

Time horizons

Men and women have different time horizons over which they view the interweaving of career and personal life interests. This difference can be illustrated by contrasting several observations. One has to do with what our professionals tell us about taking time off from work following the birth of a child (see Table 4c in Additional Tables). Unlike the more routine, often day-to-day decisions we make about allocating time for work, family, and other interests, taking a big chunk of time off from work for birth may happen only once or twice in a lifetime. It's likely to have a qualitatively different kind of effect on work and personal life outcomes.

One might assume that the more time taken off following the birth of a child, the more satisfied one is with one's family. Women in their thirties[24] are generally more satisfied with their families the more time they took off or planned to take off from work following their first child's birth. This illustrates the traditional view—apparently still relevant—that women, more nurturing and attuned to a broader cycle of time, are willing to make near-term sacrifices for the long-term benefit of their families.

Men in their twenties, however, actually feel *worse* about their families the more time they take off. It may seem like another paradox, but it's consistent with the traditional view that men (especially young men) derive family satisfaction from involvement in pursuing success in their work roles.

The time horizon difference is also made clear by these facts: it's only for men that feeling good about family is affected by satisfaction with their jobs *at the moment*; for women, it's *long-term* satisfaction with career that has a positive effect on family satisfaction. Job satisfaction is relatively short term, whereas one may hold many jobs over the course of a career.

The differences between the sexes also come through when we observe men and women attempting to manage the boundaries between their work and their families. Take, for instance, the case of a man who actively juggles his work schedule to meet day-to-day family demands—one important way of managing the work–family interface. It's not just the family that benefits; that man increases his satisfaction with family in the process. A woman, though, is likely to find that juggling her work schedule has neither a positive nor negative effect on her family satisfaction. Why? Again, it's a matter of time horizons: juggling is a short-term activity, but women—unlike men— have a long-term view. They may do far more juggling than men each day, but what matters most to women in terms of building family satisfaction are the long-term relationships they build with their families and their social networks at work.

Balance and Boundaries

What we discover about time allocations, the effects of various career experiences, and the impact of work interference are consistent with our observations regarding life role priorities and other career and life values. That is, the relative emphasis we give to career, family, self, or society influences how we feel about our personal growth, *but in different ways for men and women*. Perhaps this results from the traditional imbalance between roles taken in society by men and women.

For both sexes, satisfaction with personal growth is enhanced when we value an aspect of life that has been undervalued in traditional gender roles: for men, investment in family; for women, investment both in career and personal development. The increase in personal growth satisfaction here may represent some kind of beneficial balance being struck among different life pursuits. We think people benefit from investing in the parts of themselves that don't often get exercised: men as nurturing parents, women as hard-driving executives. In these roles, men and women express more of their potential, and are thus more satisfied with their personal growth.

The Choices We Face

Look for ways to invest in the good qualities our society says your gender traditionally undervalues—and gain the benefits that come with valuing all aspects of your self.

Balancing our masculine and feminine sides, though, is only one element in making allies of work and the family. Are there other steps we must take? How can we overcome the problem of excess psychological involvement in career? What steps can be taken to lessen the detrimental effects of role conflicts? One thing is that each of us needs to create and maintain psychological boundaries between career and our other life interests.

Our evidence on role conflicts shows that establishing and maintaining boundaries between these two life domains is essential. This means being able to

- protect one role from interference by another
- shift from one frame of mind to another as needed
- act in a way that is appropriate to the role we're in at the time.

Meaningful boundaries help resolve role conflicts and help make us available to those who matter to us in our non-work roles—not only behaviorally, but also psychologically.[25] And establishing those boundaries is one of the prerequisites to success in the changing jobs of the next century.

> **The Choices We Face**
> *An important step in making allies of work and family is to establish and maintain meaningful boundaries between those two life domains.*

The earlier in life we establish healthy boundaries between the different domains of life, the better equipped we will be to confront and conquer the psychological pressures each role puts on the other. The stakes get greater over time: as we get older, the sources of our satisfaction change.[26] The varying demands we face in our different life roles change, and pressures from multiple role demands can increase over the course of our lives—making the management of our boundaries even more important.[27]

Boundaries between and balance among our different life roles are major components of "getting a life." Each of us must choose to establish boundaries. Each of us must also make choices about what we value most, and understand the potential consequences of those choices—for instance, that choosing to value career above all else may mean sacrificing satisfaction with family.

We think there's a reason people whose life role priority puts them in the career + family group seem to have more of a life than do all others. For them, balance means something very specific. It is the same level of commitment to the domains of work and family. This balance seems to make career + family people the most likely to be able to get a life; that is, to feel satisfied with their families *and* their careers.

However, the many differences we observed—between men and women and between people who hold diverse values—suggest that it would be unwise, if even plausible, to prescribe universal fixes to the challenges faced by business professionals seeking to lead integrated lives. Much of the solution is really a matter of individual choice. To increase the quality of our lives beyond work, we must be able to express to people *at* work what is really important to us *outside* of work. We need to build the skills and secure the resources that will enable us to achieve our life goals. One of those resources is the support we can secure from the people in our social networks at work—a resource women are more adept at using to benefit their families than are men. Like members of our families, people in our social networks can help us clarify our boundaries and help keep us on track as we seek to align our actions with values; and in turn, help make work the ally of personal life.

Establishing limits and striking a balance are especially critical as information-based work fast becomes the norm. The physical boundaries that once separated work and personal life have come under tremendous pressure. In fact, they are rapidly disappearing. Whereas once the natural order (the physical world) compelled people to work at some times and not others, in today's wired world many of us find we can work around the clock, given the chance. In the future it will fall to individuals to create and manage appropriate boundaries between work and personal life so that there can be effective functioning in both domains.

To sum up, how we spend our time matters, but not as much as the psychological relationship between and among different life roles. We find that the mental struggle each of us goes through to interweave our different life roles matters far more than how time is spent. If we can in some way master that mental challenge, we are on the path to success. All sorts of career factors and experiences—authority at work, commitment to our employer, and bright future prospects, to name a few—are assets that can help create allies of work and the family.

For employers, our findings imply that helping business professionals get a life will require more than creating time for employees to spend on their life roles outside of work. Instead, the people in our study show us that employers need to see that enriched personal lives result from satisfying jobs and careers in which people are able to retain a sense of balance, and maintain appropriate boundaries between work and family.

Boundaries built on a foundation of clearly understood values help. Once established, those boundaries help provide a sense of coherence and integrity in our lives, giving us the strength to challenge the limits set by persistent gender role stereotypes both at home and at work. They help make it possible for us to overcome the conflict between our varying life roles and enjoy greater satisfaction in the different domains. They help us get a life.

As one participant in our study told us, "Better balance helps me make good decisions." It also leads to a greater likelihood that work and family will be strong allies.

5

Children: Unseen Stakeholders at Work

Researchers have historically paid considerable attention to the impact employment—the simple fact of working outside the home—has on mothers and their children.[1] Relatively few studies, however, have focused directly on how the *quality* of a parent's work life influences both the capacity to care for children and the health and development of their children.[2] Many parents today are breaking new ground by arranging their life roles in original ways—such as the dual-earner couple, both of whom work outside the home. Of course, we won't know the long-term consequences of variations in work arrangements until this generation of children grows up. We can, however, assess the impact of career and work experiences on the care that children receive and their current health and development, and use what we learn to help guide both personal action and corporate and social policy.

Few parents involve their children directly in decisions about either the design of their work or about their careers. Nonetheless, children are *stakeholders* at work—that is, parents' decisions have a significant effect on their kids' health and welfare.

How do the work experiences of our business professionals affect the care of their children? What impact does time spent at work have on a parent's capacity to care well for children? How do these issues play out differently for fathers and mothers? In what ways is work either an ally or enemy to children's health, behavior, and performance in school? These are the questions we address in this chapter.

For this examination of the effects of work and career on children, we use indicators in two categories. In the first, we look at how parents evaluate their own performance in the parental role and how satisfied they are with arrangements they have made for childcare.[3] In the second, we explore how children fare when it comes to their health in general, their behavior problems, and their performance at school.[4]

Not surprisingly, we find that children benefit when mom and dad view being a parent as important. Conversely, they suffer when their parents value career over family responsibilities. And children of career-focused parents are more likely to experience behavior problems, and do less well in school, than are those whose parents are focused on family.

One surprising result of our study is that parental performance by our business professionals suffers among those who earn the most. With all the tangible benefits money can buy for children, earning a high income still does not overcome a serious problem kids face: when their parents (especially their fathers) are so psychologically involved in work that they cannot attend well to the demands of being a parent. Behavior problems in particular are prevalent when dad's psychological involvement in his career depletes his availability to the kids—although when mom is psychologically involved in her career, the self-esteem she accrues benefits the children.

Parents reading this chapter may find some of our observations disconcerting. We are looking at the effects of parental values, life and career choices, and work experiences on our children, and some will surely recognize the negative effects we uncover in their own families. However, we also show ways in which work is an ally of the family and how the resources work provides can help parents and children. We will later address what we believe can be done by individuals, employers, and policymakers to make things better for all concerned.

We gauge here how our business professionals are affected as parents by work and career, as well as the effects on their children. We then use that information to draw some conclusions for working parents beyond our study. To begin, we present a model for understanding how work affects our performance in the parental caregiver role.

A Model for Understanding Work's Effects on Children

How do work and career affect us as parents? Several things matter: our work and career experiences, the allocations of time and attention we make to different life roles, our personal values, and our family structure. How? We believe these factors influence our self-esteem, our psychological and behavioral availability to our kids, and the resources we can use and obtain—all of which contribute to the provision of support to our children. Figure 5.1 illustrates our model, which is closely linked to the overall model we introduced in Chapter 1 (and which we detail in Chapter 8) for capturing and explaining the complex relationships between work and family lives.

Let's look more closely at how each of these elements in the middle of Figure 5.1 contributes to our effectiveness as parents, and our children's welfare.

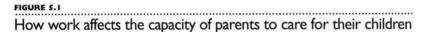

FIGURE 5.1

How work affects the capacity of parents to care for their children

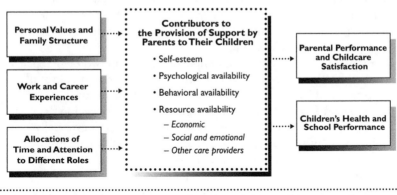

NOTE: The center box is dotted to indicate that the "contributors" are studied theoretically, but not empirically, in our research; that is, we do not have direct measures of some of these concepts.

Our self-esteem

For each of us, how we take up parenting tasks is affected by the answer we give to this question: What kind of person am I? Many elements comprise our concept of self—our self-identity—and our experiences at work and in our career certainly have an effect. These experiences can enhance or detract from whether we perceive ourselves as effective people and as useful members of the community and society as a whole—in other words, how we feel about ourselves. And it certainly makes sense that the better we feel about ourselves, the more likely we are able to care for others, children in particular.

Our availability

As parents, we need to be there when our children need us. If we're not available, we can't give them the care and attention they require. Availability, though, means more than being physically present. We must also be *psychologically* available to our children, so that we can focus our attention on them without distraction from other concerns—such as those that originate at work.

The stakes are high when it comes to psychological availability, and children are adept at figuring out whether mom and dad are paying attention.[5] As one researcher has made so clear: "So long as a child is in the unchallenged presence of a principal attachment-figure, or within easy reach, he feels secure. A threat of loss creates anxiety, and actual loss sorrow; both, moreover, are likely to arouse anger."[6]

How does this play out for our kids? Take the example of a parent who is physically present with his or her daughter but busy thinking about problems that need solving at work. That child is likely to feel a challenge to her presence. The perceived challenge translates into negative consequences for her sense of security, and in turn for her developing self-esteem.

Business professionals may face a considerable challenge when it comes to maintaining psychological focus on their children. The work of these men and women professionals is often unconstrained by physical location. Even when business professionals don't bring something tangible home in their briefcases, they often find themselves solving work problems in their minds while in the midst of their families.

Everyone finds it difficult, if not impossible, to be in two mental places at the same time. The home role and the work role each require our full attention at times, and we are called upon to do some difficult psychological juggling between the two. It is critical that working parents develop the "mental agility and versatility" to switch adeptly between roles.[7] It is especially important for those of us with work tasks that can be readily taken up just by thinking about them. In Chapter 9 we address some practical steps to manage boundaries and thus make psychological juggling easier.

In addition to being psychologically availabile, parents also have to be physically (or behaviorally) available to their children. That means not only being there to help out with homework in the evening, for example, but also to ensure that our children get to school, to the doctor, and to others to whom we entrust their well-being—even if only temporarily. Parental availability of that sort is influenced in part by the total number of hours our work requires and by how much discretion we have to arrange our work schedules.

Economic and social resources

Work and career also provide resources for our family lives. For parents, work provides resources that can make us more effective as caregivers for our children. The most obvious is economic—our income—but there are also social resources.

We discussed earlier how men and women use the social and emotional support that comes from people we meet in our work roles. These social networks can serve to enhance self-esteem. In turn, those resources help make parents more emotionally available to their families—an obvious boon for children. Enhanced self-esteem leads people to feel better about themselves in other important social relationships, such as family. Again, the kids at home benefit. We are better able to care for others when we feel good about ourselves.

Social networks at work can also provide a pool of useful information and advice that can bolster parental effectiveness, even if only by helping us realize that our child-rearing challenges are not unique. With the fabric of community looser today than in decades past, the supportive relationships we develop at work often substitute for what people once got from their neighborhoods or communities. The information other parents at work provide help keep us better informed about how to care for our children and where to find childcare resources, pediatricians, and so on.[8]

Now that we have presented our conceptual model of how our work affects our children, let's take a closer look at the impact of what is on the left-hand side of Figure 5.1 on the outcomes on the right-hand side. We'll use what we've asserted about the middle box to inform our discussion. What are the specific effects of our psychological and behavioral availability? How in particular do the economic and social resources we get from our careers affect our children? What is the impact on our kids when our self-esteem is either high or low? And what are the differences in all this between mothers and fathers?

What Affects Parenting and Child Outcomes?

At a June 1996 conference on family and work convened by Vice President Al Gore, President Bill Clinton recounted what he told his staff at the outset of his administration: If the work of the White House becomes too demanding to the point that it begins to harm your family relationships, he told staff members, you should quit. He even gave two examples of people following his advice.

Like other high-powered executives who jump off the fast track, in both cases these Clinton staffers essentially traded success in one role (work) to prevent failure in another (parent).[9] But are such trades necessary? Isn't it possible to be successful in both domains? Some aspects of work and its relation to family life make us feel as though we're performing better as parents and enhancing the lives of children. Other aspects, however, have harmful consequences for parents and their children.

Before we look at those outcomes, let's review some of our earlier observations about the impact of being a parent. Not surprisingly, among our business professionals,

- parents are more focused on their family lives, fitting their work around their families to a greater extent than do people without children[10]
- family life interferes with work for parents more than for nonparents[11]
- parents spend less time on their own relaxation

In general, having children means we have less time for ourselves. Parents also have a greater need for their work and career to accommodate family demands. Being a parent, however, affects men's careers and women's careers in different ways.

- Fathers are *more* satisfied with their careers than are men without children.
- Mothers are *less* satisfied with their careers than are women without children.
- Fathers are more committed to their organizations than are men without children.
- Mothers are less psychologically involved in their careers than are women without children.

- Fathers have reached a higher level on the corporate ladder in their organizations than have men without children.
- Mothers place more value on having a career that affords more personal time and less value on acquiring wealth than do women without children.
- Fathers have more authority in their jobs than do men without children.
- Mothers spend less time on work and more time on household responsibilities than do women without children.

Mothers also relocate less frequently for their careers than do women without children, and are more likely to work in a small company. To sum up the essence of the "bonus and penalty" hypothesis, motherhood is a career liability, while fatherhood is a career asset. Having looked at how being a parent affects work, let's turn around and consider how work and career affect parents and children, and uncover some ways in which parents' careers provide bonuses and penalties for their kids.

Our values and priorities

Parental performance and childcare. Among our business professionals, fathers and mothers are more likely to see themselves as performing well as parents the more they value family.[12] Similarly, placing high value on family translates into greater satisfaction with childcare arrangements.[13] The meaning is clear: the more our core values are bound to family, the more likely we are to think we do a relatively good job as a parent and in providing care for our children when we delegate that task to others. Let's explore this connection further.

Some parents might say, "I must be good at being a parent because being a parent is important to me." A statement like that is more than some sort of self-justifying rationalization; it is another way to understand the relationship between values and the behavior they motivate. The underlying statement might be: "Because my role as a parent is important to me I try hard to be good at it." And this applies to both fathers and mothers.

The Choices We Face

If you value being a parent, you are more likely to feel that you're good at being a parent.

But the effect of career values on perceptions about childcare cuts differently for women and men. Take, for instance, the career values of aspiring to hierarchical advancement and wealth. Mothers who want money and power from their careers see themselves as providing relatively more resources to their children; these mothers perceive that their children receive relatively higher-quality care than do mothers who have lower career aspirations and who care less about wealth.

Yet it is the opposite for fathers: the less a father aspires to hierarchical advancement, the better he feels about his performance as a parent. And the lower the value a father places on wealth, the better he feels about the care his children receive.

Our explanation has to do with the different impact career has on each gender's sense of identity. We believe that relatively high career aspirations result in high levels of self-esteem for a mother, and high esteem in turn enhances a mother's capacity both to care effectively for her children and to arrange for effective childcare from others. When it comes to fathers, the benefit to children comes from dad having relatively low career aspirations, which then produces greater availability—both psychological and behavioral—for his children. This, in turn, makes him a more effective parent.

Child outcomes. Parental values also affect the health and development of children.[14] For instance, all three of the child outcomes we looked at— health in general, behavior problems, and school performance—are enhanced in children whose mothers or fathers say that family is very important in how they judge the success of their lives. School performance is relatively good among children whose parents place higher value on these attributes of a career: flexibility, time for self, and time for family. And children's general health is higher if their parents place relatively high value on the *intrinsic* rewards of work: challenge, creativity, and enjoyment.

We find a striking difference in the children of parents who fall into two particular life role priority groups. The contrast says a lot about the effect of work on kids: children of career-focused parents are more likely to experience behavior problems than are those whose parents are in the family-focused group. These same children are also likely to be doing less well in school.

Behavior problems are indicators of a child's emotional or mental health. In explaining our model presented in Figure 5.1, we suggested that the higher a parent's self-esteem, the more the availability, and the greater the resources, the better the outcomes for children. In other words, children are less likely to have emotional problems when, for instance, their parents are more psychologically available. When career concerns invade the psychological space parents must reserve for their children, their children's emotional health is likely to suffer.

Why this happens is complex and perhaps surprising. Children's emotional health does not result directly from how much time their parents spend at work.[15] However, differences in the degree to which work interferes with family do help explain our findings. It seems that career-focused parents have children with relatively more behavior problems precisely because they experience more of such interference, or role conflict, than the other life role priority types (especially those classified as family-focused).

There are several explanations for this phenomenon. Because their work interferes more with their family life, career-focused parents may be less able to attend to their children's emotional needs—and so these kids develop behavior problems. It may also be that the more work interferes with family, the more likely a career-focused mom or dad feels emotional strain—which may reduce self-esteem and the availability to care for children's emotional needs. For career-focused fathers specifically, another possible reason is the high level of psychological involvement in careers, which implies less psychological involvement in and availability to meet the needs of a child, and hence greater behavior problems.

A parent's life role priority affects a child's performance at school in much the same way as behavior problems. The family-focused parents among our business professionals say that their children are doing better in school than the children of career-focused parents. The reason: family-focused parents are more involved in their kids' lives.

Taken together, it is clear that our values affect how well we believe we function as parents, how satisfied we are with the care our children receive, and how well our children develop. Again, we think this happens because of how our values and priorities contribute—either positively or negatively—to our sense of identity, self-esteem, and availability to meet and satisfy the needs and interests of our children.

Our work and career experiences

As our model shows, values and priorities about career and family are not all that matters in determining how we feel about our parenting and how our children are doing in terms of their health and development. Certain aspects of our experiences at work also make a difference. Some make perfect sense; others may be surprising at first, until we take a closer look at the various elements on the left side of Figure 5.1.

Parental performance. Those among our business professionals who see themselves performing well as parents share several characteristics of their careers and work experiences:[16]

- good job performance
- a high level of job satisfaction
- an employer that is supportive of family needs
- self-employment or working in a family business
- a relatively *low* annual income

Let's look first at the bottom of the list above: income. Judging from our business professionals, it turns out that perceptions about parental performance suffer among those who earn the most. We are surprised to find that high income produces perceptions of poor parental performance. After all, we've already noted that those of our business professionals with very high incomes are perfectly happy when it comes to childcare.[17] And those whose incomes appear to be higher than those of their peers' also feel relatively satisfied about childcare. So, in terms of creating a sense of satisfaction with childcare arrangements, an abundance of economic resources is clearly beneficial for both mothers and fathers. Perhaps money does allow us to buy good childcare, even if we can't purchase good feelings about our parental performance.

Why, then, does high income produce perceptions of poor parental performance? Could it be that people who earn very high incomes know deep down that they are neglecting their responsibilities as parents in favor of their work obligations, in essence making a trade of family for career? With their feet held to the fire, perhaps these parents might say something along these lines: "How else could I earn all that money if I didn't have to make some sacrifices at home, like working too many hours or being too involved in my work?"

Indeed, high income in and of itself does not result in poor parental performance. What is really operating here is that intense psychological involvement in career leads to the perception of lower parental performance by people with very high incomes.[18]

There is an important message here. Sure, a greater economic resource comes with a parent's higher income. And that parent may gain some self-esteem from that high income. However, whatever benefits children may realize from that money seem to be swamped by the lower psychological and behavioral availability of mom or dad.

Unlike high income, a satisfying job and a supportive work environment improve perceptions of parental performance. Doing a good job and being satisfied with work both contribute to feeling that we perform well as parents. So do working in one's own business or working for an employer that is supportive of family needs. In fact, other studies show that there are an array of benefits associated with family-supportive work environments, both for employees and employers.[19] In Chapter 7, we focus on the specific impacts of an employer's family-responsiveness.

Doing well at work and feeling good about our jobs contribute to high levels of self-esteem. We feel more competent, and we build confidence that enhances our capacity to meet the demands of our parental role. And when we succeed in fulfilling our work responsibilities, it leads us to feel good about being of use to our families, not to mention our communities and society. Further, being in a work environment that supports family needs—and, in the case of self-employment, allows for high levels of autonomy—contributes to our sense that we have the support of others and the requisite flexibility to be good parents.

The Choices We Face

Add children to the equation when choosing a career and selecting among job opportunities. The self-esteem that comes from a satisfying career and a job well done benefits our children.

In other words, parents with these employment conditions benefit from their access to social and emotional support. They can be available for their children. What we see here is that the quality of work affects the experience of parenting. Satisfying jobs performed well in supportive work environments help parents—mothers and fathers alike—feel that they are doing well as parents.

Childcare. Career and work experiences also affect how parents assess the care their children receive.[20] For fathers, the work factor that matters has a negative effect: whether they have recently taken developmental assignments. The more developmental assignments taken, the worse fathers feel about childcare. Why? Perhaps it's the difficulty in arranging for childcare when one has to travel—often a feature of these assignments.

For the moms, it is quite different. Several characteristics of work help mothers feel better about their childcare arrangements: when they have more authority and control in their work roles, when they feel accepted by others at work, when they have undertaken network-building activities, and when they are committed to their employer organizations.

Discretion, social attachments acquired through networking, and support from others at work provide critical resources mothers need to create and maintain adequate childcare systems. Authority at work provides discretion in how, when, and where work gets done, which helps create the flexibility mothers need to facilitate the timing and staffing of childcare by someone other than themselves. Connections to others—through feeling accepted, networking, and having a sense of commitment to one's organization—are assets for mothers in their efforts to structure their work lives while meeting critical family demands.

People at work can provide different types of support that are useful in managing childcare arrangements. For example, other parents with childcare experiences may offer needed advice or even specific ideas about where to find good providers. And when problems arise with childcare, having someone to talk with about frustrations and concerns might help a parent feel better about a difficult situation.

Child outcomes. We also learn from our business professionals that certain aspects of work generate resources that benefit the general health of our children.[21] There are three in particular: earning a high income, having authority in the work role, and achieving a high level in the employer organization.

The economic resource generated by a high income can be used to enhance the quality of a child's physical environment. For instance, this might translate into purchasing high-quality medical care or even hiring someone to dust every day. But it may not be as obvious that other resources from work—such as authority on the job and hierarchical advancement—have a positive effect on our children's physical health.

Authority at work, for instance, gives us discretion in how we as parents spend time and energy on family. This increases the likelihood that we can be behaviorally available to attend to the needs of our children when they are sick or have a doctor's appointment. And when we have authority, and when we have achieved a high level in our organization, we may also feel greater self-esteem. This comes in part from a heightened sense that we control our own destiny. When our children observe us—their adult role models—feeling bad about ourselves, they in turn are less likely to feel good about themselves. And when they feel bad about themselves, they are less likely to take as good care of themselves, including physically.

There are other work factors that affect children's health in different ways, depending on whether it is something mom or dad experiences. For example, children have relatively few health problems when their working mothers are more involved in network-building activities, presumably because these mothers gain some knowledge about how to obtain high-quality healthcare through their networks. And a kid whose dad is better able to restructure his work life to accommodate family needs (such as meeting healthcare needs) has fewer health problems than other kids.

As with general health, some aspects of work improve children's mental health and behavior.[22] In most cases, however, the effect is different for mothers and fathers. Relatively speaking, children have fewer behavior problems if their moms have a high degree of control or authority in their work roles and if their dads are highly satisfied with their jobs and feel they perform their jobs well. Yet again, the gender contrast in the impact of work and career experiences is most apparent when it comes to *psychological involvement* in career. Children have fewer behavior problems if their mothers are psychologically involved in their careers; mom's self-esteem is enhanced, and the children benefit. And children have fewer behavior problems if their dads are not highly involved psychologically in their careers; psychological involvement depletes a dad's psychological availability to his children, which works against the children's interests.

As with satisfaction with childcare, authority or control at work is an important factor for mothers in its effect on children's emotional health. The flexibility that comes with authority allows mothers greater discretion to attend to the emotional needs of their kids. That authority may also help bolster a mother's sense that she is respected and seen as capable, which in turn may make her more effective in providing competent nurturing for her children. Plus, many kids feel good about themselves when they see their mom as someone with authority. Mom becomes a positive role model.

Men, as we've noted, seem to derive different benefits from work when it comes to their self-identities. When it comes to kids' emotional health, there seems to be a benefit when dad has a highly rewarding job at which he feels he is performing well.[23] We think it's because fathers in that situation have higher self-esteem.

Children's school performance is enhanced when either mom or dad achieves a high level of responsibility at work, independent of how much income is earned. Again, we think it has to do with parental self-esteem. When certain aspects of career, such as hierarchical advancement, benefit a parent's self-esteem, children are more likely to see the value of applying their own efforts at school. These kids, in turn, perform better. For mothers, this effect is likely even greater. Furthermore, a strong network in her professional life likely enhances her self-esteem and her capacity to serve as a positive role model. A mother's career network may also provide social and emotional support and information about professional resources in the area of education.

Our time allocations

Continuing with the left-hand side of the model in Figure 5.1, we come to time allocations and how they affect parents and their children. We have argued that how we spend our time doesn't matter as much as the psychological relationships among different life roles. For business professionals, we are convinced that getting a life requires more than finding time to spend on life roles outside of work.

Nevertheless, time does matter—but in ways that might seem surprising. What is most critical is our behavioral availability to our children and how that affects the quality of care our kids receive and their health and welfare.[24] For parents, time is one of the most precious resources. Committing time to the responsibilities of parenthood can be a great dilemma for working mothers and fathers. And some of the choices we make have a greater impact than do others.[25]

Routine time allocations. Let's look first at the more routine (or weekly) allocations of time and their effect on how well our business professionals are doing as parents and on the health and development of their children. Much to our surprise, hours devoted both to work and to children do not influence how mothers and fathers feel about their performance as parents.[26] This runs counter to the widespread belief that people spend too much time on work, with negative consequences for their kids.

In addition, time spent at work and on children has no effect on how the people in our sample feel about childcare arrangements, nor do they determine whether kids are healthy or how they do in school. Even when we totaled up the time spent by mom *and* dad, the effect on their children was not significant.[27]

When it comes to routine time allocations, what mom spends on relaxation is the most important. The more time mothers take for their own relaxation, the better they feel about themselves as parents, the better they feel about their childcare arrangements, and the fewer their children's behavior problems. Relaxation results in rejuvenation, and time for self helps build self-esteem. With that comes an enhanced capacity—both psychologically and behaviorally—to attend to kids' needs.

The Choices We Make

To be better parents, moms need to make the choice to take time for themselves, and they need the support of their spouses, their employers, and society as a whole to do so.

Time after childbirth. As for nonroutine time allocations, more than a week off work after childbirth or adoption seems to make a big difference, again especially for mothers. Mothers who take more time perceive themselves as better parents (as do fathers, though the impact for mothers is much greater). For postpartum mothers, this time commitment to a newborn baby increases availability and self-esteem.

For both men and women, the end of the first week after childbirth or adoption seems to be a critical juncture. Among our business professionals there is a significant jump in parental performance ratings from those who took a week or less compared to those who took more than a week. Why is a *week* so important? Could it be that there is some biological imperative that newborns need direct and constant attention of a parent in that period immediately following birth?

The issue of returning to work part- versus full-time after childbirth or adoption is quite different from the amount of time taken off. The reason is related to something we've said repeatedly: men and women are taught to have different expectations and assumptions about gender roles. Not surprisingly, then, mothers and fathers feel differently about parental performance depending on whether they return to work full-time or part-time. The effect for mothers of returning to work part-time is the same as when taking time off after childbirth: they feel they are performing better as parents.

Fathers who return part-time, however, report extremely low performance as parents.[28] Among our business professionals, not one father who returned to work part-time said he was performing well as a parent. We believe these fathers feel they are not adequately fulfilling their paternal obligation to work full-time—something they see their peers doing. In other words, these fathers may have been at a low point in self-esteem because they weren't meeting traditional expectations as the breadwinner.[29]

When it comes to satisfaction with childcare, gender differences emerge depending on how much time is taken off. As with parental performance, the more time men take off the worse their perception of childcare quality. For women, on the other hand, the more time off, the better their feelings about childcare.[30]

Our attention to work and to our families

We have already explored a host of issues beyond time at work that influence our children. We've seen how our life role priority, the psychological involvement in careers often associated with high incomes, and the amount of control and discretion we may have at work can influence the care and health of our children. We've also seen how behavioral availability—how much time we devote to children and to work—has no direct impact on a surprisingly large range of outcomes for kids.

What also matters is the degree of attention we pay to our different life roles and the *role conflicts* we experience. How do role conflicts between work and family affect our performance as parents? How do they affect our psychological availability to our kids? What do these conflicts mean for our children's care, and for their mental health?

The relationship is quite clear: the more work, family, and relaxation interfere with each other, the less effective our business professionals see themselves as parents.[31] For mothers and fathers, parental performance is lower the more they think work interferes with family and with relaxation.

Our conflicts between life roles do not, however, affect our children's general health or school performance. But kids are more likely to have behavioral problems if their parents' work interferes with family life, if their parents' (especially their fathers') work interferes with relaxation, or their parents' work behaviors spill over into their family life. Our conflicts between work and other life roles—which are as much a matter of psychology as anything else—affect our kids' behavior. And, clearly, a child's mental state is affected by the mental state of his or her parents.

The Choices We Face

Find ways to minimize your role conflicts and your kids are less likely to have behavioral problems.

The psychological intertwining of work, family, and relaxation poses a substantial dilemma for parents. Managing the psychological boundaries between different life roles is important because of the effects the interplay among life roles has on the unseen stakeholders at work—the next generation, our children. Rapid advances in telecommunications technology are reducing the physical boundaries between work and personal life, which make finding ways to manage boundaries among roles all the more imperative. In Chapter 9 we'll get to some suggestions for about how to do this—not only on an individual and family level, but also for employers and the broader society.

Summing Up

"Parenting is an emotional experience."[32] So, too, is work. This helps explain why the amount of time we spend at work and with our kids doesn't matter as much as we would have expected. Instead, what creates the negative feelings we may have about the care our children receive and about our kids' health and development are the effects of both psychological and behavioral interference between work and family life.[33]

The gender differences in these effects make clear that mothers and fathers live in two different worlds. Yes, there has been some progress toward egalitarianism in the social, cultural, and political milieu surrounding contemporary gender roles.[34] But numerous differences remain for mothers and fathers in the effects that their personal values, choices about careers, and work lives have on children. Those effects are consistent with a traditional view of the relationship between being a parent and career experiences: fathers gain greater career satisfaction and achievement, while mothers limit their investments in career and work.

Parents' work and career do provide benefits for children, though in different ways for mothers and fathers. Similarly, numerous aspects of how work is organized facilitate the tasks of parenting in different ways for men and women. Working mothers' networks provide social, emotional, and instrumental support in the care of children, while men's flexibility in work arrangements allows them to care for their children as needs arise on a day-to-day basis. If mothers are highly involved in their careers, and if they have a great deal of control at work, their children are psychologically better off. Children have fewer behavior problems if their fathers perform well and are satisfied with their jobs. But if fathers are too involved in their careers, their kids' behavior suffers.

Children are the unseen stakeholders in the workplace, and that has an important implication. Corporate responsibility to kids and parents must go beyond providing childcare facilities and benefits, as important as these are. Yet childcare may do no more than make it possible for parents to have the *time* to be at work. Parents need work designed so that they can also be psychologically available to their children. They need work experiences that build self-esteem. And they need the resources, both economic and social, that good careers and enriching jobs can provide.

Let's now take a close look at the dynamics of relationships between spouses and partners, and the effects these relationships have on both work and personal life outcomes.

6

Support from Our Partner

For many men and women, juggling work and family responsibilities is a substantial source of stress. Fortunately, few of us have to face work–family stress alone. Or, perhaps we should say that the *fortunate* among us do not have to face work–family stress alone. People can—and do—benefit from *social support* provided by other individuals and by institutions.[1]

By social support, we mean some sort of exchange of resources between individuals that is intended to help the person receiving the support.[2] These resources take a variety of forms, including information, direct help with daily chores, understanding, and even praise. Support also comes from several different sources. Our family, our local community, and our employer can all provide resources that help us cope with the pressures of integrating our work and family lives. In this chapter we focus on the support people receive from their family, specifically from their spouse or partner.[3] In the next chapter we explore the kind of support employers can provide.

We have discussed the importance of being available to our children not only behaviorally—that is, by spending time with them—but also psychologically, by being attuned to their emotional and physical needs. The support partners provide each other breaks down into similar categories (see Figure 6.1). Behavioral support includes help with household activities such as cleaning, cooking, household repair, car maintenance, and yard work, as well as help with the children such as playing, feeding, carpooling, and the like.[4] Such support serves as a resource to partners by freeing up time that would otherwise be devoted to home and family. We can then devote that time to other parts of our lives, such as our careers. Behavioral support is an indirect means of support. In other words, partners are not the direct recipients of the assistance.

The other categories of partner support, where the person receiving the support is directly affected, are emotional types of support. We distinguish between two forms of emotional support: personal support, which provides assistance with our personal and family problems; and career support, which helps us deal with work-related problems.[5] A partner who provides emotional support expresses concern about our welfare, listens to our problems and worries, offers us advice and praise, and respects our accomplishments. Emotional support enables us to feel wanted, loved, and appreciated, and can be a rich source of useful information and counsel.[6]

This chapter answers two central questions. First, *why* do partners provide support? Given the highly touted benefits of support, it's surprising that so little research has explored the conditions under which partners provide support to one another.[7] We identify three such conditions:

- our partners support us when we need their support to achieve important life goals
- our partners give us support when they believe we deserve it
- our partners support us when they care deeply about the family and participate actively in family life—in other words, when they are psychologically involved in family

We explore whether some people are more likely to receive support from their partners than are others, and whether certain partners are more likely to provide support. We find, for instance, that men and women who are very involved psychologically in their careers (and hence may need the most support) actually receive somewhat limited partner support. We explain in more detail below how this affirms our view that the psychological interference of one domain with the other is a greater enemy of work–family integration than is time.

FIGURE 6.1
Our partners provide support in many different ways

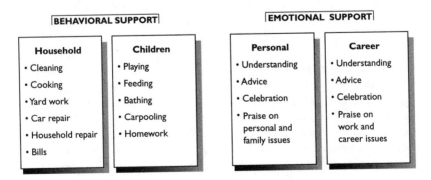

BEHAVIORAL SUPPORT		EMOTIONAL SUPPORT	
Household	**Children**	**Personal**	**Career**
• Cleaning	• Playing	• Understanding	• Understanding
• Cooking	• Feeding	• Advice	• Advice
• Yard work	• Bathing	• Celebration	• Celebration
• Car repair	• Carpooling	• Praise on personal and family issues	• Praise on work and career issues
• Household repair	• Homework		
• Bills			

The second question we examine is: How does partner support help men and women with their work and family responsibilities? We show that partner support can reduce work–family stress and increase the well-being of the partners and their children. In general, help with personal and family issues has a more powerful effect on our lives than behavioral support. That is not to say that behavioral support doesn't help—for instance, our partners' assistance with the children can increase our level of career success along with benefiting the kids.

We also find something surprising here: that the *timing* of support matters a great deal. Support that does not initially prevent the interference of work, family, and leisure on each other may be of little or no use. It may even worsen the situation.

As has been our primary focus in this book, we concentrate on cross-domain effects—here, the effect of partner support at home on work and career. However, we do discuss the effect of a partner's support on family and personal lives, to give a fuller understanding of the overall importance of such support. And we highlight the differences and similarities between men and women when it comes to receiving support and benefiting from support.

When Do Partners Receive Support?

Before we explore the conditions under which partners receive support, let's look at the prevalence of support. When it comes to behavioral support, the partners of our business professionals spend more time with their children (25.5 hours a week on average) than with household activities (16.7 hours per week). This should surprise no one: after all, few would deny that spending time with children is a more important (and more enjoyable!) activity than working around the house.

We also find that partners are more likely to provide a high level of personal support (80 percent) than a high level of career support (32 percent). Partners may need more help with personal and family problems than with career dilemmas, and partners may feel more comfortable seeking and providing empathy, information, advice, and praise on personal and family concerns than for career-related issues.

Impact of gender and family structure

As with most everything we've looked at in this book, there are differences in partner support depending on gender and family structure (see Table 6.1). Men receive more help from their partners with the household and children than women receive from their partners. (Recall that some men among our business professionals have stay-at-home wives; the husbands of all our women work.) More women, however, receive high levels of both personal support and career support from their partners than do men.

These differences are a bit misleading, because family structure plays as large a role as gender in determining how much support people receive from

TABLE 6.1

Gender and family structure affect the support we receive from our partners

▶ **TYPE OF SUPPORT**

	All Men	All Women	Dual-Earner Fathers	Dual-Earner Mothers	Dual-earner Men with No Children	Dual-earner Women with No Children	Single-Earner Fathers
Hours per week partner spends on household	20.2	8.5	19.8[a]	9.2[b]	12.2[b]	7.9[b]	25.8[c]
Hours per week partner spends with children	28.4	16.5	23.7[a]	20.0[a]	--	--	36.4[b]
Percent receiving extensive personal support	78.1	86.3	76.1[a,c]	81.3[a,b,c]	90.6[a,b]	90.0[b]	73.8[c]
Percent receiving extensive career support	32.1	40.0	32.3[a,c]	30.4[a,b,c]	39.6[a,b,c]	47.2[b]	26.7[c]

NOTE. All differences between men and women are statistically significant. Regarding the effects of family structure, groups in the same row with any of the same letters in superscript are not significantly different from each other.

their partners. For example, there is hardly any difference in the amount of household help received by dual-earner men and dual-earner women who don't have children. It is when children enter the picture that we see a difference: women providing more help with the household than men. Of course, this is consistent with our findings that dual-earner mothers substantially reduce the number of hours they spend at work so they can spend more time on home and family responsibilities.[8]

Single-earner fathers receive the most behavioral support from their partners. Why do these fathers receive more assistance with the household and children than any other group? The most obvious reason—that their full-time housewife partners have more time to spend on home and family activities—is only part of the story. There is also a psychological consideration: since these wives are more psychologically involved in their families than the partners of dual-earner men and women, they are probably more inclined to spend extra time on home and family chores.[9] These wives may even believe they are obligated to spend more time and provide greater partner support because of a quid quo pro with their husbands, who earn more money than do husbands whose wives also work.

On the emotional side, however, single-earner fathers do not fare so well. This is especially true with respect to career-related support, and there are a few possible explanations. Perhaps the wives don't feel these men require a great deal of career support; after all, single-earner fathers (as a group) are already quite successful at work. Or, it could be that because these wives are not part of the workforce, their husbands don't feel they have much to offer them in the way of career-related support. It could also be that these women feel ill-equipped to provide such support if requested. Another possible explanation is that there is a greater differentiation of roles in these single-earner families, and consequently there is more segmentation between work and family.

Independent of gender and family structure, we receive support from our partners under three primary conditions:

- when we *need* their support to achieve important goals and values in life
- when we *deserve* their support
- when they are *psychologically involved in family life*

Let's examine each of these conditions in more detail.

When we need support

There are many reasons we need the support of our partners, as Figure 6.2 shows. For instance, people who work long hours need help with the kids and around the house, as well as support that can help them deal with issues at work. Often, we provide support to our partners because we believe they

FIGURE 6.2

When do we need support?

When the Individual	The Partner Provides a Great Deal of
Works long hours ·············▶	• Help with household • Help with children • Career support • Personal support *(only for women)*

AND

When the Individual Values	The Partner Provides a Great Deal of
• Challenge in career ·················▶	• Career support
• Personal growth ···················▶	• Personal support
• Wealth ·······························▶	• Career support • Personal support
• Status in career ··················▶	• Career support
• Social relationships in career ·······▶	• Personal support
• Security in career·················▶	• Personal support *(only for men)*
• Time for self in career·············▶	• Personal support *(only for men)*

BUT

When the Individual	The Partner Provides Only Limited
Is psychologically ·············▶ involved in career	• Help with children • Personal support

need that support to satisfy their personal values and improve the family's well-being.

Our values determine the different types of partner support we receive, particularly when it comes to the emotional types of support. For instance, people who value personal growth, wealth, and status receive such support from their partners. Undoubtedly, the understanding, praise, and advice that make up this support can help build these individuals' self-confidence to pursue new challenges. This, in turn, helps them achieve success and recognition at work.[10]

It is the same situation for men and women who place a great deal of importance on social relationships. To achieve satisfying social relationships at work, many people receive personal support from their partners in the form of understanding, respect, and information, which helps them deal effectively with the interpersonal relationships they value.

Two things we may look for in a career—achieving security and having time for ourselves—bring personal support to men but not to women. And working long hours brings personal support for women but not for men. Why? Remember that by personal support we mean assistance with personal and family problems, not career problems. We think that people whose behaviors or values differ from traditional gender role norms may require additional understanding, reassurance, and encouragement from their partners. Among such people may be men who value security and free time in their careers (values which may be considered traditionally feminine) and women who work long hours (a traditionally masculine behavior).[11] Going against the grain, then, may require some additional help—a need partners recognize and then fulfill.

In short, men and women provide support to their partners when they believe their partners can benefit from the support. One partner is most likely to provide behavioral support when the other partner works long hours and thus needs help with household and children. One partner provides emotional support to help the other partner align his or her actions with important career and life values—wealth, status, personal growth, and social relationships.

There is, however, something curious in what we find: men and women who are very involved psychologically in their careers actually receive somewhat *limited* personal support and help with children. Why? Perhaps the same people who are quite willing to provide a great deal of support to hardworking partners tend to withhold support from partners who are too psychologically absorbed in their work. Put more bluntly, they'll put up with long work hours, and even support that, but preoccupation with work is another matter. This affirms our earlier observation that when it comes to work and family being allies or enemies, the problem is not time so much as the psychological interference of one domain with the other.[12]

How do people decide whether their partners require a lot of support? There are two possible answers. Perhaps the more obvious one is that indi-

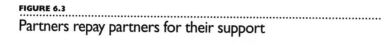

FIGURE 6.3

Partners repay partners for their support

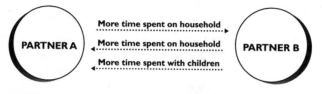

NOTE: The diagram above indicates that the more time Partner A spends on household chores, the more time Partner B spends on the household and the children.

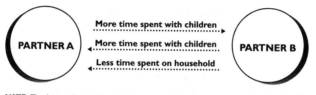

NOTE: The diagram above indicates that the more time Partner A spends with the children, the more time Partner B spends with the children but the less time Partner B spends on the household.

viduals are very direct and quite active in communicating the need for partner support. People who work long hours, for example, may explicitly seek relief from childcare responsibilities or may request information or advice on personal or family problems.

But it is also likely that we are highly sensitive to our partners' needs. We understand each other's values and how satisfying those values contributes to happiness and family well-being. In such situations, partners do not have to request support explicitly; after all, given this loving relationship, which is a relationship unlike any other, it should come as no surprise that our partner may have already anticipated our need for support and be willing to provide it. In any respect, those who require partner support—because they work hard and hold certain values—tend to get it.

When we deserve *support*

What makes us think our partner deserves our support? Most of us want to help those who've helped us, like the old adage that "no good deed goes unrewarded." So, a powerful principle governing the exchange of support is that of equity or reciprocity (see Figure 6.3).[13]

Men and women who provide behavioral support to their partners find that they receive behavioral support in return. The more help we provide our partner with household chores, for instance, the more household assistance we receive from our partner. When we chip in with the housework, our partner is willing (or feels obliged) to take on a share of the household chores too. We respond to our partner's household support by spending more time with our children as well. Could it be that one good deed deserves *two* in return?

The Choices We Face

Choose to help your partner out with the kids or around the house, and he or she will likely return the favor.

Another exchange of support not only illustrates reciprocity, but probably also reflects partners' shared values. That is, the more time one partner spends with the children, the more time the other partner spends with the children. And, the more time one partner spends with the children, the *less* time the other partner spends on household activities. People are likely to be attracted to partners who have the same sense of commitment about children, with the result that one partner matches or approximates the time the other makes available to the children. It seems that families in which both partners spend a great deal of time with the children have set priorities such that the children take precedence over household chores.

Men and women who are psychologically involved in their families and who attach great importance to family relationships also get personal support in return from their partners. Again, this illustrates the principle of reciprocity.[14] Perhaps we say: "If my partner cares strongly about the family, the least I can do is provide my partner with understanding, encouragement, praise, and advice." And men who go against traditional gender role expectations by having a high level of psychological involvement in family are also rewarded with behavioral support: their partners are likely to spend more time on household activities.

When our partners are involved in family life

Why are family-involved partners so supportive? The high value they place on their families, we believe, motivates them to help their partners and their children lead rich, satisfying lives. Indeed, for family-involved people, providing support to other family members may be a crucial part of their self-identity, defining who they are and who they want to be.[15] Men and women who are highly involved in their families may just be very comfortable in interpersonal situations, finding it easier than most—and even enjoyable—to provide behavioral help and to express their emotional support openly to their partners. This may even come from a sort of predisposition to family life.

Readers at this point may be asking: Does this support we see among family-involved partners suggest that career-oriented partners are *unlikely* to provide support? Or can career involvement create resources that enable partners to provide support? The answers depend in part on the type of support. They also depend on gender.

Let's look first at behavioral support. Both men and women who are psychologically involved in their careers do *not* provide much behavioral support to their partners. They are probably so absorbed and preoccupied with their own careers that they are less available to pay attention to home and family activities. Moreover, men who spend a great deal of time at work are not heavily involved in home and family activities. Women who work long hours, however, do not restrict their involvement with household chores or child-care. In other words, men end up allowing work to intrude into family responsibilities, while women do not.[16]

Does involvement in work limit our willingness to provide personal and career support to our partner? Both men and women who work long hours provide their partners with high levels of personal support, perhaps because they feel guilty about being absent from the home. They may allay their guilt by helping their partners with personal and family problems. Men who work long hours are also likely to provide their partners with a great deal of career support. We think that heavy time commitment to work gives these men expertise on work-related matters their partners seek out.

Women who are psychologically involved in their careers provide their partners with a great deal of emotional support, both personal and career. Although they may not be inclined to do much around the house or have time for this, these women do provide their partners with encouragement and advice in their attempts to solve personal, family, and work-related problems.

These women may feel more competent to provide this kind of support because of their empathy or expertise accrued as a result of their career involvement. Empathy and expertise serve as resources by making these women feel competent to provide both personal and career support—and in this respect work becomes the ally of family. It is directly analogous to what we discussed in the previous chapter about how a parent's work experiences can create resources that positively affect children.

Now let's turn our attention to some particular ways in which partner support benefits men, women, and children.

Are There Benefits to Partner Support?

Figure 6.4 illustrates a model to explain how partner support can, in theory, help people in three distinct yet complementary ways.[17]

The first is partner support's *stress-prevention* function, represented by Arrow 1 in the diagram. Support from our partners may lessen the pressure from time and emotional demands that we face in our work and family lives. A spouse caring for a sick child at home, for instance, may allow us to attend a crucial meeting at work. Similarly, our partners might explore with us ways to seek a more flexible work schedule so our jobs don't interfere as frequently with family responsibilities. In both examples, the result is to ease the severity of conflicts between work and family.

Second, partner support may aid our overall well-being, represented by Arrow 2 in the diagram. Even if we don't experience high levels of work–family stress, partner support may increase our well-being. When we receive support from our partner, we may find we feel better about our family situation, our career, and ourselves. By bolstering our feelings of confidence and self-esteem, personal and career support may help us solve career-related

FIGURE 6.4
....

Support from our partners has potential benefits

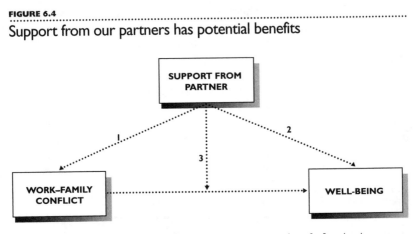

NOTE. Arrow 1 reflects the stress-prevention role of partner support. Arrow 2 reflects the role of partner support in well-being. Arrow 3 reflects the buffering role of partner support. Adapted from Greenhaus & Parasuraman (1994).

problems and become more satisfied—possibly even more successful—at work.[18] Behavioral support may also help us feel better about our relationship with the partner who provides that support.

Finally, partner support may serve a *buffering* function (represented by Arrow 3) by helping us cope with work–family conflict. In this way, support may act as a shield that protects us not from work–family stress itself, but rather from the devastating effects such stress can have on our health and well-being. For example, the understanding and advice our partner provides may help us grasp how a particular problem at work is hampering our capacity to pay attention to family, and in doing so help us find a way to mitigate the impact of the conflict at home.

So, partner support *may* benefit people in their work and family lives. But does it? The matter is more complicated than it initially appears. Partner support, whether behavioral, personal, or career, can—but does not necessarily—help in all of the ways we've just described.

Work–family conflict

Let's look first at Arrow 1 in Figure 6.4. We find that *personal* support consistently helps reduce work–family conflict.[19] When we receive a great deal of personal support from our partner, there are at least three noteworthy results:

- Our work is less likely to interfere with our family life.
- Our family is less likely to interfere with our work.
- We experience relatively little behavioral interference.

Surprisingly, though, career support from our partner (the other type of emotional support) does not reduce work–family conflict. Because career support deals specifically with work-related issues and problems, it may simply be too limited in scope to help us when work and family interfere with one another.

Why is it that personal support reduces work–family conflict? The concern a partner expresses about our personal and family problems, and the listening and advising they do, enables us to make changes in our work and family lives that ease the conflicts between the two domains. Take, for example, a man who has very high expectations about how much he can accomplish at home or work. His supportive partner may encourage him to relax some of his standards, or set expectations that are more reasonable. As a result he may experience less work and family pressure. Or consider a woman who needs more flexibility at work. Her understanding and supportive partner may help her develop enough self-confidence to approach her boss and work things out favorably.

The perspective and insights of our partners—and the feelings of acceptance and respect they give us—can make the difference in our ability to clarify and confront difficult situations head on, before they produce work–family conflict. A partner's advice can help make it possible for us to adjust our behavior when crossing boundaries between work and family. Partners remind us to be focused on family life when we come home. And by being good listeners, they help us let off steam that might have built up at work and this helps make us better able to focus on our families—to be psychologically available—after work hours.

In contrast to personal support, *behavioral* support provides little relief from conflict between work and family. Take the case of a man who helps his partner out around the house. This may afford his partner some time, but it does little to encourage any discussion of long-term solutions to work—family conflicts. It is a surprising and interesting example of how yet again the issue of time spent (quantity) does not matter nearly as much as something that is psychological in nature; that is, the quality of the experience of support.

Well-being

Turning to Arrow 2 of Figure 6.4, we find that different types of partner support affect, in diverse ways, the various components that make up "well-being."

Family and personal satisfaction. Emotional support from a partner communicates love, respect, and concern. This, in turn, produces positive feelings. That is why those of our business professionals who receive a great deal of personal and career support from their partners are very satisfied with their family lives.[20] Such support also helps us develop greater self-esteem and confidence, and as a result we might well seek new challenges and thus experience greater satisfaction with our personal growth and development.

Help with the household and the children (behavioral support) is of little consequence when it comes to this component of well-being. Again, as with its impact on work–family conflict, additional time in the form of assistance with household and children does not, in and of itself, produce positive feelings toward family and personal life.

Healthier children. Personal support not only enhances satisfaction with family life; it also affects the well-being of our kids.[21] Our business professionals who receive a lot of personal support from their partners report that their children have relatively few behavioral and health problems. We think this important effect stems from the fact that personal support promotes satisfaction with family life, which in turn radiates to the children. Kids benefit from growing up with satisfied parents, and feelings of satisfaction and personal fulfillment that accrue from our partner's understanding and advice may enable us to interact in a more positive way with our children.[22] It is also true that parents who provide personal support to their partners are likely to be more attuned to their kids' needs, thereby nurturing healthy and well-adjusted children.

That personal support from our partner enhances our performance as parents should come as no surprise. If that same support reduces the incidence of children's behavioral and health problems, it seems quite natural that, as a result, we take a better view of our parental performance.[23] Career support, however, creates no significant benefit for kids.

Behavioral support, however, influences the well-being of children, but in only one way: when partners provide help with the children, the kids experience relatively few behavioral problems. The time and attention devoted to children by the partner may communicate care, love, and concern that help meet the children's emotional needs and reduces the likelihood of behavioral problems.

Career success. Career success is another element of well-being. We measure career success from two perspectives: the objective indicators of money and power (that is, income and level in the organizational hierarchy) and the subjective indicator of career satisfaction. Previously, we identified some of the key work experiences that are dominant influences on career success. We now look at those same experiences (coaching, networking, and authority on the job) to help us understand *why* a partner's support has the effects it does on career success. Could it be that partner support promotes these work-related experiences, which in turn affect the level of career success that is achieved?

Both men and women who receive extensive personal support or career support from their partners are more satisfied with their careers than those who receive relatively little of these two types of emotional support. These men and women also tend to have a high level of authority in their jobs, receive a lot of coaching at work, and feel accepted by other employees. Those who receive a great deal of career support from their partners also engage in extensive networking and take many developmental assignments.

It's not clear whether these men and women are specifically advised by their partners to seek out these work-related experiences, or whether the confidence they derive from their partner's support enables them to pursue these experiences. In either case, both types of emotional support foster these kinds of positive work experiences, which in turn promote career satisfaction.

In addition to the impact of partner support on career success, we also observed that a partner's personal support improves the job performance of women, but not men. We think women are better able (or more willing) than men to accept and use the information and advice from their partners to enhance their performance at work.[24] This fits with our assertion that women might well be better suited to the career environment of the future, one in which there will be a continual need for learning and rapid adaptation to new environments.

When it comes to behavioral support, we find that men (but not women) whose partners spend a great deal of time with the children reach higher levels in the organizational hierarchy than men whose partners spend limited time with the children. The explanation is straightforward: receiving that help enables men to devote long hours to work and to achieve a high level of job performance, both of which contribute to their rise in the organizational hierarchy.[25] In other words, receiving help with the children frees men to spend more time at work and pursue their career with fewer distractions and a higher level of proficiency.

Why doesn't behavioral support benefit women in the same way? We think it is because women are still preoccupied with the kids even when dad spends time with them. Consistent with what we've been saying about gender stereotypes, mothers have ultimate responsibility for the children, and so they are always at least somewhat distracted psychologically.

Both men and women whose partners spend a great deal of time with the children also earn more money than those whose partners spend relatively little with the children. How can we explain this result? Frankly, it is a bit baffling. Although they also receive extensive coaching in the organization, achieve high levels of job performance, and rarely need to adjust their work schedules to meet family and personal needs, none of these factors explain why income rises when partners spend more time with the children. We can't rule out the possibility that a high salary already existed, which enabled the partner to spend more time with the children in the first place.[26]

When partner support is not *beneficial*

We've looked at the stress-prevention and well-being functions of partner support—behavioral, personal, and career—and have seen that partner support can enhance our careers and our personal and family lives. Personal and career support, the two types of emotional support, are particularly powerful: they reduce work–family conflict, increase satisfaction with family and personal growth, enhance the well-being of our kids, and produce high levels of career satisfaction.[27] Behavioral support—especially help with the children—has other benefits: reducing the incidence of children's behavioral problems, promoting financial success, and helping men to rise in the corporate hierarchy.

Remember, though, that there is a third potential function for partner support: its buffering function. Does partner support do any good as a buffer? In fact, we find little evidence for the notion that high levels of partner support shield or buffer a person from the negative effects of work–family stress. On the contrary, there are a number of instances of what has been called "reverse buffering" in which partner support actually *reduces* the well-being of individuals experiencing high levels of work–family conflict.[28] Figure 6.5 illustrates what happens when reverse buffering occurs.

Notice that the well-being of people who experience high levels of work–family conflict is actually lower when they receive a great deal of support than when such support is more limited. Prior research attributes this reverse buffering effect to a number of factors. There is speculation, for example, that support when we are experiencing intense work–family conflict may actually make us feel guilty, because it makes us more aware of how we are neglecting our family responsibilities, and in turn our sense of well-being declines. And high levels of partner support—especially personal and career support—may have another negative result: it may cause recipients to feel dependent on their partners, induce them to dwell on the very problem the support is aimed at helping get them past, and in turn render ineffective any coping with work–family stress.

The Choices We Face

If you are going to provide support to your partner, remember that it best serves before *work-family conflicts become overwhelming. After the fact, it may actually do more harm than good.*

FIGURE 6.5

Paradoxically, when we're stressed by work–family conflict, support may *reduce* our well-being

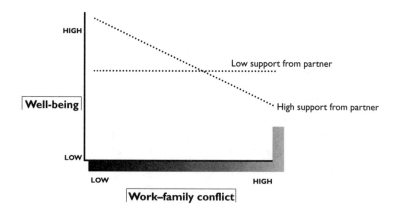

In summary, we found no buffering effects, but did find the reverse in some instances. So, although we don't fully understand why support can backfire, it is clear from what we find with our business professionals that support from a partner is more effective in *preventing* work–family conflict than in helping people cope with the aftermath of such conflict.

Four Conclusions About Partner Support

In previous chapters, we have explored the choices people make, how family affects work, and how work affects family. Here we've explored how support from our partners affects our personal life and career outcomes—and reached four major conclusions.

Support is more effective in preventing work–family conflict than in alleviating it once it occurs.

Individuals who receive a great deal of personal support from their partners generally experience relatively little work–family conflict. But people who *do* experience intense work–family conflict are no better off—indeed, they are sometimes worse off—when they receive support from their partners.

In other words, support may prevent a partner from experiencing work–family conflict, but timing is everything. If the support does not *initially* prevent the interference of work, family, and leisure on each other, it may be of little or no use—or even make things worse. So, we need to be aware of our partners' work and family demands if we are to provide enough support (especially personal support) *before* the conflict becomes debilitating. We are not suggesting that people should withhold support to partners who already experience intense work–family conflict, but rather that the support is likely to be more useful if it is provided before matters get out of hand. Moreover, if support is provided after the partner experiences intense conflict among roles, we should take care to ensure that our partner does not end up feeling guilty or dependent or in some other way resentful.

The benefits of personal and career support are more pervasive than the benefits of behavioral support.

Empathy, praise, information, and advice regarding personal and family concerns—what we call emotional support—have far-reaching benefits. They reduce work–family conflict, enhance satisfaction with personal development and family life, heighten the well-being of kids, and promote a high level of career satisfaction. Personal support communicates concern, love, and respect that nurture the recipient's self-confidence and self-esteem. And dialogue that brings new information and a fresh perspective can help partners solve problems in the work–family arena.

This is not to reduce the value of behavioral support. It conveys that we care. When we assist with home and children, we provide our partner with time and energy to devote to other activities. He or she can pursue career advancement and even earn more money.

Behavioral support works best—it is most beneficial and most powerful—when it is accompanied by emotional support, because it puts it in the context of affection, caring, and empathy. The combination of different types of partner support creates a whole greater than the sum of the parts. Our partner's assistance with the kids reduces our work–family conflict *only* when he or she also provides a lot of emotional support. Similarly, our partner's assistance with home chores reduces children's behavioral problems only when it comes with substantial emotional support.[29]

The very nature of partner support makes the family an ally of work.

The support we get from our partner—which essentially originates within the family—has many of its roots *and* consequences in the workplace. We see cases where the number of hours one works influences the support provided by the partner—an instance of the workplace affecting family dynamics. And we find that support from a partner crosses boundaries to affect career experiences (such as opportunities for coaching and developmental assignments) and career success. Family creates resources for work life and vice versa. What we've learned about partner support reinforces the importance of understanding the interdependencies between our work and family lives.

Our final conclusion concerns the role of gender in partner support. Do men and women receive support for different reasons? Do they reap different benefits from support? These questions are not easy to answer. Certainly, women devote more time to home and family than do men. And while gender differences in behavioral support may be diminishing, women still bear primary responsibility for the well-being of the household and the children. We're surprised to find that women receive more personal and career support than do men—although we attribute this difference in large part to the modest level of such support received by single-earner fathers.

In general, men and women receive support for the same reasons and experience the same benefits of support.

There are a few exceptions.[30] Several of these exceptions suggest that men and women whose values or behavior run counter to gender role expectations receive more support than those who are more in synch with traditional expectations. Take men who value security and free time in their careers and who are psychologically involved in their families. They receive extensive support from their partners, as do women who log many hours at work. If the desires for security, free time, and a high level of family involvement are not traditionally expected of men, and if putting in long hours at work is not traditionally expected of women, then the one thing these people have in common is an inconsistency with gender role expectations. Perhaps individuals realize that partners who go against gender role norms need and deserve their support. In Chapter 9 we address how some people are challenging traditional gender roles—a difficult path to follow alone. Partner support could mean the difference between success and failure.

Partner support isn't the only kind of support that can benefit our work and family lives. In the next chapter, we explore *employer* support—organizational policies and practices with respect to life at work and life beyond work. Just as partner support can make family the ally of work, so can employer support have a substantial impact on whether we succeed in making work the ally of family.

7

Support from Our Employer

O ver the past few years in this country, society at large has begun to look more closely at the family-friendliness of employers.[1] A family-friendliness movement has sprung up, driven by social and cultural forces pushing for gender equity, a sense that society may be neglecting the needs of children and of our communities, and a heightened awareness of the importance of personal and spiritual development. This movement's focus on the workplace stems from an increased sensitivity to the role employers play in shaping their employees' personal lives. More and more, people are realizing that employer policies and practices dealing with work and life outside of work can have a substantial impact beyond the workplace. In fact, they are among the deciding factors in whether people succeed in "having it all"—in living lives that are fulfilling and productive.

In this chapter we demonstrate the importance of employer support for their employees' family and personal lives, commonly referred to as family-friendliness. We focus on three questions: Why are some firms family-friendly and others not? Under what conditions are firms more or less likely to be seen as supportive of family and other life interests? And what is the impact of family-supportiveness on the work and personal lives of business professionals?

Our exploration is in some respects the inverse of what we looked at in the preceding chapter. The observations here build on the earlier material not only about partner support, but also in general about the impact of work and family experiences on the personal lives and careers of our business professionals. We show, for instance, how a firm's family-friendliness helps alleviate the family penalty suffered by working mothers. We explain how family-friendliness affects parents' work experiences and how children benefit. And we explore whether the beneficial effects of a partner's support on personal and professional life are different when the recipient works in a family-friendly environment.

In general, our findings provide some very good and promising news for those vanguard employers that are developing new solutions to the challenge of work–family integration. People who perceive their organizations as family-friendly *are* better off in terms of their lives beyond work and their feelings about their jobs and their organizations. And while these same people spend less time on work and more on other life interests, their job performance is no different from those who see their employers as unsupportive of their personal life needs. On top of this, these people are *more* committed to the long-term interests of their organizations. Family-friendliness appears to be win–win for employers and employees alike.[2]

What Do We Mean by Family-Friendliness?

Typically, whether an employer is designated as family-friendly depends on the answers to several questions.

- Do formal programs and policies exist that allow for flexible work options such as flex-time, flex-place, and job sharing?
- Are employees assisted in meeting their childcare needs, either through development and maintenance of on-site childcare facilities, financial support for off-site childcare options, or resources devoted to developing greater capacity in the community to provide for childcare? To what extent?
- Are employees getting help to meet their elder care needs? To what extent?
- Are consultation and referrals available to employees to help them cope with personal life issues (especially childcare and eldercare, but also including physical and mental health needs)?
- How much time can employees take for family and medical leaves, and how much are they paid during such leaves?
- Are there employee-assistance programs? Wellness and fitness programs? Adoption assistance? Retirement planning? What other benefits exist?

These questions largely measure company policies, which are objective factors. We think, though, that while these policies and programs are important, even necessary, they are not sufficient. Family supportiveness cannot be judged so simply, and in our study we went beyond formal measures to explore whether employees *perceive* their employers as family-friendly— whether, in effect, employees take advantage of such policies and programs and find them useful. Rather than assessing the full range of employee benefits options available in the organizations in which our business professionals work, or exploring such things as the ratio of daycare center slots to working parents, we asked our business professionals whether they experience their organizations as supportive of their family needs.[3] After all, the best policies and programs are worthless if the organization's members don't find them useful. That is why we focus on the impact of the perceived family-friendliness of an organization on employees.

We think this is the best way to assess the family-friendliness of an organization.[4] As several reports and analyses have noted, it is *utilization* of programs and not the existence of the programs per se that matters in determining whether they can and do have an impact.[5]

We assessed an employer's support for family needs according to the responses of our business professionals to five items on our survey instrument.

1. The level of commitment expected by my organization requires that employees choose between advancing their careers and devoting time to their family (reverse scored).
2. My organization is understanding when employees have a hard time juggling work and family responsibilities.
3. Career advancement is jeopardized if employees do not accept assignments because of their family responsibilities (reverse scored).
4. My organization has a satisfactory family leave policy.
5. My organization allows for flexibility in work scheduling.

We look at the average of these five items as a single indicator.[6] It is useful to see the exact words in the survey instrument so that it is clear that the composite measure assesses the extent to which an organization is seen by employees as providing flexibility and control, the two factors we have identified as critical to integration between work and other life interests.[7]

We think it's likely that more and more employers will adopt family-friendliness as an explicit goal over the next several years. It's not just the growing social pressure on employers to be friendlier to the family needs of their employees. Employers in the vanguard of such change are beginning to demonstrate that family-friendliness actually can improve economic outcomes for firms. In other words, family-friendliness comes with bottom-line benefits to the firm.

Why Are Some Employers Family-Friendly?

Some firms are keen to establish policies and practices that are supportive of the family needs of employees, while others are not.[8] Why do some organizations take the steps and not others?

There are several explanations for why some employers are family-friendly. Foremost among these is that employers see family supportiveness as a way to

- deal with absenteeism, turnover, productivity losses, and other work-force problems that result when the stresses employees feel from family and other personal problems spill over to the job
- attract and retain talented (particularly younger) employees who express their interest not only in making a contribution and maintaining high-quality job performance but want to "have a life" while doing so
- build commitment to an organization

Among our business professionals, the perception of whether an employer is family-friendly depends on whether we ask men or women.[9] Fifty-nine percent of the men we asked rate their employers as supportive of their family and personal lives, compared with only 46 percent of the women.[10] Why the disparity? One reason is that women are more acute in the way they judge

FIGURE 7.1

Some industries are more family-friendly than others •

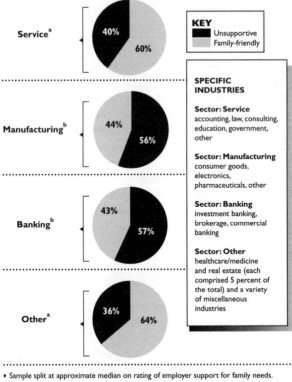

Service[a]

40%

60%

KEY
■ Unsupportive
▨ Family-friendly

Manufacturing[b]

44%

56%

Banking[b]

43%

57%

Other[a]

36%

64%

SPECIFIC INDUSTRIES

Sector: Service
accounting, law, consulting, education, government, other

Sector: Manufacturing
consumer goods, electronics, pharmaceuticals, other

Sector: Banking
investment banking, brokerage, commercial banking

Sector: Other
healthcare/medicine and real estate (each comprised 5 percent of the total) and a variety of miscellaneous industries

• Sample split at approximate median on rating of employer support for family needs. Percentages are proportions of people in relatively unsupportive and in relatively supportive organizations, respectively.

a,b Industries with different letters in superscript are significantly different from each other on employer family-friendliness.

FIGURE 7.2

Who works for family-friendly employers?*

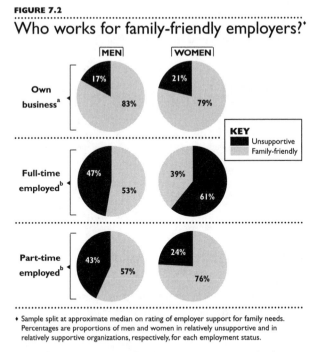

♦ Sample split at approximate median on rating of employer support for family needs.
  Percentages are proportions of men and women in relatively unsupportive and in
  relatively supportive organizations, respectively, for each employment status.

a, b Types of employment status with different letters in superscript were significantly
  different from each other on employer family-friendliness for the total sample.

their employers. After all, women bear the greater burden of responsibility for family life, and are more keenly aware of whether their organizations support their lives beyond work.

Whereas small firms are as likely to be seen as supportive of family needs as are large ones, perceptions of family-friendliness do vary across industries and depend on whether one works for oneself and on whether the work is full- or part-time. As Figure 7.1 shows, those of our business professionals who work in the service sector and the miscellaneous group of industries (which includes healthcare and real estate in proportionally high numbers) see their employers as more family-friendly than do those working in manufacturing and banking. The impact of industry sector is the same on both men's and women's perceptions.

Figure 7.2 shows how employment status influences perceptions of an organization's family-friendliness, and how this works differently for men and women.

Not surprisingly, self-employed people—those who own their own businesses—are much more likely to see their organizations as supportive of their families than are those who work for someone else (whether part-time or full-time). Self-employment allows us greater discretion over virtually all conditions of employment. While the benefits of self-employment seem to be enjoyed by both men and women, proportionally more men in our sample run their own businesses (22 percent) than do women (10 percent)—another reason men in general are more likely to feel their organizations are supportive of their lives outside work.

A man's employment status (full- or part-time) makes no difference in his perception of whether his employer is supportive of family needs. Women who work part-time, however, feel more supported by their employers than do women who work full-time.[11] Indeed, among our business professionals, most of the women who are employed full-time—the majority of women in our study—feel relatively *unsupported* by their organizations. This, coupled with the flexibility and control that come with self-employment, helps explain the trend towards women bailing out of the traditional corporate track to pursue their career goals either as entrepreneurs or in alternative work arrangements in organizations that allow for such flexibility.[12]

Benefits of Employer Family-Friendliness

We have explored whether support from our partners is beneficial in making allies of work and family, and we can ask the same question of employer support. Does working for a family-friendly employer make things better for our business professionals? How so?

We've already seen in earlier chapters that people who work for family-supportive employers fare better than those who work in relatively unsupportive organizations. For instance,

- they feel less compelled to make tradeoffs between work and family
- they are more satisfied with their personal growth and development
- they feel they perform well as parents

Figure 7.3 provides a closer look at the full range of the effects of a family-friendly work environment on careers and on family and personal lives.[13]

It turns out that people who place high value on flexibility and time for themselves are more likely to work for family-friendly employers. Why is not so clear. Do business professionals adopt these values as a result of working for employers that encourage them to do so? Or do they consciously seek out family-supportive employers? We can't say for sure, because we didn't ask. Whatever the reason, we're not surprised to find that people who value flexibility are more likely to be employed in organizations that are indeed seen as flexible.

We also see that people in family-friendly organizations are more likely to aspire to senior management positions and are more likely to believe they will achieve their aspirations for hierarchical advancement. This indicates that being in a supportive organization affects how a business professional feels about his or her future with that employer. It also increases commitment to their organizations. When people feel their employers are supportive of their lives beyond work, they are more likely to align their future career plans with the firm's future direction.

FIGURE 7.3

Employer family-friendliness benefits career as well as family and personal lives

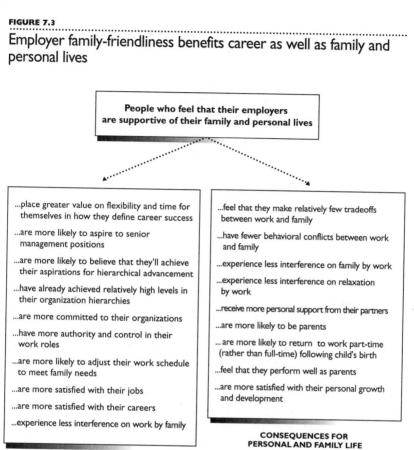

People who feel that their employers are supportive of their family and personal lives

...place greater value on flexibility and time for themselves in how they define career success

...are more likely to aspire to senior management positions

...are more likely to believe that they'll achieve their aspirations for hierarchical advancement

...have already achieved relatively high levels in their organization hierarchies

...are more committed to their organizations

...have more authority and control in their work roles

...are more likely to adjust their work schedule to meet family needs

...are more satisfied with their jobs

...are more satisfied with their careers

...experience less interference on work by family

CONSEQUENCES FOR WORK AND CAREER

...feel that they make relatively few tradeoffs between work and family

...have fewer behavioral conflicts between work and family

...experience less interference on family by work

...experience less interference on relaxation by work

...receive more personal support from their partners

...are more likely to be parents

...are more likely to return to work part-time (rather than full-time) following child's birth

...feel that they perform well as parents

...are more satisfied with their personal growth and development

CONSEQUENCES FOR PERSONAL AND FAMILY LIFE

People who work in organizations they feel are family-friendly are more likely to have achieved relatively high levels in their organization hierarchies, and they have more authority or control over their work. Because they work in family-friendly organizations, they are more apt to alter their daily work schedule to accommodate family needs. In short, people who feel their organizations to be supportive of their personal lives have greater control over and flexibility in how they go about pursuing their work and career objectives.

As for satisfaction, people who perceive their employers as supportive are more satisfied with their jobs *and* more satisfied with their careers.

Better use of time

One obvious benefit of working for a family-friendly employer is that people spend their time more wisely—in ways that are good for them personally and for their organizations (see Table 7.1). For instance, both women and men

TABLE 7.1
....
Employees in family-friendly organizations make better use of their time*

Hours allocated per week
FAMILY FRIENDLINESS

	LOW	HIGH	LOW	HIGH
Work*	◄ 54.5	51.4	52.6	46.6
Relaxation●	◄ 14.0	17.2	15.4	17.9
Household■	◄ 9.5	9.8	10.8	12.3
Children*	◄ 12.8	14.2	37.3	45.1
	MEN		WOMEN	

....

★ Sample split at approximate median on rating of employer support for family needs. Numbers on table are hours per week.

✦ Main effects of sex and employer family-friendliness, as well as interaction of sex and employer family-friendliness, are significant.

● Main effect of employer family-friendliness is significant.

■ Main effects of sex, as well as interaction of sex and employer family-friendliness, are significant.

spend less time on work and more time on children when they work in organizations they feel are supportive of their lives outside of work. These differences are greater for women than they are for men. In addition, women who work in family-friendly firms spend more time on household responsibilities than do their counterparts in unsupportive organizations (the time men spend on household chores is hardly affected by the supportiveness of their employers).

Both men and women are likely to spend more time on relaxation when their organizations allow for flexibility and provide support for life interests outside of work. And, as we noted earlier, while time spent on work is less in family-friendly organizations, job performance is just as high and commitment to organization goals is even greater. How is it that they perform as well while putting in fewer hours? They're working smarter.

One recent analysis asserts that some employees choose not to take advantage of family-friendly policies because work is an easier, less emotionally challenging and complicated place to be than home. That is the thesis behind Arlie Hochschild's important and provocative work.[14] She contends that people *escape* to work—in other words, that people exchange the messy entanglements that are the stuff of families for the surface camaraderie of the modern, worker-friendly workplace.

Were this true, we would expect to see people who are relatively dissatisfied with their families and who receive relatively little personal support from their partners spending more time at work in supportive organizations—in a sense, substituting the work environment for what they *don't* get at home. But it turns out that the people who spend the most time at work are those who work in unsupportive organizations and have *highly* supportive partners.[15] So, contrary to Hochschild, it's not that friendly, supportive organizations create an attractive, home-like place to which family-stressed people want to escape. Instead, we see that having a supportive partner allows people to respond to rigorous work demands.[16]

People who truly feel their employer supports the pursuit of harmony among, and engagement in, different life roles arrange their time in ways that integrate work with their interests—family, community, and so on—that lie beyond the bounds of the workplace. Nothing we found fits Hochschild's notion that business professionals use a supportive work environment as a refuge from the intense pressures of other life demands.

Offset career penalties for working mothers

We have discussed the "bonus or penalty" (BOP) hypothesis—that men gain a career bonus and women suffer a career penalty from being married and having kids. To recap: fathers earn more and are more satisfied with their careers than men with no children, while mothers earn less and are less satisfied with their careers than women with no children. Men, in fact, realize a career asset just from being married, whether or not they are fathers. Marriage (without children) neither benefits nor hurts a woman's career. Because they tend to have more authority in their work roles than single men and men without children, married men and fathers enjoy competitive advantages in their careers. And in comparison to women without children, mothers suffer a penalty in part because they have fewer opportunities to develop their careers, spend less time at work, and are less psychologically involved in it.

Working for a family-friendly employer has a significant effect on these bonuses and penalties, especially for women. In supportive organizations, the gap between mothers and women without children is considerably smaller (see Figures 7.4 and 7.5). In other words, a supportive work environment reduces the negative impact motherhood seems to have on women's career outcomes.

The career penalty for mothers is reduced in organizations seen as family-friendly. Why? We think it has to do with how family-friendly employers alleviate the disadvantages faced by mothers working in unsupportive organizations, where employers hold on to the stereotype that mothers are uncommitted to their work and careers just because they have children, that they tend to work fewer hours, and that they make greater adjustments to accommodate family interests. Family-supportive employers provide flexibility and understanding to mothers, viewing mothers not as liabilities but as valuable contributors to the business.

An employer's family-friendliness affects men, too, but not to the same extent as women. For instance, the career satisfaction of fathers is enhanced in organizations they feel to be supportive of their personal lives. Several factors may be at work here. Fathers enjoy the gratification of fruitful work without it being quite as diminished by the pull of family demands. These men spend fewer hours at work and more hours on relaxation and family.

FIGURE 7.4

Career satisfaction of women working for supportive and unsupportive employers

▸ **PERCENTAGES REFLECT THOSE REPORTING A HIGH LEVEL OF CAREER SATISFACTION**

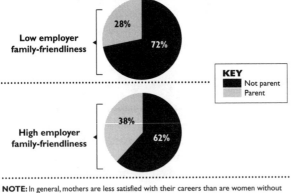

NOTE: In general, mothers are less satisfied with their careers than are women without children, and this difference is significantly smaller in organizations that are supportive of family.

FIGURE 7.5

Income of women working for supportive and unsupportive employers

▸ **PERCENTAGES REFLECT THOSE WITH HIGH INCOMES**

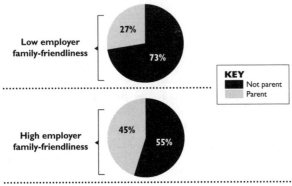

NOTE: In general, mothers earn less than women without children, and the income gap between these two groups of women is significantly smaller in organizations that are supportive of family.

Their organizations offer understanding and flexibility, just as they do for women.

The impact of employer family-friendliness on men, however, ends at career satisfaction. It does nothing to close or widen the income gap between fathers and men without children. Similarly, it has no impact on the differences in career outcomes between married and single men and between members of single-earner versus dual-earner couples (see Chapter 3).

Improved quality of life beyond work

One of the motivations behind the family-friendliness movement was to attract and retain people who demanded a better quality of life outside of work, and who were unable or unwilling to keep up with the demands of the time-consuming modern corporation.[17] And just as family-supportiveness helps people in their careers, it can improve the quality of life beyond work.

We touched on this subject earlier. People who work in organizations they see as supportive of their family and personal lives feel they make relatively few tradeoffs between work and family, are more satisfied with their personal growth and development, and perform well as parents. And in Figure 7.3, we detailed other benefits.

Parents are most likely to report that their employers are supportive of family needs; after all, we would expect parents to be most aware of company policies that have an impact on their children. But parents are not the only ones who benefit from the reduced psychological conflicts between work and personal life that result from flexible and supportive work environments. Indeed, people who work for family-friendly employers report less of every type of role conflict we measured: they feel less interference on work by their families, they experience fewer behavioral conflicts between work and family, and they worry less about work when they are spending time with their families and when they are relaxing.

It cannot be stated too many times: an employer's family-friendliness, when really felt by employees, has a positive impact on people's lives, in part by allowing for—even encouraging—the flexibility needed to integrate work, family, relaxation, and other pursuits.

Better parental performance

In Chapter 5, we explored how work experiences affect parents and their children. We concluded that feeling satisfied with our jobs, performing them well, aspiring to senior management positions, and taking time for relaxation all enhance our performance as parents, although differently for mothers and fathers. What role is played by an organization's supportiveness of family needs?

Women perform better as mothers when they are satisfied with their jobs. When we sharpen our focus and account for the impact of family-friendliness (see Figure 7.6), it turns out this finding is true only in organizations seen as

FIGURE 7.6

Whether job satisfaction leads to good parental performance depends on whether mom works for a family-friendly employer

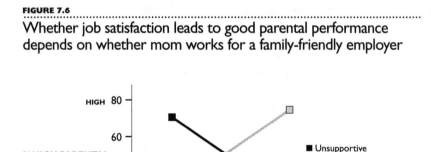

NOTE: There is a significant interaction between employer support and job satisfaction. In unsupportive organizations high levels of job satisfaction result in poor performance as a mother but in highly supportive companies, it's just the opposite: being satisfied with your job goes hand in hand with good performance as a mother.

family-friendly. In fact, for mothers in unsupportive organizations we see the opposite effect: they are more satisfied with their jobs the *less* well they perform as mothers. In other words, mothers who are highly satisfied at work rate themselves relatively low as parents if they work in organizations that do not accommodate their family interests, but rate themselves as good parents if their firm is family-friendly.

So, employer support for family needs reverses the ill effects of a forced tradeoff for mothers torn between trying to be a good mother *and* have a satisfying job.

Another aspect of work we have observed is that men aspire to senior management to the detriment of their parental performance. The lower a father's career aspirations, the better he tends to rate himself as a parent. Factor in whether the organization is supportive of personal life, however, and we see something different: if a father who aspires to a high position works for a family-friendly employer, he does *better* as a parent.[18]

Employer Support + Partner Support

Clearly, working in a family-friendly organization has benefits. So does the support we get from our partners. But we have questions about the combination of these two kinds of support, and the effect support in one domain might have on support in the other.

Does a supportive work environment result in partners being more or less supportive? Does having a supportive spouse result in our seeing our employer as more or less supportive? It depends on which type of partner support we're talking about. For instance, business professionals who receive relatively high amounts of personal support from their partners also get the most employer support for family needs. There is no connection, though, between an employer's family-friendliness and a partner providing either career support or behavioral support (assistance with household responsibilities or help with the kids).

What explains these findings? People who have both a supportive employer and a partner who provides personal support probably place a high value on receiving social and emotional support in general. They are, therefore, less likely to remain in an organization or in a relationship that does not provide personal support.[19] It may also be that people in supportive organizations are more likely to receive personal support from their partners because their work environment allows them to be more psychologically open to receiving such support.

We have discussed the role of partner support in terms of its functions. We explored how it can lessen the time pressures and emotional demands we face in our work and family lives—its stress-prevention function. We also examined how it can aid our overall well-being—personal, family, and career success. Now we want to consider whether the family-friendliness of our employers affects how partner support may or may not fulfill these two functions.[20]

Figure 7.7 shows that we find two kinds of interaction between employer and partner support. There is a *compensation* effect. In other words, the impact of partner support on the outcome is greater if the family-friendliness of the employer is relatively low. We see this effect on the psychological outcomes of work interference with family, family interference with work, satisfaction with personal growth, and career satisfaction. Partner support, in other words, is needed more when we work in organizations that are not supportive of our lives beyond work. There is also an *enhancement* effect, or synergy—the beneficial effects of partner support are greater in family-friendly firms. We see this effect on both behavioral interference and parental performance.

Alleviating the stress of work–family conflicts

Working for a family-friendly employer has beneficial effects on all forms of perceived role conflicts, as does personal support from one's partner. Both forms of support help reduce the stress of role conflicts. But is the impact of personal support different depending on whether it's given to a person who works in either a supportive or an unsupportive work environment? As Table 7.2 illustrates, the answer depends on the form the role conflict takes.[21]

For two forms of psychological interference—work-to-family and family-to-work conflicts—there seems to be a compensatory effect. In other words, the impact of partner support is greater when our business professionals feel their organizations to be unsupportive of their lives beyond work. In these

FIGURE 7.7

The combination of employer support and partner support works in two ways

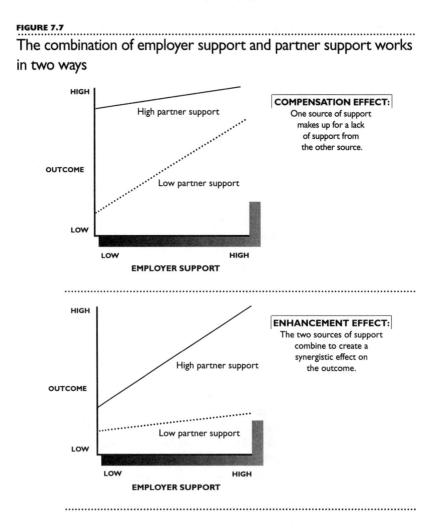

COMPENSATION EFFECT:
One source of support
makes up for a lack
of support from
the other source.

ENHANCEMENT EFFECT:
The two sources of support
combine to create a
synergistic effect on
the outcome.

instances, partner support seems to makes up for the absence of employer support. Conversely, for people with relatively unsupportive partners, employer family-friendliness reduces these same types of role conflicts to a greater extent than for those whose partners are supportive. Those with greater need for support in one domain search harder for support in the other—and that more motivated, focused search results in greater support. One source of support compensates for a lack of the other.

A different picture emerges when we look at behavioral interference of work on family (when people act at home in ways that are more appropriate to the work environment). Here, the whole is greater than the sum of its parts—the combined impact of partner and employer support results in a greater reduction in conflict than we see for either of these two sources of support taken independently. More specifically, while behavioral interference on family by work is lower for people who work in supportive organiza-

TABLE 7.2

How partner support + employer support affects different role conflicts·

▸ **LOW EMPLOYER FAMILY-FRIENDLINESS**

	Percent who experience relatively high levels of:		
	Psychological interference of work on family★	Psychological interference of family on work ★	Behavioral interference of work on family ■
Low personal support ◂	48	67	57
High personal support ◂	41	54	54

▸ **HIGH EMPLOYER FAMILY-FRIENDLINESS**

	Percent who experience relatively high levels of:		
	Psychological interference of work on family★	Psychological interference of family on work ★	Behavioral interference of work on family ■
Low personal support ◂	32	48	59
High personal support ◂	26	41	36

♦ Main effects of employer family-friendliness and partner's personal support, as well as interaction of both employer family-friendliness and personal support, are statistically significant for all three forms of role conflict in this table.

★ Interaction between employer family-friendliness and partner's personal support resulted in a compensation effect.

■ Interaction between employer family-friendliness and partner's personal support resulted in an enhancement effect.

tions—even if they have unsupportive partners—it is *much* lower if their organization is supportive also. One source of support enhances the other.

Why do things work out this way? It may be that business professionals are better able to take advantage of the benefits—flexibility and understanding—they get from family-friendly employers when their partners at home make relatively few demands that require them to adjust their behavior to fit the norms of a family domain that might be different from, or even in conflict with, the norms of their work world. And it could be that the supportive partners are able to confront issues more directly and are therefore better able to help their partners shift gears and manage the transition from work to home.

In other words, partner support, coupled with flexibility and understanding from an employer, enables business professionals to move freely between work and family roles—in effect, to be themselves wherever they are and manage their boundaries better. In the case of behavioral interference of work on family, then, there is an enhancement effect—the combined impact of partner and employer support results in the greatest reduction in role conflict.

Boost to well-being

As with role conflicts, employer support both enhances (in some cases) and compensates for (in other cases) partner support when it comes to our well-being—the components of which are family and personal satisfaction, the health and behavior of children, and career success. Take the example of our performance as parents. Personal support from a partner improves our parental performance to an even greater extent when it is given to a person who feels he or she works for a supportive as opposed to an unsupportive employer; an enhancement effect.

We have seen that we are more satisfied with both our personal lives and our families when we have a partner's personal and career support. Oddly enough, while working for a family-friendly employer improves satisfaction with personal growth, it has no impact on family satisfaction. And it neither enhances nor compensates for personal support from a partner (which itself increases family satisfaction).

FIGURE 7.8

In their influence on personal growth satisfaction, partner and employer support compensate for each other

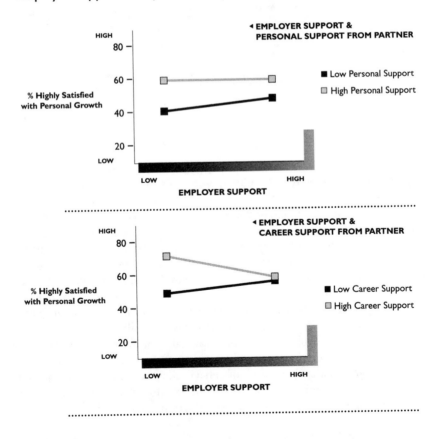

As Figure 7.8 shows, there is a compensation effect on personal growth satisfaction in the cases of both personal and career support from a partner. In highly supportive organizations, there is virtually no difference in personal growth satisfaction between those who do and those who do not receive personal and career support from their partners. It's mainly for those business professionals who work for unsupportive employers that we observe the benefits of a partner's personal and career support on how they feel about their own growth and development.

Finally—and not surprisingly—the pattern of results for career satisfaction is essentially the same as those we just observed for satisfaction with personal growth. Both personal and career support make more of a difference in increasing career satisfaction when it is given by partners to business professionals who work in unsupportive organizations. In other words, there is a compensation effect operating here as well.

Summing Up

Family-friendly firms have a significant impact on the lives and careers of the business professionals who work in them. We've shown that the supportiveness of employers for the family and other life interests of employees makes a difference beyond the quality of life employees experience. There are important work and career outcomes as well.

We hope our findings will encourage a greater effort to create family-friendly work environments—and not only for the sake of the personal lives of employees. It turns out this makes good business sense. Employer family-friendliness builds commitment and satisfaction among employees. Corporations ought to welcome that outcome.

Perhaps even more important, it turns out that although people in family-friendly organizations work fewer hours, their job performance is equal to those in unsupportive organizations. In other words, they are working more efficiently—a win-win situation for employees and employers alike. Firms that provide understanding and flexibility for the whole lives of the business professional create environments in which people work smarter.

Family-friendliness is one among a number of important building blocks in what we call an *infrastructure for flexibility*—a web of social, political, and economic support needed if work and the family are to be allies in our society. Constructing such an infrastructure must be a central task of businesses and individuals; we offer ideas for how to do this in Chapter 9.

And what makes a family-supportive organization? It is more than policies and official programs about family and personal life. These are important, but they go only so far. What really affects people is an organization's culture, its values in practice. Measure family-friendliness according to formal policies and programs (as most studies to date have done) and the assessment is likely to be off by a considerable degree. That is why we focus on how people actually feel about the degree to which their organizations are supportive.

Our use of a subjective measure led us to find that family-supportive organizations do not, as some assert, compel people to use work as an escape from the challenges of intimacy and family life. To the contrary, we see that business professionals who feel supported take advantage of the flexibility and understanding their organizations provide, using those benefits to live more satisfying lives.

Support from our employers goes a long way toward alleviating the penalty mothers in particular face in the workplace. It can either compensate for or enhance the support we receive from our partner at home. It seems that for people who feel supported by their organizations in their life interests outside of work, the role played by emotional support from a spouse or partner in reducing work–family conflicts and in increasing satisfaction with personal growth and career is less critical than in those organizations where work dominates personal life. A partner's support makes a difference for psychological well-being when it is given to someone who needs it because his or her organization doesn't seem to care. On the other hand, there is a synergistic effect in the case of the happy combination of working in a supportive organization *and* having a supportive spouse. This situation makes for greatly reduced behavioral interference of work on family life and results in very high levels of parental performance. Partner support and employer support together enhance the value of each kind of support on these important behavioral outcomes.

As we saw in the previous chapter, we again see the cross-domain effects of social support. Work can generate resources for personal life, just as personal and family life can generate resources for work and career.

This brings us to the end of our analyses of findings about how family affects work and how work affects family for men and women. Our final two chapters present a synthesis of our observations and choices for individuals, employers, and society—all geared toward making allies of work and the family.

8

What Have We Learned?

The business professionals we surveyed are doing quite well. About half have very satisfying careers, more than seven in ten are highly satisfied with their family lives, and 53 percent feel very good about their personal growth and development. But the combination of career and family life doesn't translate into overall satisfaction for every group. Single-earner men, for example, are most pleased with their careers but least satisfied with their families. Dual-earner mothers are pretty much the reverse—satisfied with their families but not so much with their careers. Dual-earner fathers are reasonably satisfied with career and family.

We raised several fundamental questions in Chapter 1, and they have guided our study. What is the relationship between work and family? Do work and family stand in opposition, competing for time and attention, draining energy, evoking conflict? Or do people draw on their experiences in each sphere of life, enriching the other parts of their lives in a process of integration? Do women and men experience their work and family lives in similar or different ways? One thing was certain to us going in: that work and family touch one another in profound ways, and their relationship is neither simple nor straightforward.

Chapters 2 through 7 have presented the major findings of our study. Now it's time for synthesis. Here we present a model that captures what we've brought to light: a highly complex relationship between two often disparate spheres of life, work and family. This chapter is the necessary prelude to our recommendations that follow, where we address what individuals, employers, and society must do—the choices they face—to make allies of work and the family.

A Model of Work–Family Relationships

More than anything else, our research has demonstrated the *interdependence* of work and family lives. We may not always know what causes what—which is the chicken and which is the egg—but we do know that work and family are intertwined in myriad ways. Knowing this, however, isn't much different from what we knew from the outset. It certainly doesn't answer the question of whether these connections between work and family are positive or negative. This knowledge alone won't reveal for us whether work and family enrich each other or whether they place obstacles and constraints in each other's way. Now we've come to the overarching question: All things considered, are work and family allies or enemies?

To find the answer, we reflected on all our findings. We looked for where the work–family linkage represents a positive impact, and where it is negative. In other words, we looked at the conditions under which work or family promote well-being in the other domain (which makes them allies) and those where work or family create difficulties or conflicts for each other, spurring tradeoffs (which makes them enemies). Then we sought to determine which domain was "calling the shots." In other words, we asked which is more plausible in a given situation: that work influences family or that family influences work.

This analysis proved illuminating. Work and family indeed conflict with each other—especially for women—and limit success and fulfillment in important ways. We hear about this conflict all the time. But work and family also serve as allies, providing positive experiences and feelings that spill over to affect each other in helpful ways. The positive interdependencies between work and family can be just as extensive and important as the more harmful effects. From our analysis, two key concepts emerged:

> *Allies in integration.* Work–family integration occurs when participation in one role enhances the quality of life within the other role. When work is family's ally, it improves our experiences and outcomes within the family. When family is the ally of work, our family life strengthens our experiences and outcomes at work.

> *Enemies in conflict.* Work–family conflict occurs when participation in one role detracts from the quality of life within the other role.[1] When they are enemies, our work lives interfere with satisfaction and success in the family or our family lives interfere with our satisfaction and success at work.

Figure 8.1 shows when work–family integration and conflict are most likely to occur. Figure 8.2 is our general model of work–family relationships, a picture of a process we're about to describe. It shows three key components

FIGURE 8.1

When are integration and conflict most likely to occur?

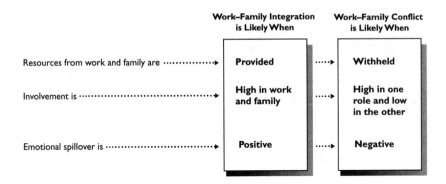

FIGURE 8.2

A general model of work–family relationships

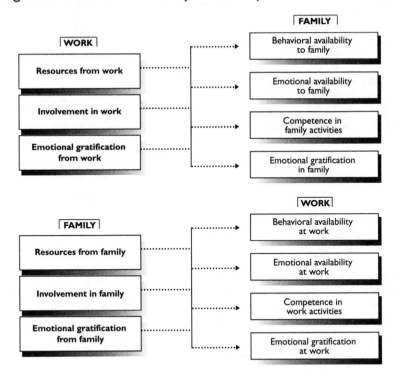

FIGURE 8.3
....
Ways in which work and family help each other

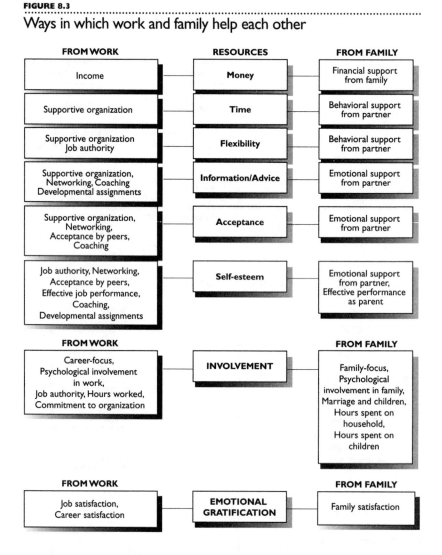

of Figure 8.1—resources, involvement, and emotional gratification—that affect our availability, competence, and emotional gratification in each domain.[2] In Chapter 1, we introduced this general model and provided brief definitions of its key components. Figure 8.3 provides some specific examples of the three key components in our work and family domains. Let's look more closely at each of the three key components in our model and how they work.

Resources

A resource is a supply of support or aid that helps make us more capable of dealing with a situation or meeting a new difficulty. Some resources are tangible, such as time or money. Many other resources are intangible. Information, acceptance, and self-esteem are all examples of important, but less tangible, resources.[3]

We obtain resources in both our work and family domains. In the work domain, a wealth of resources comes as a result of family-friendly policies and practices. Others come from our daily work experiences, which are also a rich source of resources. Partner support—behavioral, personal, or career—provides resources from the family domain.

Figure 8.4 offers an overview of how resources in one role affect behaviors and feelings in the other role. For instance, the resource of flexible control over work time enables an employee to be available behaviorally to family members—that is, to be physically present when a partner, child, parent, or other relative needs assistance. This in turn leads to good feelings (shown as "emotional gratification" in the figure). Similarly, the monetary resource can allow behavioral availability to family members through the purchase of the services of outside help, for example, also leading to emotional gratification.

As we've discussed so often in this book, however, availability isn't only about behavior, or physical presence. It has a psychological aspect as well; it means being attentive and sensitive to another person's emotional needs. The figure shows that being understood and accepted at work and possessing high self-esteem allows a person to be psychologically, or emotionally, available to a family member. The better we feel about ourselves in one domain, the more able we are to give emotional support to others in another setting. The outcome is emotional gratification in the other role.

FIGURE 8.4

Resources in one role affect our availability, competence, and emotional gratification in the other

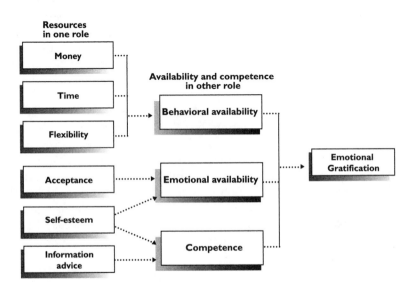

High self-esteem also promotes competence in family activities, because self-confidence gives us the power to attempt—and persist at—challenging tasks.[4] Of course, information and advice provided at work also provide us with the knowledge and counsel to achieve greater competence in dealing with family demands.[5] Plus, being available and competent in the family domain is likely to enhance the emotional gratification we get from family life, since we feel useful and capable in family matters.

The more resources, the better: an abundance of resources promotes work–family integration, and makes allies of the two domains. Time, flexibility, knowledge, acceptance, and self-esteem received within a role enable us to become available and competent in the other role. Of course, the opposite is also true. Work or family environments that provide little time flexibility, that drain our energy, that hinder our feelings of acceptance, and that erode our self-esteem increase the likelihood of conflict between work and family. Without flexibility, it is difficult to resolve time and scheduling problems effectively, and feelings of rejection and low self-esteem hamper our development of skills that can be applied fruitfully in the other role. Work and family become enemies.

Involvement

Involvement refers to the time and psychological energy we devote to our various social roles—parent, employee, neighbor, Little League coach, and so on. Some of our roles are more central to our concept of self than are other roles. And the more involved we are in a particular social role, the more intensely we invest ourselves in that role and the more extensively we participate in role-related activities.[6] Achieving success in a highly meaningful role is a powerful source of self-esteem.[7]

Imbalanced involvement—where we are much more involved in work than family, or vice versa—creates such a preoccupation and absorption in the more involving role that it weakens our behavioral and emotional availability in the other role.[8] Our limited availability to other people can prove harmful to our own competence and emotional gratification in the role getting short shrift.[9] Imbalanced involvement thus produces extensive work–family conflict (see Figure 8.5).

If we are highly involved in *both* work and family, however, we're likely to experience work–family integration. Just as resources serve as enablers in efforts to make allies of work and family, so does balanced involvement. When we embrace balanced involvement—that is, when both work and family are important to us and we care deeply about both roles—we will be highly motivated to apply the resources derived from one role to enrich the other. Those of us strongly involved in both roles, for example, may actively seek more flexibility at work to enable us to meet our family needs. We may also be better at using partner support to help us meet our work-related challenges.

FIGURE 8.5

Imbalanced involvement in one role has negative effects on the other

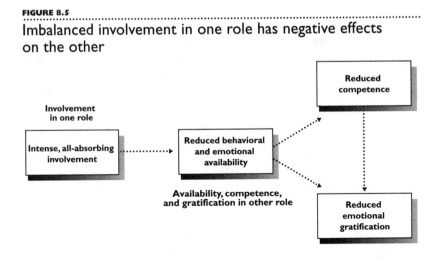

Involvement in one role

| Intense, all-absorbing involvement | ┄┄⟶ | Reduced behavioral and emotional availability |

Availability, competence, and gratification in other role

Reduced competence

Reduced emotional gratification

Emotional gratification

In our work roles, emotional gratification is what we feel when we are satisfied with our jobs and careers, when our work experiences satisfy important goals, and when our work lives are interesting and rewarding.[10] We get emotional gratification in our family roles when we experience satisfaction with our families, when important social and emotional needs, values, and goals are met at home.

The level of emotional gratification we experience in one domain directly affects our level of emotional gratification in the other, as Figure 8.6 illustrates. In other words, this "emotional spillover" can be positive *or* negative, producing integration *or* conflict. When it is positive, it is because we are able to transfer our good mood from one role directly to the other. Satisfaction with our family lives can make it possible for us to enjoy our work more—we feel less pressured, less distracted by stressful family situations. Likewise, a satisfying career can allow us to enjoy our family lives more fully. The negative spillover produces work–family conflict—when, for example, dissatisfaction at work causes frustration and stress that we just can't shake when interacting in the family domain.[11]

FIGURE 8.6

Our emotional gratification in one role affects our emotional gratification in the other

| Emotional gratification in one role | ⟵┄┄┄┄┄┄┄ ┄┄┄┄┄┄┄⟶ | Emotional gratification in the other role |

Positive emotions experienced in a role promote work–family integration, and help make allies of the two domains. Integration makes it possible to participate in our life roles with less stress and distraction. The converse is obvious: frustration and dissatisfaction within one role can produce work–family conflict—as negative emotions spill over, they interfere with our satisfaction and success in the other role. Clearly, emotional gratification in one role is important to the other.

Now that we have an idea of how these three elements in our model help determine whether work and family are allies or enemies, let's look specifically at their effects at work and at home. The two accompanying boxes provide an overview of what we've learned and what we'll be discussing in this chapter.

How Work Affects Family Life

WORK LIFE	FAMILY LIFE
Resources from Work*	**Lead to . . .**
High level in organization	Healthier children Children do better in school
High income	More satisfied with childcare Healthier children

Family-friendly employer	Spend more time on home
	  and children
	Spend more time relaxing
	Return to work part-time after child
	Experience few work–family
	  tradeoffs
	Experience few work–family
	  conflicts
	Perform better as parent

Authority	Healthier children
Networking	More satisfied with family
Effective job performance	Perform better as parent
Men Only Adjustment of work schedule	Healthier children
Women Only Authority	More satisfied with childcare Children have fewer behavioral problems
Acceptance by peers	More satisfied with childcare
Networking	Children do better in school More satisfied with childcare Healthier children

*Factors that produce resources at work.

Involvement in Work	Leads to . . .
High psychological involvement in work	Lower psychological involvement in family
	Less satisfied with family
	Perform worse as parent
	Partner provides less personal support
	Partner provides less assistance with children
Career as life role priority	Spend less time on home and children
	Take less time off following children
	Lower psychological involvement in family
	Less adjustment of work schedule for family
	Less satisfied with family
Men Only	
Long work hours	More satisfied with family
High job performance	Children have fewer behavioral problems
High psychological involvement in work	Children have more behavioral problems
Women Only	
Long work hours	Less satisfied with family
Committed to organization	More satisfied with childcare
High psychological involvement in work	Children have fewer behavioral problems
Emotional Gratification from Work	**Leads to . . .**
Satisfied with job	Perform better as parent
Satisfied with career	More satisfied with family
Men Only	
Satisfied with job	Children have fewer behavioral problems
Women Only	
Satisfied with career	Children do better in school

How Family Affects Work

FAMILY LIFE   WORK LIFE

Resources from Family   **Lead to . . .**

Partner helps with children   Higher income
                                     Higher job performance
                                     More coaching
                                     Fewer adjustments of work schedule
                                       for family

Partner provides extensive   More authority
  personal support   More coaching
                                     More accepted at work
                                     More satisfied with career

Partner provides extensive   More authority
  career support   More developmental assignments
                                     More coaching
                                     More networking
                                     More accepted at work
                                     More satisfied with career

Men Only
Partner helps with children   Higher level in organization

Women Only
Partner provides extensive   Higher job performance
  personal support

Involvement in Family   **Leads to . . .**

High psychological involvement   Lower psychological involvement
  in family   in work

Family as life role priority   More adjustment of work schedule
                                        for family
                                      Lower psychological involvement
                                        in work
                                      Lower career aspirations
                                      More relocations for family reasons

Men Only
Marriage and children   Higher income
                                      Higher level in organization
                                      More satisfied with career

Women Only
Presence of children   Lower income
                                      Less satisfied with career

Extensive family responsibilities	Work fewer hours
	Lower psychological involvement in work
	More adjustment of work schedule for family
	Fewer developmental assignments
Emotional Gratification from Family	**Leads to . . .**
Satisfied with family	More satisfied with career

Resources and Their Impact

Resources at work have a profound effect on family life and vice versa, as we've seen from our business professionals. Let's delve deeper into what we've learned about how resources from one domain affect our lives in the other.

Resources from work affect the family

Our business professionals have better family lives when their work provides resources. Jobs that provide few of the resources we've been discussing can have negative consequences for family life by detracting from the quality of family life and producing work–family conflict. Clearly, whether work is an ally or enemy of family depends in large part on the resources available in the workplace—which is precisely why we call so much attention to these resources. Let's look more specifically at the effects.

We find that individuals who occupy high-level positions in the organization, and who earn the substantial income that usually accompanies such responsibilities, have healthy children who do well in school and have satisfactory childcare arrangements. So, *financial* resources from work are important. While it is still the case that money and power cannot buy happiness or guarantee that we perform well as parents, they do seem to enable people to acquire high-quality services for their children, and perhaps even provide a home environment that contributes to the kids' academic accomplishments.

As we've noted several times in earlier chapters, *flexibility*—discretion over the methods, timing, and location of work—is a resource critical to work–family integration. Through alternative work arrangements, employers furnish the time and flexibility employees need to juggle work and family responsibilities. People who work for family-friendly employers use that flexibility to devote more time to home, children, and relaxation; they're also more likely to return to work only part-time after the birth of a child. Further, these people experience fewer tradeoffs and work–family conflicts and feel better about their parenting than people who work in less supportive organizations.

Authority is another resource at work. People with high levels of authority on the job tend to have healthy children—perhaps because they have the flexibility to attend to their kids' health needs in a timely manner. The fact that women with authority are highly satisfied with childcare and have children with relatively few behavioral problems suggests these women are even more likely than men to use their job authority to better their families.

We expect that authority at work also boosts self-esteem. The additional responsibilities associated with jobs that have high levels of authority make them more challenging, and when we meet those challenges we feel better about ourselves.[12]

One intangible, but extremely important, set of resources is the information and advice that come from networking with—and feeling accepted by—other people in our work organizations. Although networking promotes a feeling of satisfaction with family for men and women, networking and acceptance generally have a stronger impact on children for women than for men. Children's health and school performance improve when their mothers network extensively, and the quality of their childcare arrangements depends on whether their mothers network a lot and feel accepted by their peers. As we have suggested, women may use networking not only for instrumental, career-enhancing purposes but also to meet their emotional and social needs. It's clear that the information, advice, and perspectives provided by other people at work help women improve the quality of their children's lives.

Family-friendly employers also provide information and advice, often through referral services and work–family counseling. The resource of acceptance often comes through company practices that acknowledge the difficulties of managing work and family commitments.

As noted earlier, our self-esteem can also be enhanced when we perform well on assigned tasks—especially those involving a great deal of authority—and when we participate in particularly challenging special assignments that stretch our capabilities and promote the development of new talents. We've already seen the impact of authority on family life. It's also interesting that individuals who perform well in their jobs feel they perform well in their parenting role. Some of the skills we need to achieve high performance in professional jobs—listening, coordinating, mentoring, and leading teams—are also relevant to being an effective parent. Moreover, the self-esteem we derive from high job performance can give us the confidence to learn and apply effective parenting skills at home.

Resources from the family affect work

Just as resources at work can strengthen family life, resources in the family can improve work. One of the family's primary resources is the support partners provide for each other.[13] Behavioral support from our partner—in particular, help with the kids—can provide us with time and flexibility at home that makes us better able to meet the demands of work. Those of us who receive behavioral support from our partners find we make relatively few family-imposed adjustments in our work schedules. In turn, we are more available behaviorally to work colleagues. And when we can give that extra time and attention to work—time less distracted by family concerns—we get more opportunities for coaching, our job performance is enhanced, and, at least for men, there's more rapid ascent through the organizational hierarchy.

Partners who bolster us emotionally with personal or career support also provide resources. Emotional support from our partners—through their love, concern, empathy, and advice—provides information, guidance, and acceptance that help build our self-esteem and self-confidence.[14] With higher self-esteem, we're better able to seek out experiences like coaching, networking, and key assignments that ultimately develop greater competence at work, not to mention higher career satisfaction. For women, receptiveness to a partner's support is particularly useful in promoting a high level of job performance.

The scarcity of family resources that results from having little or no partner support reduces our availability, development, and satisfaction at work. Under these circumstances, the family can be an enemy to work.

There is another way in which family resources can enrich people's careers, although we did not look at it specifically in our research. It has to do with skills and social connections developed and reinforced outside of work. For example, managing a household, coping with interpersonal difficulties, and teaching children are skills and talents we develop at home, and are resources that can be applied to the work setting—they can help us become more effective managers and developers of people in the workplace.[15] Our attentiveness to the emotional needs of family members, for example, attunes us to the importance of being emotionally available to work colleagues, and can help us become more competent in solving problems and resolving conflicts at work. Household management—with its financial, interpersonal, entrepreneurial, and administrative requirements—has many applications to the management of a business enterprise. This educational spillover can make family experiences and accomplishments strong allies of work.[16]

Men and Women Use Work Resources in Different Ways

There are some important differences in the impact of work on family for men and women—reflecting somewhat distinct social identities for men and women. Most men view work first and foremost as a vehicle to success, placing more emphasis on achieving status and wealth than do most women. Devotion to work reinforces a man's self-image as a good provider. Men who work long hours and perform well in their jobs are satisfied with their family lives; their children have relatively few behavioral problems; and they feel good about themselves and their role in the family.

Women are more likely than are men to value growth and challenge in their work, without the emphasis on money, status, and power we see among men. Women also view work positively when they see it as an opportunity to care for others through their work. Also, women more than men seem to use authority and flexibility at work to provide better care for their children, with the result that the kids have relatively few behavioral problems. Not unexpectedly, women are more likely than are men to value time for themselves and their family in their careers.

Women generally place a higher value on social relationships at work than do men, and use these relationships to a greater extent. For example, when women network extensively in their jobs, they are more satisfied with childcare arrangements and their children have fewer school and health problems. Networking by men has no such effect. Similarly, women who feel accepted by their peers at work also express satisfaction with childcare. Taken together, these findings strongly suggest that women use work relationships—at least in part—to enhance the well-being of their families. We're not certain whether women intentionally utilize these relationships to help solve family problems or whether family well-being is an incidental by-product of sharing family and personal concerns with colleagues. But what is clear is that women leverage social relationships at work for the betterment of their families.

The Effects of Involvement

Involvement in work affects the family

A disproportionately high level of psychological involvement in work can have several negative effects on the family. It generally detracts from the quality of a person's family life. In this respect, work can be an enemy of the family. People who are involved in work to the point of preoccupation tend to be uninvolved in—and dissatisfied with—their family lives. Among our four life role priorities, people in the career-focused group are least satisfied with their families.

Absorption in work reduces availability to other family members. People absorbed in their work have little energy or inclination to give their time or attention to others. Their partners are reluctant to provide much of any kind of support. The expectation of reciprocity discourages individuals from providing behavioral or emotional support to partners who give little in return.

Career Success: Ally or Enemy of the Family?

Do people who are successful in their careers inevitably pay a price for that success—in the way of unhappy family lives? We don't think so. Achieving career success can be a *boon* to family life. People who are satisfied with their careers are also satisfied with their families. And earning a high income certainly promotes children's health and parents' satisfaction with childcare. Moreover, individuals who achieve a high-level position at work have kids who are healthy and perform well at school. There are few indications that a high income, a responsible job, and a satisfying career—our three measures of career success—have harmful effects on the family.

If career success is not the enemy of the family, what about career is harmful? The answer is crucial: the *preoccupation with work* that some people deem necessary to achieve a successful career. We have shown repeatedly that people who pour most of their psychic energy into work simply have little left for their families. In effect, these people are making a trade—a satisfying family life for intense absorption in their work.

Undoubtedly, success in certain career fields requires an intense preoccupation with work. It may well be that the energy and sacrifices expected if one is to achieve success in these particular fields are themselves the culprits. But some occupations—and an increasing number of family-friendly employers—do not impose work demands so severe that family and personal life inevitably suffer. Indeed, if we are to make allies of work and family, it is critical that we select careers and employers compatible with the kind of life outside work that fits our values.

There's a vicious circle at work here, as well. The less available work-absorbed people are to family members, the less competent they're likely to be in family life—which explains why they view themselves as ineffective parents. Opportunities to master parenting skills simply do not arise when we are emotionally and physically withdrawn from our children. Moreover, people who are unavailable and incompetent in the family domain are unlikely to meet the needs usually satisfied in healthy family relationships, such as the intimacy we experience in loving relationships in which we have the opportunity to nurture others. This helps explain why career-focused people, highly involved in their work, tend to be dissatisfied with their family lives.

Involvement in family affects work

The effects we've seen from work to family tend to be replicated in the other direction. When we are deeply involved psychologically in our family lives, we tend to reduce our involvement in work. Recall that family-focused people are not strongly involved in their careers, do not aspire to senior management positions, frequently adjust their work schedules to meet family and personal needs, and relocate for family reasons. We have seen that people in the family-focused group restrict their career involvement to avoid extensive conflicts between work and family. However, the impact on work of involvement in family responsibilities is more pronounced for women than men.

Involvement in Family and the Careers of Women and Men

Extensive involvement in family life can be an enemy to work, especially for dual-earner mothers with young children. These women carry heavier family responsibilities, work fewer hours, and adjust their work schedules more than all others—which means they limit their behavioral availability at work. Their diminished psychological involvement in work may render them less emotionally available on the job as well. These dual-earner mothers also receive less coaching and fewer developmental assignments at work, in part out of choice and in part because of stereotypes. Absent the career development opportunities other women may have, these moms have fewer chances to strengthen their competence or develop new skills at work. They end up being less satisfied with their careers than women without children.

Women—dual-earner mothers in particular—are generally more involved in their families than are men. They spend more time with the children and less time at work than men. Perhaps most significantly, women are more willing than men are to *trade* career success for the well-being of the family. It is the woman, not the man, who suffers the family penalty when children enter the picture. It is the woman with family responsibilities who adjusts her work schedule for family reasons, and it is the woman who turns down developmental opportunities at work. In short, the woman—specifically the dual-earner mother— often experiences a substantial tradeoff between family and work.

Men, conversely, receive a family bonus that enables them to achieve high levels of career success. This is especially true for single-earner fathers. Although we don't rule out that fathers are especially motivated to achieve success, the more plausible explanation lies with the favorable stereotypes of family men held by many employers. It is less a case of the families providing resources to single-earner fathers than it is biases among employers that result in fathers being given more authority (and achieving greater career success) than men with no children. This bias even extends to fathers with stay-at-home wives being paid more. Clearly, in this situation, the single-earner father's family is an ally to his work.

Is family simply more important to women than to men? Or do women view their role in the family differently than men? We believe it's more the latter. Men who are highly involved in their families do believe their family is very important to them. But they take an instrumental view of their role as husband and father; that is, their function is tied to the breadwinner role by which they provide financial security to their partners and children. This is one reason men's satisfaction with their family lives seems to go hand in hand with the number of hours they spend at work. Although men—especially dual-earner men— probably spend more time on home and family activities than their own fathers did, they often find it difficult to escape the division of labor by gender that has been reinforced for generations. Marriages that begin with an egalitarian orientation often revert to a more traditional separation of tasks for men and women once children enter the picture.

In most cultures, women have traditionally assumed primary responsibility for assuring the family's emotional wellbeing. No wonder, then, that women have a more stringent and demanding conception than men do of what it takes to be a good partner and parent. In contrast to men's roles, being a wife and mother generally means something more than—or different from—bringing home the bacon. It means being available to family members and being attuned to their varied needs.

The Dynamics of Emotional Gratification

Because emotions can spill over from one role to another, the emotional gratification we get in one domain can have a direct effect on the satisfaction we experience in the other sphere of life.

When it comes to emotional spillover, work can be either an ally or an enemy to the family. Work is an ally when it produces satisfaction and other positive emotions that promote satisfaction in the family domain: the more satisfaction people experience in their careers, the more satisfied they are with their family lives. People who are satisfied with their work feel good about themselves and their role in society and transfer these positive emotions—satisfaction, optimism, and self-esteem—to the family domain.

Work that is dissatisfying, that leaves us frustrated and anxious, is an enemy to family life. The negative emotions from the work domain are transferred to the family domain.

Similarly, men and women experience positive and negative emotional spillover from family to work. People who are satisfied with their family lives find they are satisfied with their careers; the positive emotions in the family domain spill over to enrich the work domain. When we are satisfied with our families, we feel better about ourselves and we approach our work with fewer family-related stresses and distractions. This makes us better able to derive greater satisfaction from our careers.

But just as a happy family life can be an ally to work, a stressful, dissatisfying family can impede satisfaction with work. Here family is the enemy of work.

What Causes Conflict Between Work and Family?

Time is often invoked to explain the conflicts people experience between their work and family lives. Most of us have heard the argument before: if only people didn't work such long hours, they'd have a more satisfying family life. Or, if they didn't devote so much time to home and family, their careers would flourish. But is time the culprit? The short answer is: Not as much as most people think.

To be sure, we did uncover several examples where time spent in one domain detracts from the other.[17] However, time spent working has no bearing on children's behavioral, health, or school problems, and does not determine parental performance, although it reduces family satisfaction for women over 30.

What matter more are the psychological conflicts we experience between our work and family lives. When are our family and personal lives likely to suffer? It's when the demands of work interfere with our family responsibilities, and when we find it difficult to adjust our behavior as we move between work and home. It's when our intense absorption in work intrudes into the quality of family life.

People who are preoccupied with work are uninvolved and dissatisfied with their family, are dissatisfied with their performance as parents, and find it difficult to get partner support. Children and adults alike sense when their parents or partners are consistently distracted by their work—and relationships can suffer as a result.

Here are some examples of statements reflecting our measure of the interference of work with family (the first four are about psychological interference; the last two are about behavioral interference):

- When I spend time with my family, I am bothered by all of the things on my job that I should be doing.
- Because of my job responsibilities, I have to miss out on home or family activities in which I should participate.
- Because of my job responsibilities, the time I spend with my family is less enjoyable and more pressured.
- Pursuing a demanding job makes it difficult for me to be an attentive spouse/partner.
- My partner complains that I treat family members as if they are work associates or subordinates.
- I find it difficult making the transition from my job to home life.

With the possible exception of job responsibilities intruding into family activities, these conflicts have little to do with time. Rather, they involve preoccupation with work, pressure from work experienced at home, inability to be a thoughtful partner because of work demands, and difficulty turning off work behaviors at home. What we've learned about these conflicts points to the importance of managing the boundaries between work and family. We must learn how to create greater flexibility to minimize the schedule conflicts between work and family, and then use that flexibility. We must learn how to leave work behind and enjoy family life when we're at home—in other words, to separate or segment our work and family roles at certain times. We have to learn that behaviors that may be effective at work are inappropriate when we're at home dealing with family members. The need to "switch gears" when traversing the great divide between work and family is paramount. We have more to say about managing role boundaries in our final chapter.

Recurrent Cycles of Influence

When work and family are integrated, one role strengthens and enhances the other role. But work–family integration doesn't necessarily mean both roles strengthen each other at the same time. For some, work may strengthen family; for others, family may improve the quality of work. The same can be said about work–family conflict. For some people, work interferes with family, while for others it is the reverse.

Individuals who are highly satisfied with their careers are also very satisfied with their family lives. Perhaps a satisfying career enables us to relax and enjoy relationships with family members. It is also easy to imagine how a satisfying family life can, over time, promote a high level of career satisfaction, since we may be able to pursue our work relatively free of distractions caused by family stress. But which is the cause and which the effect? Does our career satisfaction initially enhance our family satisfaction, or is it the other way around? We don't know. But it is likely that a recurrent cycle eventually occurs in which satisfaction with work and satisfaction with family mutually reinforce each other over time.[18]

There is a similar situation when work and family are enemies. Individuals highly involved in their work may become be uninvolved and dissatisfied in their family role. Does absorption in work make it difficult to become involved in family, or do people run away from dissatisfying family situations by throwing themselves into their work? Undoubtedly, both situations occur. Regardless of the initial cause, however, an ongoing cycle can appear in which high involvement in work not only compensates for low involvement in family but also makes future involvement in family less likely.

There is another example of this recurrent cycle. In our discussion of the family bonus or penalty, we showed that women with children often suffer a family penalty that detracts from their career success, specifically in terms of lowered income and career satisfaction. This can prompt a woman to involve herself even more deeply in her family to compensate for the lack of success and satisfaction in the world of work. Although a woman's family responsibilities may initially affect her career, her unsatisfying experiences at work can subsequently heighten her involvement in family life.

In summary, we believe there are recurrent cycles of influence between work and family lives. These cycles, which may be positive or negative, make it difficult to determine whether the influence originally resides in the workplace or in the family domain.[19] Regardless of its origin, however, work–family linkages take on lives of their own that perpetuate over time.

In Praise of the Career + Family Focus

We've shown that psychological absorption in work or family often results in interference between the two roles. The role in which we are absorbed and preoccupied crowds out rich and fulfilling involvement in the other role. This suggests that equal involvement in both work and family may result in fulfillment in both roles. Let's look at what happens when *both* work and family are prominent parts of our lives—that is, when we are psychologically involved in both work and family domains.

In Chapter 2 we introduced life role priorities and provided an overview of four groups among our business professionals:

- Career-focused, in which the greatest importance is placed on career
- Family-focused, in which the greatest importance is placed on family
- Career + family-focused, in which dual importance is placed on career and family
- Self/society-focused, in which the greatest importance is placed either on personal development or community

Throughout this book, we have returned to these life role priorities to help explain how work and family affect people in different ways. Now, as we attempt to answer the big question—whether work and family are allies or enemies—we return to life role priorities to take a special look at one group: career + family. Why? People in the career + family group display the highest level of work–family integration, which we've suggested may be the key to finding fulfillment in both domains of life.[20] These people

- are the most satisfied with their careers
- are among the most satisfied with their family lives
- are among the most satisfied with their personal growth and development
- have children who are doing well physically, emotionally, and academically
- are among the most satisfied with their overall lives

We believe people whose life role priority is career + family achieve satisfaction in both spheres of life because their work and family roles are integrated rather than conflicted. Their work interferes with family far less than it does for their career-focused counterparts. Their families interfere with their work far less than it does for the family-focused group. Their value for *both* work and family prevents one role from consistently being accommodated in favor of the other. In fact, the career + family group experiences fewer work–family tradeoffs than do any of the other groups.

Contrast this with a family focus. Family-focused individuals give of themselves freely to their partners and children, and they have much to show for it. They have satisfying family lives, and their kids are healthy and well-adjusted. But their careers—in which they invest relatively little of themselves—suffer. Their extensive involvement with family responsibilities interferes with work; consequently, they have to make many work–family tradeoffs. With the restrictions family-focused individuals place on their career involvement—so that they can accommodate their families—these people end up relatively dissatisfied with the direction their careers have taken.

However, family-focused people are satisfied with *something*, while career-focused people seem to have the worst of both worlds. Predictably, they express little satisfaction with their family lives, probably because they give so little of themselves in that arena. But they're not especially satisfied with their personal growth and, most surprising, do not experience the high level of career satisfaction we might expect of people so focused on work. The self/society group has its share of problems, too. Their kids may be doing relatively well, but these people are the least satisfied with their careers and their personal growth, and lag behind most of the other groups in satisfaction with their family lives.

The self/society group is deeply involved neither in work nor in family. Indeed, they're among the least likely to be married or have children. No surprise, then, that they experience little career or family satisfaction, at least in comparison to the other groups.

Contrast again the career + family types, who invest heavily in work *and* family. Sure, they work long hours and are psychologically involved in their career but they also spend time with their families and are psychologically involved in the lives of their partners and kids. And they reap benefits from this dual involvement: satisfying careers *and* rewarding family relationships.

One general principle that emerges from our research is that the more we invest in a life role, the more we receive from that role in return. The career-focused group, though, is the most perplexing of all. Apparently, these people are the exception to this principle of increasing returns from high involvement. By all accounts, they should be exceptionally successful and satisfied in their careers, given the time and attention they invest in work. But they're not.

It's interesting to compare the career-focused group directly with the career + family group—people who *are* satisfied with their careers. Both work long hours, are psychologically involved in their work, and hold ambitious career aspirations. Both groups have similar experiences at work in terms of authority, career development opportunities, and networking. And both groups value similar rewards in their careers. Why, then, are the career types less satisfied with their careers?

One possibility is that career-focused people place so much importance on work that they have overly exacting standards for career success. Their lives are so imbalanced, and they demand so much of themselves at work, that it is difficult for them to find satisfaction with their accomplishments in the work domain.

It's also possible that career-focused people receive so little satisfaction from their family lives that they just can't enjoy their careers. A satisfying family life might well be a necessary (although, in and of itself, insufficient) ingredient of a satisfying career because of the positive emotional spillover that can take place from one's family to work. Is it just a coincidence that the people most likely to be very satisfied with their career—the career + family types—are also very satisfied with their families?

It is tempting to recommend that business professionals adopt a career + family focus as their life role priority. After all, we are praising their dual involvement in work and family because the evidence shows it is likely to bring substantial returns in both domains. We can say with conviction that although a career + family focus is not the most common (about 30 percent of our sample), it can lead to a rich, satisfying, integrated life.[21] People in this group demonstrate that it is possible to be involved in work and family without becoming victims of destructive work–family conflict. It is, in short, a good lifestyle choice for those individuals who want to be emotionally engaged in—and reap substantial rewards from—both work and family domains. That said, praise does not necessarily lead to prescription. Our primary aim in this book is not to prescribe one set of values, but rather to understand the implications of different patterns of work and family involvement.

Summing Up

So, it appears that work and family can be close allies. Resources derived from one role can be fruitfully applied to the other, and positive emotions initially experienced in one part of life can spill over to enrich other domains as well. When our experiences, behaviors, and feelings cut across life roles in favorable ways, work and family are allies, and are integrated.

Work and family can also be enemies. When work and family fail to provide resources (or deplete them) and when we experience dissatisfaction and frustration, our lives suffer. And we can be so involved in work or family that our absorption and preoccupation prevent us from participating fully and happily in the other role. Work and family are enemies when they consistently conflict with one another.

All of us can live happier and more balanced lives when each part of life benefits from the other—when enough flexibility, information, acceptance, and self-esteem are derived from work and family to help us become involved, competent, and happy in other parts of our lives. How do we achieve this work–family integration? Most of us need some support to get there—from employers, from families, and from society itself. In our closing chapter, we turn our attention to how such support can be provided, how people can be helped in crossing great divides, how we can increase the odds that work and family are indeed allies.

9

What Can Be Done?

Throughout our book, we've pointed to the choices about work and family that affect the quality of men's and women's lives. We've presented our data and our model for understanding the relationship between work and family (see Figure 8.2). Now new questions loom, which put the choices into a more action-oriented context: What steps can achieve work–family integration? What should individuals do? What should employers do? What about the public policy arena? Can work be made the ally of family, and family the ally of work? And do we—our employers, our families, and society—have the will to change?

We believe there are things that *must* be done. In this final chapter, we become advocates for creating what we call an infrastructure for flexibility, the broad implication drawn by our findings. What we suggest in this chapter also flows from the model in Chapter 8, and our recommendations should be taken in the context of that model. Some of the suggestions we endorse here come from others. We're glad to report that at least some of what we advocate is already being implemented in one form or another.

Our advocacy in this chapter is also tied directly to the themes we first presented in Chapter 1. Here, the implications embedded in those themes become an agenda for action for individuals, employers, and society—which we believe is a prerequisite for creating the opportunities for men and women alike to shape their work and family lives in ways that are consistent with their personal values. This is the way to make work the ally of the family, and to make family the ally of work.

Every one of our recommendations, in one way or another, either overtly or not, is about creating options. In turn, those options are meant to create an infrastructure for flexibility. And that infrastructure can be seen as a framework for our entire action agenda.

What we endorse, first and foremost, are *integration* and *conflict reduction* between family and work. Forging the alliance between work and family requires understanding, and it requires options. At present, corporate and social policies in general don't support options because they are based largely on outmoded gender role stereotypes, employment models, and cultural values that emerged in the days of a different workforce demography—with dad at a job away from home, mom back with the kids, and the boss keeping a close eye on employees to make sure they were adding value.

Every component of our action agenda is based on our conviction that greater diversity in options is necessary, and that providing this diversity is consistent with the needs of business—indeed, of society as a whole—to have committed, motivated employees both now and in the workforce of the future. Options will also help men and women pursue the things that are important to them—not only as productive players in the economic system, but also as members of families and communities.

Benefits

Why bother? What are the benefits of work–family integration to individuals, families, employers, and society? It is our hope that by now readers will have a good idea of our answer. But let's take another look at these benefits.

We are convinced that work–family integration affords people a greater opportunity to achieve personal goals and lead more satisfying lives. For adults, it can promote career success and more satisfying relationships at home. It means we can be more available to deal with eldercare issues. It's a common observation that reductions in role conflict reduce stress for nearly everyone—single men and women, as well as parents in the workforce. All of us can have more satisfying personal lives when work is our ally.

For children, work–family integration means parents can be more available. In turn, parents can be more involved in their children's lives.

Think of the implications for education. Richard W. Riley, the U.S. Secretary of Education, put it this way: If parents paid more attention to being involved with their children's learning, "it would revolutionize education in America. When parents are involved, children get better grades and test scores, are more likely to graduate high school and go on to college, and are better behaved in class."[1]

Then there's the issue of childhood development. We need parents to be available to their children (especially when they are very young), and work–family integration is a way to make that happen—because it's an investment in parents. The stakes are high. Former U.S. Surgeon General Dr. C. Everett Koop, speaking of the importance of parental availability for infants, sums ups the research on child development: "The best thing to do is be the best possible parent—bond, touch, talk, cuddle—make your baby a part of you."[2] Children need to know and feel the love of their parents, and we as a society need to provide those opportunities for parents to give that love to their children.[3]

Employers also need to pay attention to family issues. It's a business concern with bottom-line implications. In a global economy, with heightened competition, American employers perhaps more than ever need the advantage of committed employees. That advantage can give the employer an edge in dealing with some of the features of the new economic landscape.

The new workplace for business professionals is becoming one where workers are less likely to stay with one employer over the course of a career, where there's a sort of "free agent" mode of thinking. Employers have an incentive to keep their employees, however. Long-term employees in an organization, if they're satisfied with their jobs, are loyal workers. They're morale-builders. They know the business and the customers, and they know what quality means in the specific context of that employer. They have what labor economists call "firm-specific knowledge." That makes these employees a particular asset to the company.

As business professionals increasingly come to expect the kind of flexibility we've been describing, they're sure to seek out those employers who offer it. Employers who fail will experience greater unwanted turnover. Reducing that unwanted turnover can translate into a competitive advantage. Parents, especially, are looking for flexible employers. As one researcher has put it, flexibility "is the major enabler for working parents to participate successfully in the labor force."[4]

There are other benefits. Businesses should view creating a flexible environment for employees as an investment. Investments bring returns. In this case, the investment can enhance a company's image among current and future employees, not to mention customers, and improve the quality of the workforce now and in the future. Employees will not only give a greater personal commitment to employers who demonstrate a willingness to be flexible, they're likely to find ways to work smarter too.

Society also benefits from making allies of family and work. Surely, more committed workers means greater productivity for the nation as a whole. And surely the nation benefits from well-adjusted kids who do well in school and exhibit fewer behavioral problems. Individuals who are satisfied with their lives make for more active, more contributory citizens. These are but a few examples.

Our findings about the benefits of work–family integration for men, women, children, and employers have broader societal implications. That's why society has a big stake in affecting the sort of change we advocate. We propose some specific action items for the public sector.

Three Principles for Creating Allies of Work and Family

What happens at home has a profound effect on work. Take partner support, for example. Receiving *behavioral* support from a partner makes it possible for us to devote more time to work and make relatively few family-imposed adjustments to our work schedule. In turn, we can be more available behaviorally to work colleagues. *Emotional* support from a partner provides the information, advice, acceptance, and self-esteem we need to seek out the experiences and opportunities that ultimately develop greater competence at work.

Similarly, experiences at work have a profound effect on family life. Flexibility is one important example: if we work for a supportive employer that provides flexibility, we can devote more attention and energy to home, children, and relaxation. We experience fewer tradeoffs and work–family conflicts. We feel better about our parenting than do people who work for less supportive employers.

Our experiences in each domain, the resources provided by work and family, the gratification we get from our different roles—all can serve to make work the ally of family and family the ally of work. Put to optimum use, they support work–family integration.

What does it take to make this happen? We believe there are three basic principles that should guide individuals, employers, and society.[5]

Clarify what's important

The first principle is to *clarify what's important*. It's about understanding our values, our life role priorities. From that understanding, we can see how the choices we make in the work and family domains have consequences across the divide between the two domains.

We can't overstate the importance of clarifying what's important. We'd like to see fewer regrets like the one expressed by Laurel Cutler, vice chairman of Foote Cone & Belding: "I wish I had known sooner that if you miss a child's play or performance or sporting event, you will have forgotten a year later the work emergency that caused you to miss it. But the child won't have forgotten that you weren't there."[6]

A large part of clarifying what's important is for each individual to let others know what's important to her or him. This is the key to taking a focused and intelligent approach to negotiating for authority on the job, which is a source of flexibility. Goals that are articulated and understood are more likely to be met—and meeting goals generates greater self-esteem. We are more likely to acquire information and advice (two of the resources we identified earlier) if our vision and values are clearly known.

Clarifying what's important isn't only for the individual, however. Employers, too, need to apply this principle. Those that do so make business priorities clear to employees. They also encourage their employees to be just as clear about personal interests and concerns. They ask their employees to speak up. And they listen, and seek to understand work's place in the overall life of each employee. This is the way to achieve *both* business and individual goals.

Vice President Al Gore, in a 1997 speech to a group of corporate leaders gathered at Microsoft, spoke to the issue of clarifying what's important. He pointed out that "CEOs who have found ways to honor and respect their employees' loyalties to their spouses and families and communities have reduced turnover and absenteeism, and increased creativity and productivity. Family-friendly workplaces, family and medical leave, flex time, and other measures to bolster employees' emotional satisfaction are proving to be extremely valuable to earnings, revenues, and profits." For these employers, *results*—and not "face time"—are what count.

This principle of clarifying what's important applies to the public sector as well. Society needs to choose to value quality of life and the development of the next generation to a greater extent than we do now. Our leaders need to place more importance on societal values such as quality of life and human dignity. And we should reward those who provide resources that allow for flexibility.

Vice President Gore's focus was on how the private sector can and should capitalize on our "core capacities as human beings—spirit, creativity, and heart." This, coming from a national leader, helps to build a sense of value for what's important, not only to the national "soul," but to our nation's economic well-being.

Recognize and support the whole person

For individuals, the second principle—*recognize and support the whole person*—requires that we respect different life roles, including work, family, community, and others, and that we focus on building supportive relationships at work and in our personal lives. Strong relationships, combined with a healthy respect for the diverse needs that arise from different roles, work together to create the foundation for that infrastructure of flexibility we need to integrate work and family. They also strengthen our commitment to achieving both work and personal life goals, in part by helping us to manage boundaries between roles. Supportive relationships are a necessary resource in both domains.

This principle has relevance for employers, too. Employers who recognize and support the whole person are open-minded. They go beyond the mere recognition that their employees *have* a life beyond work—they celebrate that life. They don't just know that this or that employee is married or single, has children or not. These employers recognize and support their employees in their varied life roles: not just a "mother" or "father," for instance, but the parent of a particular child with a unique identity; or a coach in the local Little League; or a volunteer providing meals for the homeless.

And they seek to take advantage, in good ways, of the things that employees' lives beyond work bring to the workplace. Think about the skills required to achieve high performance in professional jobs—listening, coordinating, mentoring, and leading teams. Aren't they also relevant to being an effective parent? Plus, skills developed and reinforced at home are resources that can be applied to the work setting. Attentiveness to the emotional needs of our family members, for example, can attune us to the importance of being emotionally available to our colleagues at work, and can help us become more competent in solving problems and resolving conflicts at work.

The management of a household, with its financial, interpersonal, entrepreneurial, and administrative requirements, has many applications to the management of a business enterprise. These spillovers can make family experiences and accomplishments strong allies of work. Doesn't this suggest that employers ought to recognize and *value* the skills family people bring to work? And doesn't that in turn suggest that employers ought to encourage their workers to be effective in their families—because it translates into economic benefits for the firm?

Society can take steps as well to recognize and support the whole person. Social policy should be developed that supports the needs of people to manage boundaries between work and family and to enhance the value of family to work and of work to family—and in turn to increase the chances that they'll function as allies and not enemies. Further, society needs to loosen the constraints on choices available to men and women, through education and models that demonstrate the varieties of legitimate roles each of us can play.

Continually experiment with how goals are achieved

The third principle—*continually experiment with how goals are achieved*—points to the need to learn from our experiences and those of others. There are no simple solutions, and what works now may not work later. In our agenda for action, we're prescribing a major cultural shift. The outcomes aren't certain, and all of us will need to experiment if we're to secure the best results. We need to continually reexamine our goals, try new strategies, question stereotypes we hold, and be willing to adopt new ways of looking at our work and our lives outside of work.

For employers, this principle is about new approaches to increased efficiency and productivity. Adopting this principle means encouraging employees to question basic assumptions and to learn about new possibilities in every aspect of the business, particularly in how work is designed. It means putting technology to work as an enabler of organizational and employee flexibility. And it means seeking out the ways in which work and personal life can be connected to benefit both, and win greater attention and commitment from employees.

Again and again, as we review the literature on creating family-friendliness in work organizations, the same motif emerges: employers have to challenge assumptions, and they have to change their cultures. These are at the core of any effort to make work–family integration an effective business strategy.[7]

As several researchers have noted, one of the most common assumptions in corporations has been that work and private lives are separate and conflicting, that what's personal is personal and shouldn't intrude on work-related decisions. Another is that most employees don't want to take responsibility for improving business processes. These two assumptions end up being an obstacle to changes that can make work more family-supportive. Even many of the employers who have introduced work/life programs have continued to let these assumptions stand unchallenged. In fact, many people *welcome* the challenge of improving business processes when they're given freedom, flexibility, and encouragement to put their personal interests on the table in coming up with constructive changes in how work is accomplished.

With respect to experimenting continually with how goals are achieved, we need at the societal level to question the old assumptions about what should be, particularly with respect to gender roles. By doing so, we can open society to embracing new ways of getting things done. This, in turn, can help prepare our citizens for a future that promises different models for career and family.

An Action Agenda

We believe that making allies of work and family requires that choice be available and supported. We also believe that this integration can be achieved only if individuals, employers, and society are committed to seeing that happen.[8]

In her important book, Susan Chira puts the importance of choices in perspective.[9] While her book is about mothers, the ideas behind what she says can be applied to all working people—not to mention employers and society as a whole. Chira writes: "The right balance of work and mothering can only be decided after struggles with our own hearts. In the end, individual decisions will and should vary. Is giving up a job so painful that doing so will sour time with children and make mothers feel their lives are failures? Is giving up time with children so painful that doing so will poison the hours at work and torture mothers with the belief they've failed their children?"

Of course, we've tried to show that tradeoffs aren't always necessary, and that there's a way to build alliances between work and family so they are mutually enriching. But, ultimately, choices are necessary, because we don't have limitless resources.

Chira argues, as do we, that there needs to be a broader range of discretion available for people. Again, she's talking about working mothers, but it's easy to substitute women without children, or men, in these sentences: "Mothers must be given the freedom to make choices without being blinded and hounded by the false debate, the confining ideal of the perfect mother, and the taunts of the self-righteous. Only then, unencumbered, can mothers make the decision that works best for them. . . . I only ask that no mother should curb her dreams—whether to be at home or at work—out of baseless fear or guilt."

We believe this same freedom of choice must be available to all individuals: freedom to establish priorities and find the right mix of commitments to different life domains. It implies that part of clarifying what's important, for those who value harmony between work and family, is to choose an occupation, employer, or industry that is supportive of integration. And it implies further that any activity that helps us find supportive organizations is a good thing, be it counseling, mentoring, talking to friends, and so on.

The Choices We Face

In earlier chapters, we offered several suggestions for the types of choices individuals, employers, and society face in the struggle to make allies of work and family. These were presented in boxes peppered throughout the text. Now, in the context of our action agenda, we recap those choices.

- As a society, we must choose to correct the problem of unequal access to success in both work and family roles. This will require creating the options that allow more of us—especially women, but men too—to match our values with our actions.
- Employers that choose not to support life beyond work create an imperative for their employees: choose between career advancement and devotion to family.
- Tradeoffs between work and family are inevitable. The downside of these tradeoffs can be mitigated, at least in part, by seeing them as opportunities to choose among life priorities; to become clearer about our values.
- With the way things are now, unfortunately, choosing motherhood can mean not only decreased financial success for women, but a career satisfaction penalty as well.
- Experiment with how time is allocated between work and relaxation, seeking a balance that supports a sense of satisfaction with family *and* personal growth.
- Look for ways to invest in the good qualities society says your gender traditionally *under*values—and gain the benefits that come with valuing *all* aspects of your self.
- An important step in making allies of work and family is to establish and maintain meaningful boundaries between these two life domains.
- If you value being a parent, you are more likely to feel that you're good at being a parent.
- Add children to the equation when choosing a career and selecting among job opportunities. The self-esteem that comes from a satisfying career and a job well done benefits our children.
- To be better parents, moms need to make the choice to take time for themselves, and they need the support of their spouses, their employers, and society as a whole to do so.
- Find ways to minimize your role conflicts and your kids are less likely to have behavioral problems.
- Choose to help your partner out with the kids or around the house, and he or she will likely return the favor.
- If you are going to provide support to your partner, remember that it best serves *before* work–family conflicts become overwhelming. After the fact, it may actually do more harm than good.

Now let's look at what needs to be done to create greater "freedom of choice." Our agenda is organized by the themes first presented in Chapter 1.

1. We can have (much of) it all, but it's especially tough for working mothers.

It *is* possible to have a fulfilling career and a satisfying family life, but it requires balanced involvement in both these spheres of life. Traditional values, though, continue to shape the division of labor at home, which means that it is easier for men than women to invest time and energy in both work and family. Working mothers are the most vulnerable to suffering career penalties and work–family stress.

Women—especially mothers—end up having to make more tradeoffs than do men to manage the demands of work and family. These tradeoffs have a particular effect in the work domain: women in general are less involved in work because they're more involved in family, spending more time on household activities and far more time on children than men do. Women have to make the bulk of the adjustments in work schedules.

It *is* possible, though, to have a fulfilling career and a satisfying life in both work *and* family. To create options that allow for work–family integration, we need to change the traditional gender roles. Mainly, men must take up more of the childcare and household responsibilities.

But the first step involves making a choice.

Choose to live a balanced life. To enjoy a fulfilling career and a fulfilling family life, we must establish balance as a priority. Balanced involvement in the two domains occurs only if we want it to. Once that choice is made, we—as individuals, as employers, as a society—can move on to tackling the other things that have to happen.

Employers and society need to facilitate that choice, by broadening the range of options available to men and women who want to enjoy a balanced involvement in their different life roles. Much of our action agenda involves creating those options.

Once we've clarified what's important, we need to live our lives accordingly. Each of us needs to claim as legitimate both our values and the choices we make associated with those values. This may require constant negotiation, not only with our employers but also with our families, on issues such as how we spend our time. We may find we must go up against not only traditional expectations in our work and family roles, but the demands other people make of us—including those rooted in traditional stereotypes that govern what men and women should do.

Reshape the division of labor at home. Put simply, men need to take more responsibility at home and with the kids.[10] This is critical if dual-earner families are to function effectively.

We're glad to see some evidence that men are doing more at home. The Families and Work Institute conducted large-scale research in 1997 to follow up on the U.S. Department of Labor's 1977 Quality of Employment Survey.

The Institute's study, the *1997 National Study of the Changing Workforce*, finds that employed fathers spend about a half-hour more with their children per day than their counterparts twenty years ago.

The report has a number of important findings. The Institute finds that the roles of married men and women are changing. For instance, the gap in time spent on household chores is narrowing. Men spend 2.1 hours per day (an increase of almost an hour over the 1977 study) compared to 2.9 hours spent by women (a half-hour decline). This is important evidence that there's a trend toward greater gender equity.[11]

Of course, there's always the option of leaving the workplace altogether—though that's not an option available to the average wage earner or even the great majority of business professionals. It is, however, an option fathers are taking more and more, reflecting a growing interest in spending more time with families.

"The trickle of top business and political figures who say they are resigning to spend more time with family has widened to a stream," writes Sue Shellenbarger in her "Work and Family" column in *The Wall Street Journal*.[12] Her newspaper database search turned up 296 such stories. With the U.S. Bureau of Labor Statistics reporting that professionals and managers are working 37 percent more hours per week since 1985, executives are leaving after soul-searching and "have used family as a starting point for overhauling all their priorities."

Should we applaud these men? They are, after all, clarifying what's important—as we advocate. But their decision to quit the workplace is based on a tradeoff mentality, not an integration mindset. People don't have to leave work in order to find family—they can have both. There are ways to achieve fulfillment in both domains.

In fact, employers can play an important role by *encouraging* men to take more time for family and personal life. One way is through formal training, and the support of role models who blaze the path for male employees. Another is by making it easier—for instance, through paternity leave policies that serve the interests of fathers who seek a more balanced life. But perhaps most important is the redesign of work itself, so fathers can be available to their families (behaviorally and, more importantly, psychologically) as well as productive in their work. Working fathers and their employers stand to gain from changes that create flexibility in how, when, where, and with whom work gets done.

Change society's gender ideology through education and socialization. Beyond the steps above, we need to encourage the legitimacy of new social roles available for men and for women. It's part of continually experimenting with how we as a nation can achieve the goal of building an infrastructure for flexibility.

Socialization, education, and training are prime media through which values are shaped. We're glad to see that traditional assumptions about gender roles are being challenged in many different ways throughout the socialization process in our country. Take innovative summer camps as examples. Some summer camps are de-emphasizing traditional forms of competition and instead are embracing cooperative, gender-neutral forms of interdependent action among kids. One observer found that "since it's not competitive, a lot of girls play sports because they don't feel dominated on the court."[13] Other girl's camps teach entrepreneurial skills.[14] One way to change cultural values and expectations for women is to demonstrate, early on, that it's normal to have economic and social power.

Society needs to go further. In our families and in our schools, let's open our children's minds to challenging the traditional gender roles. Kids need to see that egalitarian relationships between men and women are viable and laudable.

We must adopt a model for education that sees schooling as a cooperative effort, something that teaches our children not only facts and figures but to accept diversity, to challenge stereotypes, to work cooperatively, to become good citizens. Let's train these kids to create the environment for success in the twenty-first century.

Educate young people about choosing careers that fit their values. The next generation is about to enter the workforce. Society has an obligation to teach young people in high school about the importance of choosing careers that allow them to live integrated lives. We need to arm our kids with the means through which they can clarify what's important to them and then assert those priorities, both professionally and personally.[15]

Celebrate the new breed. There are employers today who are providing support—through policy and real management practices—for men and women who are staking claims to new tracks, ones that run counter to the traditional norms and expectations based on outmoded gender roles. We'd like to see the press celebrate these progressive companies, and we'd like to see government play a more active role by creating the incentives to make this even more of a trend.

2. Work and family can be allies.

Work creates assets for personal life and vice versa, although sometimes they're different for women and men. Those assets can help affect integration between work and family, and make the two domains mutually enriching.

Individuals and families should seek new and creative ways to make this integration a reality. Employers should strive to create work environments that promote integration by respecting the whole person and allowing for flexibility. Society, too, has a stake in enhancing opportunities for work–family integration.

Establish networks of support at home and at work. Key to making each domain an ally of the other is to utilize partner support and support from coworkers and managers. Each of us can benefit from a network of support both at home and at work that includes people who value what we do and who we are in our different roles. Integration can't happen on its own; each of us needs some help from people who care about us.

We've identified *partner support* as a resource particularly important in work–family integration. It reduces work–family conflict, helping us to maintain boundaries between the two domains and adjust our mentalities when we cross those boundaries.[16] We need to strengthen partner support, and take advantage of the support that's potentially available to us. Couples need to talk about their values and needs, and get support from each other.

Children stand to benefit here, too. Partner support, especially of the emotional sort, makes for better-adjusted kids, because their parents have a better relationship.

Recall that we find that partner support is best when it is given to *prevent* rather than alleviate the stress that comes with work–family conflict. We should strive to anticipate our partner's need for support. This requires listening, actively and persistently, to the subtle and not-so-subtle cues our partners give us about what's important. That's how we can be the most helpful. And one other point to recall here: we found that one way we can get more support from our partner, as it turns out, is to be involved in hammering out new roles, to challenge the existing norms and assumptions about what men and women are supposed to do.

Educate employees about the value of support from others. Employers ought to build the concept of partner and coworker support into formal career development programs, as well as into mentoring initiatives. One way is to help employees focus on their individual life role priorities and the role of social support in achieving integration of work and personal life.[17]

Invest in what employees do outside of work. Managers should view their employees' lives beyond work as potential business assets, and look for ways to invest in what people do when they're not on the job.

We know of a great example of how such an investment can pay off. One company turned the intense dedication of one of its sales reps to her alma mater into a win-win situation for employer and employee. It seems the sales rep spent much of her free time actively fundraising for the school, and recruiting local high school students. With her permission, her manager worked things out so she could be assigned as the company's liaison to the school in its recruiting efforts there. In the end, the employer benefited by recognizing and supporting the whole person in that employee. The employee benefited as well. Recruitment efforts improved substantially in the hands of this booster for the school and company, and the employee was more committed than ever to her employer.[18]

Create work environments that value employees as whole people. Companies need to get away from the notion that people who are serious about their families are not serious about their careers. Charles Romeo, the director of employee benefits at ConAgra, Inc., puts it well: "When we make our employees choose between work and family, we lose every time."[19] The Johnson & Johnson credo gets it right: "We must be mindful of ways to help our employees fulfill their family obligations."[20]

Family-friendly employers make a tremendous contribution in the struggle to make allies of work and family. Those of us—men and women—who feel that our employers support our lives beyond work experience less conflict and more opportunities for integration between work and family. Family-supportive organizations create greater employee commitment and career satisfaction, and everyone wins.

Companies should take an activist approach to this recommendation. Supervisory personnel need training if they are to become business leaders capable of capitalizing on the skills people develop outside work. They need to be supportive supervisors who know the company's work–family policies, apply those policies fairly, and believe work–family programs and policies are a legitimate part of the workplace and a means of creating long-term value for the company.[21]

Creating an Organization that Supports Work–Life Integration

Joan Kofodimos is a creative thinker in the work–family area, with a keen eye for how to deal with the practical dilemmas of work–family conflict. The author of numerous works on the subject, she is now a freelance consultant based in the Boston area.

One of her most important contributions to this field of study is her book titled *Beyond Work-Family Programs: Confronting and Resolving the Underlying Causes of Work-Personal Life Conflict*. It is a great piece on the cultural underpinnings of resistance to change.

Kofodimos points out that most work–family programs are "a product of the value system they seem to be trying to change and . . . as a result, they cannot accomplish their intended purpose of enhancing individual well-being and organizational productivity." Employers are usually concerned with treating the symptoms of work–family conflict, rather than addressing the fundamental causes. These programs, she argues, would be more effective "for both individuals and organizations if they were reframed around a broader context of creating a balance-supportive culture."

How can we get there? Kofodimos has a plan. To create an organization that supports work-life balance, employers must support

- *Time-and-energy balance across life areas*—recognize that those who are involved in areas outside of work bring valuable skills and creative ideas, are more likely to be adaptive, and less likely to burn out; find new ways to define contributions from individuals (these provide an ongoing standard against which to choose activities and behaviors that add value)
- *Collaborative connected leadership*—embrace power-sharing and consensus decision making; be more sensitive to changes in the environment and supportive of others' life balance needs, which will lead to more widespread commitment and ownership
- *Self-realization*—value the personal development of employees as

much as valuing organizational outcomes; provide opportunities for identifying personal goals and talents and integrating them for the common purpose

Creating change, Kofodimos notes, requires that change agents model behavior. There must be a climate for safe dialogue and support to others seeking to balance their lives. It must be a collaborative process, with widespread involvement and consensus on the vision and associated interventions. And employers need to think systemically—look at the organization as a whole and all its component parts and practices.

Where should employers consider new practices? Kofodimos recommends a number of important areas:

- *Work design and staffing*—optimize existing strengths; provide cross-training so co-workers can cover one another; eliminate low-value activities; manage staff reductions collaboratively
- *Measurement, compensation, and incentives*—focus measurement on behaviors and outcomes that contribute to the organization's value creation rather than hours spent at work; develop measures collaboratively with members and stakeholders; "assess the extent to which the individual has acquired critical knowledge or skills or the extent to which the individual's output has created value for the organization as a whole, rather than basing compensation on hierarchical level or seniority"; create a menu of incentives from which employees can pick those most valuable to them; provide incentives for non-work behavior that create value for the organization; stop rewarding behaviors such as overwork and unilateral decision making
- *Performance management*—assessments should be collaborative and focused on value creation; collaboratively develop criteria and include items focused on "collaborative-connected" orientation
- *Training and development*—help supervisors develop flexible styles for administering work–family programs; consider the developmental value of nonwork activities; help individuals develop strategies for balancing their lives
- *Career development*—paths should offer alternatives and flexibility, focusing not on hierarchy but on contribution; involve and assist other family members; allow for leave without penalty

To sum up, Kofodimos warns that balanced organizations must manage their boundaries and guard against being pressured to adopt their old ways. Work with partners "so that all organizations interacting along the value chain operate according to congruent principles."

Train managers to take a new look at work processes. Firms should train managers in the principles and skills that will help them see that redesign of work processes—experimenting with how goals are achieved—is an opportunity to enhance business results and the personal lives of employees. As these employers set on the road to developing this kind of family-friendliness, they need to ask how work gets done and what about that makes it difficult (or easy) for employees to juggle work and personal life so that neither suffers. These questions must be raised in a safe environment where employees who might acknowledge their difficulties balancing involvement in the two domains aren't concerned that they'll be "branded as less committed or undependable."[22]

Training of the sort we're recommending can help dispel two distortions managers may promulgate. One is that if the boss doesn't have a life, neither should workers. This is a costly error for employers. The other is that paying one's dues—through face time, for example—equals results. It doesn't.

That last point is especially important, because employers have a tendency to measure employees according to how much time they are visibly on the job. Women *and* men do spend less time at work and more with kids when they work for family-friendly employers. At first blush, it would seem that we're confirming the greatest fears hard-nosed businesspeople have about introducing personal life considerations into the workplace. But we find that workers in family-friendly organizations perform just as well as those in non-supportive organizations. And they perform as well in less time—they've experimented with how goals are achieved, and now they're working smarter. And they bring greater commitment to the workplace. For forward-thinking CEOs, then, there should be little doubt about which is the better choice.[23]

Promote family-friendliness in the terms of employment. Family-friendly firms should also establish policies that govern the conditions of what might be called the "contract" between employee and employer. Many companies have implemented policies such as those in the following list:[24]

- Travel policies that avoid last-minute trips, so families can plan ahead for the absence of mom or dad. Use of technology—such as video-conferencing—to avoid travel.
- Sick-leave policies that allow mom or dad to care for children home from school or childcare.
- Personal days that mean employees don't have to present their "excuses" and ask for permission to do personal things that are important to them but are in conflict with work schedules.
- Paid parental leave for both mothers and fathers (and encouragement to fathers so they use the benefit).
- Vacation policies that discourage the mindset of employees who feel they can't use vacation time because they can't afford to get away from the job, and that make it possible for parents to take more time off with their children, who have nearly three months off school.

- Policies that avoid "macho meetings" at 7 A.M. or on the weekends and which concede that it's poor management if everyone must stay in the office until midnight.
- Family-friendly relocation policies which first question whether relocation is really necessary, which offer job relocation assistance for spouses, and which guarantee that employees who are reluctant to move don't lose their prospects for future promotion.

IBM has the right idea. Lou Gerstner, the company's CEO, explains why IBM has become one of the leading employers committed to work–family integration: "I don't want IBMers worried about who's watching their children. I don't want them worried whether they'll be able to leave early to attend their child's first recital or take elderly parents to the doctor." That's from an IBM booklet called "We the people @ IBM."

The booklet is filled with great examples of the many initiatives IBM is supporting that are aimed at fostering integration of work and personal life. It includes a letter from Ted Childs, the company's director of workforce diversity, in which he talks about the benefits of investment in diversity, which includes the diverse needs of people with various work–family demands: "In the final analysis, workforce diversity is about real change in our corporate culture. It's about replacing old assumptions. With our individual and collective commitment to diversity, by offering all of our constituencies the opportunity to attain their full potential, and the rewards that come of it, we will provide our employees, our customers, and our shareholders the very best chance to succeed."

In other words, IBM recognizes the bottom-line value—the economic value—of family-friendliness. It's an excellent example of private sector commitment to work–family integration.

There are a growing number of concrete examples of family-friendliness steps taken by employers, big and small. When Mobil Oil was losing more and more employees who didn't want to relocate, the company implemented placement assistance for spouses and created career development programs at hub locations to minimize geographical relocations.[25] Having received a quick education in the connection between work and family, and the need to find ways to integrate the two domains, Mobil took action.

Merck, the pharmaceutical firm, is an innovator in work–life initiatives. Early on, the company responded to growing work–family conflict by expanding childcare assistance, flexible work hours, and parental leave policies. The company inaugurated lunchtime seminars on family matters, and introduced training programs to encourage manager sensitivity to family concerns and awareness of accommodations they can make.[26] It has continued to lead with initiatives in work redesign and a full range of options for flexibility.

At Xerox, a leader in family-friendliness, benefits include flexible schedules, uninterrupted quiet times, childcare and eldercare referrals, adoption subsidies and counseling, and education information. The company also offers "benefits credits"—$10,000 for an employee to use over the course of his or her career for specific life needs. Credits have been used as mortgage assistance for first-time buyers, childcare subsidies, and healthcare benefits have been extended to parents and siblings.[27]

These are only a few of the many examples we have noted as we survey the landscape of American business.[28] The monthly *Work and Family Newsbrief* provides a very useful way to keep track of what corporations are up to across the country.[29]

Demonstrate the value of investing in family-friendliness. Companies need to demonstrate to their shareholders that investing in policies and practices that encourage integration between work and family has a positive effect on the bottom line. Researchers can help here by studying the beneficial impact on employee health, retention, productivity, and commitment. Even the hard evidence of positive economic benefits to corporations is increasing.[30]

A Note to Researchers

The issues we've raised in our book require ongoing exploration, both at the level of theory and at the level of their practical impact. For instance, we show that career satisfaction and commitment to the work organization are affected by the experience of work–family conflict. Further research into how satisfaction and commitment are linked to job performance can provide a better understanding of the effects of work–family relationships on organizational effectiveness. There also is a crying need for more research into the ways in which work and family affect one another over time.

We have other suggestions, too, for what future researchers can do. One critical area is gender differences. Researchers ought to explore the differences between men and women that must inform policymaking. For instance, how do women and men apply work-related resources to their family lives? What factors may lead to greater involvement of men in child-rearing and other household responsibilities?

Other gender-related questions deserve closer scrutiny. Do men and women attribute different meanings to their involvement with and their role in family life? How does the role of gender in work and family life change over the course of men's and women's lives? We believe that analyses incorporating family or life stage may reveal when the linkages between the two domains are similar *and* different for both sexes.

So much research to date has focused on the individual. We think there's a critical need for more research at the level of the dual-earner couple or family. How do dual-earner partners make decisions about their role, and that of their partner, in family and career? What are the consequences of those decisions? What happens to one partner when the other is stressed, or when work or family strains the relationship?

A great deal of attention has been paid to understanding work–family conflict. We believe it's time for researchers to examine work–family integration more thoroughly. What are the mechanisms that integrate work and family lives? Through what process are work and family experiences utilized as resources in each domain?

In this area of work–family integration fall several of the practical implications researchers should explore. We'd like to see research help establish the business case for why employers ought to be family-responsive. What is the financial impact of family-friendly policies on businesses? What happens when employees are treated as whole people with lives beyond work? We'd also like to see documentation of the costs of turnover, absenteeism, and, more subtly, benefits of commitment and motivation towards organizational goals. And are there public-image benefits for corporations that take a highly visible role in advancing a socially responsible agenda like work–family benefits? A quantification of the bottom-line possibilities would be a tremendous contribution to the discussion.

At the societal level, research can help identify the societal costs of *not* changing cultural values and norms towards greater family-responsiveness? What is the impact of work–family conflict on societal costs like healthcare and productivity? For instance, recent studies have demonstrated that clinical depression costs society billions of dollars.

These are but a few of the contributions researchers can make to understand how to make allies of work and family.

Enact even more flexible family leave legislation. The Family and Medical Leave Act (FMLA) is the prime example of the public sector recognizing and supporting the whole person. The first bill signed into law by President Clinton, the FMLA is an important federal social policy initiative with a profound impact. As the Department of Labor's Interim Final Rule for the law states: "The FMLA—like similar State laws and employer policies—is intended to promote a healthier balance between work and family responsibilities, ensuring that family development and cohesiveness are encouraged by this nation's public policy."[31]

The FMLA has benefited large numbers of working Americans while imposing minimal burdens on employers. A Congressional report in 1996 noted that "The Family and Medical Leave Act has had a positive impact on employees overall. It has succeeded in replacing the piecemeal nature of voluntary employer leave policies and state leave statutes with a more consistent and uniform standard. The FMLA has not been the burden to business that some had feared."[32] In fact, Andrew Scharlach's analysis suggested that family leave legislation actually contributes to economic growth.[33]

The Congressional report continues: "For most employers, compliance is easy, the costs are nonexistent or small and the effects are minimal. Most periods of leave are short, most employees return to work and reduced turnover seems to be a tangible positive effect. The FMLA, with its signature features of guaranteed job protection and maintenance of health benefits, begins to emerge, even now, as a significant step in helping a larger cross-section of working Americans meet their medical and family caregiving needs while still maintaining their jobs and their economic security—achieving the workable balance intended by Congress."

Clearly, at least some of our nation's leaders see a role for the federal government in creating conditions that promote "balance." And while the FMLA of 1993 was an important step, we have much further to go.[34]

This country lags sorely behind other nations in the provision of support for parents, including leave.[35] Recent data indicate that paid leave is available at 100 percent in Austria and Finland, 90 percent in France and Sweden, 80 percent in Italy, and 60 percent in Canada and Japan.[36] As we write, the changing global economic situation is bringing these social gains under attack. We hope they're not lost, and that the United States will catch up.[37]

3. Time is not the major problem.

The time bind is real, no doubt, but a more subtle and pervasive problem is the *psychological* interference of work with family and of family with work. This makes it critical that we acquire the skills to manage the boundaries between these two spheres of life.

Clarify what's important so we can find the ways to manage our boundaries. This is the first of the principles we introduced earlier. Here, it relates specifically to the need for each of us to continually assess and reassess our needs at work and at home. We need to make this assessment not only in terms of time, but also in terms of the psychological attention we need to pay to the people and things about which we care.

Each of us needs to be able to function in a more fluid, turbulent social structure in which boundaries will shift and become more permeable. That's what we face in the careers of the future. We'll need to make sure we unwind, taking personal time to prevent psychological strain from accumulating.[38]

One way to manage boundaries effectively, to protect them, and thus to reduce conflict is to make them *less permeable*. Work and family roles require different frames of mind, for most of us. Managing the boundaries means leaving the work frame at work—and in turn being more psychologically available to our families. It also means learning to be mentally agile, with the ability to move quickly from one frame of mind to the other, particularly for those who work at home. Parents, especially mothers, seem to acquire this skill particularly well. If we don't learn this skill, the family is the likely victim. As the ancient Chinese philosopher Lao Tze cautioned, "In family life, be completely present."

In her landmark study, Ellen Galinsky found that managing boundaries is important for our children. "Kids said they wanted their parents to come home from work not so wired. They wanted their parents to really be with them when they're at home instead of being there physically but thinking about work."[39]

How can we as parents get past being wired? One way is to take time out. It will make a difference. As Penn State psychologist Peter Crabb says, "When human beings don't get enough time to themselves, they become stressed, sick and they can't function well. There are clear benefits to having private times and spaces."[40] And as we found in our sample, the more time mothers take for themselves, the better their kids' emotional health.

Crabb's suggestion deals with being wired figuratively. But what about being wired literally? In a meeting of a taskforce on work and family, Vice President Al Gore spoke of his dislike for voice mail—it's too impersonal and too omnipresent, he said, like a slave chain. The implication is that technology can serve either to enslave or liberate, as an ally or enemy of the integration between work and family. Used wisely, it liberates us, allowing us to shift time and place in a way that can create flexibility—a key attribute of any integrative solution to work–family dilemmas.

What to do? One relatively easy step is to create a schedule (one that allows for adjustments) with actual time off from electronic and other contact with work. Add personal life commitments to our calendars, just as we would write down a professional commitment. If we indeed consider those commitments to be of value we need to give them space in our schedules.

We want people to clarify what's important to them and then align their actions with those values. This requires knowing the available choices and the consequences of a choice in one domain on the other domain. Our advocacy is for options and flexibility, so that people can achieve a level of involvement in work and family that suits them. The more that individuals find creative ways to craft their lives the more demonstrated diversity there will be—and thus the next generation will have a wider array of models from which to learn and upon which to build.

Get help staying on course with commitments. One of the keys to successful support from others is confrontation—the kind of support that comes from being held to account. Everyone can use the help of trusted advisors and friends when it comes to keeping commitments. This is no less true for maintaining boundaries than with any other aspect of life. Find people who are willing to say what needs to be said when we are straying from the path of aligning our values and our actions.

Respect the boundaries employees set. Companies should encourage their managers to respect the fact that employees have lives beyond work, and to respect the boundaries those employees set. When employees feel they are respected as whole people and can take care of their families and other personal life interests when they need to, they're less likely to be distracted at work. In turn, they can make a more focused and productive work effort—not to mention their higher commitment to work and greater career satisfaction. It's all part of recognizing and supporting the whole person.

Don't ignore issues of time. Some employers are putting our third principle into practice as they experiment with issues of time. For instance, at Xerox, a project team was regularly working long hours, but still missed a lot of deadlines. And if someone on the team finished early, it was assumed he or she had not been given enough work to do. Managers were constantly interrupting the engineers. To deal with this problem of boundary permeability, the company set up "library hours"—interruption-free hours in the middle of the day. Soon, the team was meeting deadlines on a regular basis, without having to put in extra hours.

In the administrative department of Amerco, teams worked together to schedule their hours to meet individual needs. The company learned that "team governance can increase efficiency and worker morale. ... [W]orkers can organize both their work lives and their home lives with an eye to efficiency and that they can do so without the intervention of a boss."[41] When ESI, a computer company in Oregon, was going to lay off part of its workforce, they allowed employees to take a vote. The workers chose instead to reduce their hours at reduced pay. There was no decline in productivity, and after the crisis ended the workers voted to continue with the policy of a four-day, thirty-two-hour week.[42]

4. Authority on the job is essential for work–family integration.

Authority over work—control over when, where, how, and with whom work gets done—has a major impact on both career outcomes and satisfaction with life beyond work. An essential component of an infrastructure for flexibility is greater control over work by the people who do it.

In the new century, with big changes in careers as we've described, flexibility and authority will become more and more important in empowering the employee to achieve integration between the two domains, and in helping the employer to realize the bottom-line benefits that can accrue when work and family are allies.

Authorize employees to think and act like entrepreneurs. Companies should give employees the opportunity to take responsibility for their work as competent adults with the capacity to choose and improve on the ways they get work done, within the context of their lifestyles.[43] Employees so empowered become entrepreneurial, and constantly seek new ways to make a positive business contribution to their employers.

We have seen the start of a shift by employers toward greater recognition of the work–home boundary and the need for flexibility and authority.[44] First Chicago Bank, for example, requires managers to submit written plans for expanding job flexibility.[45] While a number of companies have adopted similar policies, it is essential that more corporations do so, for the benefit of businesses and the people in them.

Five years ago, we would never have seen recruitment materials for new MBAs that spoke of how you can "have a life" at some large investment bank. Today, however, most banks and consulting firms that recruit at business schools place at least some emphasis on work–family issues—although it's still more rhetoric than reality. It's our impression that most students don't believe this rhetoric: still, the shift by companies is a sign of changing times. Employers are realizing that to attract and retain the best and the brightest they will have to adjust to create more options and more flexibility for how, when, where, and with whom work gets done. We hope this new rhetoric will turn into new reality—sooner rather than later.[46]

Radcliffe College's Public Policy Institute is involved in a well-publicized initiative to improve both work and life outcomes. It's a good example of the kind of innovative, cross-disciplinary, action-oriented research needed for the field to demonstrate the value of investing in integration of work and family life. Working with Fleet Financial Group, one of the nation's largest bank holding companies, the Institute conducted a study that focused as much on business outcomes as on employee well-being. Changes in work design were implemented, geared toward providing workers with greater flexibility and authority on the job, in collaboration with all key parties. The result: real productivity gains and less stress and a greater sense of control for employees. Turnover rates for employees who participated in the study were lower than were those for employees who did not participate.

Companies Need to Rethink How Work Is Organized

Lotte Bailyn, a professor at the Massachusetts Institute of Technology, is a seminal thinker and innovator in the work–family field. She points out that "companies are organizing work in new ways to make America more competitive in a world economy. While certain aspects of these new ways of organizing work are congruent with emerging personal needs, others create problems." Notes Bailyn in her important book *Breaking the Mold: Women, Men, and Time in the New Corporate World*, a lot of these new approaches require "more time and energy from employees than they can easily provide given the increasingly complicated pressures of their private lives. The difficult cross-pressures that result can only be resolved by new ways of relating employment to the needs of families. The separation of these domains in the traditional organization of work is no longer tenable. Public and private spheres must now be linked."

What does Bailyn propose? First, she challenges assumptions about work and control. "[F]raming the issue as a conflict between employees' private needs and the competitive and productivity needs of American enterprise is self-defeating for both. I hope to provide a different way of thinking about the link between public and private life that will allow the work of American companies to be organized to create synergy rather than conflict between these two spheres. The goal is to break the mold of traditional assumptions; the hope is that the needs of organizations and employees can be brought into a constructive harmony."

Progressive organizations, notes Bailyn, are responding to families in two general ways. Some are creating services and programs to help diverse families adapt to the corporate world designed for the father-works-mother-stays-home homogeneous workforce. Others are creating flexibility in time and place to provide employees with more discretion over work conditions. And others are doing both.

Neither of these responses is adequate, though—the first because it seeks to eliminate distractions so employees can work even harder for the company, and the second because employees are penalized for utilizing the options, creating a two-tier structure of employment. "In order for *all* employees to feel free to use the flexibilities provided, it will be necessary to link work–family issues systemically to organizational change and not deal with them in a piecemeal fashion. These issues must be accepted as an integral part of organizational life and as an important business concern."

Bailyn writes: "The ultimate goal is for companies to view [issues of balance] brought on by an increasingly diverse work force not as marginal problems, but as opportunities for productive change in the organization of work."

Rethinking Time

The first step is to rethink time—the traditional way of structuring and controlling work. In the minds of most managers, time and productivity are linked. Companies operate as if time were infinitely available and belonged wholly to the company. Managers would love to have people work smarter and longer.

Bailyn argues that it would be far better to measure productivity by output or client load rather than hours of input. Employees must learn to work more efficiently and eliminate activities that are of limited value. However, employees have little incentive to do so if the resulting extra time is recycled back into work.

An experiment in the administrative division of a company provides Bailyn with a good example of a different—and better—way to handle the issue of time. Managers lay out business goals (in a broad outline) and employees define the operations and conditions necessary to meet them. Managers set boundaries within which teams develop the whens and wheres. Managers do not set the conditions for work. Employees have operational autonomy.

"It is only a managerial assumption that one must control the work process of one's employees," writes Bailyn. "With changes in technology and the growing interdependence of work, a transformation in this mode of managing may be necessary in any case. Operational autonomy at the working level may be required for organizational adaptation to a rapidly changing environment, and it certainly will help individuals trying to mesh work and family concerns."

Rethinking Commitment

Most employers today define commitment not based on mutual respect and trust, but rather in terms that mean giving work top priority in one's life. However, when employees view the company as accommodating their personal needs, they are likely to feel greater long-run commitment. "Face time as an indicator of commitment, though clearly an imperfect rule, works because it unambiguously indicates that the work of the organization can and does take precedence over other aspects of one's life. But in the end, it is the underlying sense of responsibility for the work that really matters."

As Bailyn puts it, "If commitment is really to be based on trust and respect, then it must be interpreted differently, as the thoughtful (not preprogrammed) response to organizational need. The goal would then be to establish the conditions of work in such a way to allow employees, whatever their personal circumstances, to function in this manner as fully as possible." The manager becomes facilitator rather than boss. This in turn would force a change in the compensation system that dictates all employees must be evaluated on their output.

Rethinking Equity

Equity implies justice and fairness. It's not the same as uniformity. "An equitable society," writes Bailyn, "would equalize the impact of [varying economic and social forces] on its populace; so too would an equitable organization."

The problem, though, is that "if salary is linked to a carefully predefined job with an objectively attainable value, it is likely to perpetuate existing conditions that often entail subtle sources of inequitable rewards." Compensation also presumes that employees are oriented to moving up the hierarchy. Current systems are not designed to work equitably with employees who choose differently, for whom status in the organization is not a priority.

Prepare our children for the new world of work. High school students need to be able to define their values, think for themselves, and make intelligent choices about their future. Schools need to make this possible by helping kids with their awareness of self, to know their strengths and limitations, to know who they are and what they want to do with their lives. Beyond that, our curricula should include teaching high school students about how to explore and create opportunities, and how to network. This relates directly to our earlier call for a new model of how we educate our children.

The more we expose these young people to different kinds of ideas and to different models of what's possible for them, the more likely they are to be prepared for the entrepreneurial roles that will be demanded of them in the careers of the future. This needs to be done in an arena of psychological freedom, where kids feel safe to explore, to try things out. We need more dialogue in the classroom with teachers, with parents, and with other sources of wisdom in the community. Let's give our kids the means to think about their role in the world, the means to manage successful careers, and the ability to use authority on the job successfully.

5. Women may be better adapted for the jobs of the future.

Career success in the twenty-first century will require the ability to handle ambiguity, manage multiple tasks simultaneously, and build networks of support at work and in the community. Each of us needs to be adept at juggling career, family, and other commitments. Women seem to be more skilled in these areas than men.

Employers should be willing to invest in women as leaders for the future, and to create a work environment that values their particular skills. Men need to develop these skills as well, and organizations should find ways to aid this process.

Women—mothers in particular—benefit from working for family-friendly employers. By leveling the playing field, these employers help alleviate the career penalty for mothers. These women are more likely to stay on the job and become the role models for younger women who aspire both to career and family success. Family-friendly organizations also make it easier for work to be a resource for all parents.

Invest in women as leaders. Jobs and careers are changing, becoming more and more in the hands of the individual. Many of us are acquiring new responsibilities for organizing how we work, when, and with whom. The twenty-first century promises only more changes. We need to value, not deny, the ability many women have to integrate work and family life. Businesses that succeed will be the ones willing to invest in women, to grow new female leaders for the future. Employers should provide mentoring for women that is particularly sensitive to the differences in their lives outside of work.[47]

It's also worth the effort of companies to make a periodic assessment of whether working mothers in their employ are being given enough support in their efforts to succeed at work and at home. If not, employers ought to challenge traditional methods and mindsets and work with these moms to create the needed supports.

Keep the revolution going. The struggle for the creation of new and more varied lifestyle options is far from over. Each of us needs to enlist the aid of those who care about us, at work and at home, to support our efforts to align our values and our actions.

Elizabeth McGuire, a graduate student at the Johns Hopkins University School of Advanced International Studies, expresses the kind of thinking that bodes well for the future. In a *New York Times* op-ed piece, she states: "If Gen-Xers don't succeed in forcing a shift in the very concept of a 'career,' the balance between work and family we desire will remain out of our reach.

Instead of the traditional corporate ladder, which emphasizes stamina, we must seek a model of career progress that resembles mountain climbing, which requires flexibility, lateral moves and lengthy rests at base camp. . . . Many people may think we are nearing the end of the workplace revolution. In reality, we are only just beginning."[48]

6. Kids are the unseen stakeholders at work.

Parents' work experiences and career values influence children's health and welfare in significant ways. Corporate responsibility to kids and parents, then, must go beyond providing childcare facilities and benefits. Work needs to be designed so parents can be available—behaviorally and psychologically—to their children.

Renowned child psychologist Penelope Leach writes: "In setting and reshuffling your priorities, in making choices as you meet today's economic and parenting challenges, it's vital that you never lose sight of your child and what he needs." There are "emotional essentials that, if understood and taken into account, can assure that children will thrive, no matter what actual living and working arrangement is established by parents." Among them are this: "Children can thrive in any kind of family where they have love, security, and support, and in no kind of family where they do not."[49] Combining love, security, and support at home with the attention of competent caregivers is a winning formula—one that needs to be available to a broader segment of society.

We've shown that there is a direct link between parents' work arrangements and children's welfare. It's clear that the relationship between work and children may finally be getting the attention it deserves. As President Clinton said at an October 1997 conference, the childcare issue "is the single most important question about social policy today."

Expand and enhance the childcare options available to parents. The childcare options available today in American society are woefully inadequate. We agree with Sylvia Ann Hewlett and Cornel West, who state: "Government and businesses should significantly increase the quality and affordability of child care for working parents."[50]

Hewlett and West make some bold recommendations that deserve serious consideration: Enact tougher regulation of the childcare industry. Create subsidies to underwrite training and much higher salaries for childcare workers. Restructure federal funding to cut back the dependent care tax credit for affluent families and increase childcare block grants to the states. Make paid parenting leave a central component of childcare policy. Target tax credits and subsidies to full-time moms and dads, so that government supports parents at home as well as parents at work. And integrate childcare into our schools.[51]

In April 1998, the U.S. Treasury Department sent a powerful message about the business and social value of providing childcare for employees.[52] The report points to many ways businesses can promote access to childcare for employees: by providing on-site care; by contributing to the cost of care employees bear; by providing access to resource and referral networks; by participating in public–private partnerships; and by providing greater flexibility for working parents. "It makes good business sense to create a work environment that supports the needs of each individual, such as by providing access to childcare," the report noted. "It not only benefits the individual, but it also benefits the company by enabling it to attract and retain the best people. . . . Investments in childcare can pay off in real dividends for employers and employees. . . . Businesses [should] draw lessons from the best practices presented here to help determine what best meets their needs going forward." There are implications, Treasury Secretary Robert Rubin stated in the report, for the "well-being of our economy as we enter a new century."[53]

Create public sector–private sector partnerships. There's societal action beyond government itself, as well. Advocacy groups such as the Child Care Action Campaign, led by Faith Wohl, are making major strides in creating solutions that combine the interests of the private and public sectors in building an infrastructure for flexibility that supports the alliance of work and family. The campaign states that its goals are aimed at increasing "investment in childcare so that children can develop to their fullest potential and families can get and keep jobs. Schools, government and businesses all have key roles to play in making this a reality for American families." The strategy is to "link early care and education to the public interest in school readiness, welfare reform, family stability, corporate productivity and profitability, and community economic development."

Wohl's interest is in generating the public will to see childcare not so much as a way to support parents as "the beginning of a lifelong process by which we become good workers, good citizens, good parents."[54] This is another example of how we must, as a nation, challenge assumptions about the way things are and, instead, choose a new set of lenses through which to view the connections among major social institutions.[55]

One highly visible example of the increasing concern expressed by corporations about the quality of employees' family lives is the American Business Collaborative (ABC) for Quality Dependent Care, spearheaded by IBM's Ted Childs. Twenty-one of the nation's largest corporations contributed a total of $100 million to help their communities provide care for children and aging relatives. ABC has generated many creative initiatives, one of which is the Bridge Project. Through the creative use of technology, teachers can leave daily messages for parents about school activities, and parents can call anytime to find out what their kids have learned in school that day and what homework assignments were made.

This is a great example of how new technology can enhance the quality of communication and relationships among key stakeholders in the work–family nexus. A study of 102 schools in seven states found that parental involvement in their children's education—a key factor in student success—increased sharply through the Bridge Project.

It's also a good example of public–private partnerships. These will likely expand as it becomes more widely recognized that meeting the family needs of workers provides part of the solution to the increasingly complex business challenges corporations now confront.[56]

When Paula Rayman, director of the Radcliffe College Public Policy Institute, spoke at a White House dinner in early 1998, her words were no doubt motivated in part by her positive experience at Fleet. She called for a national commission on work, family, and community for the twenty-first century.

"This commission," Rayman explained, "would examine what new social, political, and economic institutions should be created to help families and communities. . . . We need new intermediate institutions to sustain social cohesion." We hope to see government support for this laudable call to action. It could be a major promoter of the kinds of public–private partnerships we envision.[57]

We would also like to see the creation of a national dialogue about the amount of time and energy we should be investing in family life. Arlie Hochschild takes note of how some workers respond to the lack of time by "outsourcing" home/family responsibilities such as childcare, grocery shopping, or yard work. Others "backtrack" (demote themselves) or stay in place by turning down promotions. Still others start their own business or simply abandon corporate life in search of a simpler lifestyle.

Hochschild suggests the answer may lie in collective action, a "time movement" to reclaim time from the workplace. She argues that "it is hardly prudent to rely on company executives as our architects of time [since they absorb all time which is freed]. Therefore, a time movement would need to find its center *outside* the corporation, however important it may also be to cooperate with advocates of family-friendly policies inside the company."

She suggests this time movement should ask questions that challenge the premises of work culture: Are workers judged mainly on the excellence of their performance, or mainly on the amount of time they are present in the workplace? Is there a "culture of trust" that allows workers to pinch-hit for one another as needs arise? Is there job security—"for there can be little appeal to shorter hours when employees fear that the long hours they now work may disappear entirely"?[58]

Invest in childcare as a profession. Childcare in the United States is generally a low-status, underpaid occupation.[59] It's the opposite in Europe; in countries that provide childcare at government expense, the profession has status. Those societies invest in training childcare professionals, and in turn provide a better option for parents.[60]

We need to take the same initiative here. The government should provide benefits and incentives for people seeking careers in childcare. Further, we need to establish standards of care that are monitored and enforced.

We believe each of us—society as a whole—bears responsibility for all children, even other people's children. After all, society shares the collective costs of not caring for children. How other people's kids are raised, how they're cared for affects all of us. Children who lack the care so vital in the first three years of life do poorly in school. We all bear the tax burden of special school programs for these kids and perhaps for their harmful behavior later. Society needs to ensure the provision of good care from birth, so that kids are raised well. It's the powerful message Hillary Rodham Clinton champions in her book *It Takes a Village*.

Build networks of support for childrearing, at work and at the childcare center. Parents at work have a tremendous resource available when it comes to childrearing—other parents. Women get information and gain acceptance from these networks at work, while men build their self-esteem and self-identity. In both cases, these networks are a tremendous resource. We encourage parents to talk to their coworkers about bringing up kids, about their family needs, about where to find childcare. Having someone with whom to share questions and information can go a long way toward creating a network of support that can benefit every parent at work.

We also need to recognize that the childcare center today fills a void created by the lesser emphasis in society on "communities." Often, it is at the childcare center that parents make contact with other families. Roger Brown and Linda Mason, leaders of Bright Horizons Family Solutions, recognize this and design their childcare centers to enhance the sense of community. We encourage this kind of connection—it's a key thread in the web of support children need.

Encourage and support fathers who want to be more involved with their children. Levine and Pittinsky offer many useful suggestions for fathers and for employers to strengthen their connections with their children and to enhance their parental involvement. Encourage dads to eat lunch with their children. Offer workplace education and support for fathers. Make it possible for them to become involved in their kids' schools. Create partnerships between the company and the schools attended by employees' children. And support fathers who stay home with sick children.[61]

Provide a range of benefits at work to help parents. We're convinced that corporate responsibility to kids and parents must extend well beyond childcare. Corporate America needs to embrace a redesign of work so that jobs can be more flexible and parents can be in greater control and thus psychologically (as well as physically) available to their kids.

While there's still lots to be done, some companies are blazing a new trail. As one among an increasingly wide array of examples, John Hancock Mutual Life Insurance Co. offers pre-tax spending accounts for childcare and elder care and "a benefit which allows employees to call home to check on family members (latch-key children) . . . for those who don't normally have access to a work phone."[62] The firm also offers "Kids to Go"—a program of childcare during school holidays for school-age kids—under contract with a local non-profit agency.

A word of warning: Recent initiatives by companies to support employees with families have left some employees without children feeling like second-class citizens. They complain they're expected to work later, travel more, and forfeit weekends and holidays. They feel they're less likely to be granted flexible work schedules, have to justify leaving early, get transferred more often, and pay health benefits which are less subsidized than those of coworkers with families. But, notes Michele Picard (in "No Kids? Get Back to Work!"), they're reluctant to speak out, lest they be seen as anti-family.[63]

Family supports that *are* essentially subsidized by employees without kids can cause resentment, as can preference to parents when approving leave or flex requests. It creates a sense that pay is not equitable. There are fixes, however. At Hewlett-Packard, for example, everyone gets the same amount of time off, regardless of circumstance. The company has adopted "a need-blind work time standard." And Eastman Kodak has domestic partner policies that extend benefits to committed partners of either sex living in the same household.

Summing Up

We've presented recommendations for making allies of work and family. In some cases, they have been quite specific. In others, we've concentrated on broad strokes. In general, these recommendations flow from the findings we reported in previous chapters.

Before we leave readers to play their part in creating the tremendous set of changes we advocate for society, for employers, and for individuals, we want to return to the three principles introduced earlier in this chapter. We remain convinced that nothing we recommend can be implemented successfully unless these principles for action are embraced.

Clarify what's important.

Individuals must clarify what is important to them so that they can identify their values. People simply cannot act on their priorities if those priorities haven't been clearly defined. It's the same with employers, and with society. Clarifying what's important is the first step toward making allies of family and work.

Recognize and support the whole person.

The success of future generations in the changing workplace depends on individuals and businesses embracing this principle. It is a necessary step in building supportive relationships at work and in our personal lives. Without embracing this principle, no employer will succeed in creating a family-friendly organization. Value life beyond work to get value at work.

Continually experiment with how goals are achieved.

Central to creating family-friendly organizations is treating employees like thinking adults capable of making decisions about work in a way that supports the business *and* supports their personal lives. This won't happen, though, if employers and individuals fail to adopt an experimental attitude—an *entrepreneurial* attitude—toward how work is organized, how time is organized, and how both life quality and business results are achieved.

Hope for the next generation

Much can be achieved with the current generation at work, but of course long-term hope lies with those who will next enter the workforce, and with our children still in school. We're encouraged by recent studies showing how young people see their futures—with changing values and expectations for men and women.

The Swedish firm Universum conducts an annual survey of MBA students from around the world, asking about career goals and other issues.[64] When asked to choose three from among sixteen alternatives in response to the question, "Which career goals do you hope to attain once you have your MBA?" the top response was "balance personal life and career"—chosen by 44 percent of the sample.

The implication is clear: *integrating work and family matters to tomorrow's business leaders.* And harkening back to what we said in Chapter 1 about new careers, teenagers have similar concerns. In a 1998 column in the *Wall Street Journal*, Sue Shellenbarger focuses on how teens she spoke with see their working future.[65] She points to "high hopes" and "high hurdles" as the "tense realities that frame teenagers' vision of the future . . . a different frame than the one that bounded their parents' outlook at the same age."

These teenagers see a time when careers will "evolve to meet the needs" of future families, "demanding less workday time at a desk"—thanks to technology. This is good news for the future: these teens are intent on building close families.

Most of the teens "envision themselves in dual-earner households as adults, and many plan to delay child-bearing in hopes of better equipping themselves to carve out time for their children while paying the bills." And suggesting a shift in *choices* about what men and women can do, there was little resistance in this group to the notion that dads stay at home with kids. This likely reflects changes in the values promulgated in grade and high schools as well as in the role models increasingly available to young men and women.

On working at home, one teen said: "My dad works at home sometimes, and it doesn't make any difference, or not much. He's physically there, but mentally he's isolated. Mentally there's a door between us." This young man speaks directly to the difference between behavioral and psychological availability and the need to create meaningful boundaries between work and family life, especially for those who work at home. Again, the future holds promise for addressing this critical issue; among this group, the "desire for relaxed, sustaining family relationships ran deeper" than any Shellenbarger could "recall hearing from baby boomers as teens." [66]

Kids today are thinking in ways different from their parents' generation.

They seem more conscious of the choices they face and the consequences of what they might choose. Will society meet the challenge young people place before it? Will we create the kind of world in which the next generation will indeed have greater options to adopt a lifestyle that makes sense for each individual? Will we build the infrastructure for flexibility that allows for the pursuit of satisfaction in all the domains of life, for the expression of talents, and for contributions to the world to the fullest possible extent?

Decisions individuals, employers, and society make today and in the next few years will have a lot to do with what the terrain looks like over the next few decades. Our job is to speed along the transformation. If we don't move fast and establish an infrastructure for flexibility, norms and structures that preclude choice may find their way into the lives of the next generation, set in stone.

Big changes are upon us, like it or not. The social and economic transformation we talked about in the first chapter is fast becoming a reality. We must be prepared to make the most of the brave new world, lest we fail to make the workplace revolution one that not only benefits business but families and communities as well.

Appendix One

Design and Methodology of Our Study

The design of any research project must be consistent with its aims. And our aim has been to understand the relationships between the work lives and family lives of business professionals— how work affects family, how family influences work, and how men and women experience work and family. To achieve our objective required that we

- Identify a sample of men and women business professionals
- Assess their work and family experiences, as well as the outcomes of those experiences
- Analyze the data and present the findings in a manner accessible to a broad spectrum of readers

The Survey Sample

The primary sample for our research consists of alumni of two university schools of business in Philadelphia: the Wharton School of the University of Pennsylvania and the College of Business and Administration of Drexel University. Wharton, which provided about two-thirds of our sample, is consistently ranked among the nation's elite business schools, and draws its students from throughout the United States and abroad. Drexel, which provided about one-third of our sample, has an excellent regional reputation; most students there come from the greater Philadelphia area, but many states and countries are also represented among the student body.

A total of 861 alumni from these schools each completed written surveys that were mailed to their homes.[1] Approximately 64 percent of the sample hold the MBA degree; the remainder have baccalaureate degrees in business.

We chose to study business school alumni for several reasons. First, most graduates of business schools work as managers or professionals in the private or public sector, which assured that we ended up with a large number of business professionals in our sample. Second, we wanted to avoid a sample within one particular organization; the alumni represent a wide range of organizations, including the respondents' own businesses, as well as a broad spectrum of industries. Had we sampled individuals from only one or two employers, we doubt our findings would be as representative of our target population—business professionals in general—as they turn out to be.

We chose these two schools in particular because as faculty members at the respective institutions we were granted access to the names and addresses of our schools' graduates for the purposes of this study.

FIGURE APPENDIX 1.1

Who's who in our sample? •

▸ **PERSONAL AND FAMILY BACKGROUND**

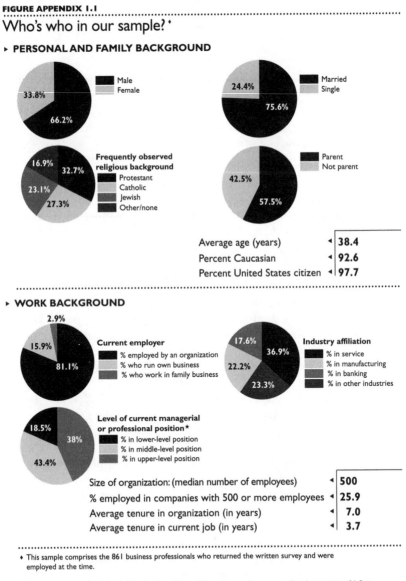

Average age (years)	◂	**38.4**
Percent Caucasian	◂	**92.6**
Percent United States citizen	◂	**97.7**

▸ **WORK BACKGROUND**

Size of organization: (median number of employees)	◂	**500**
% employed in companies with 500 or more employees	◂	**25.9**
Average tenure in organization (in years)	◂	**7.0**
Average tenure in current job (in years)	◂	**3.7**

• This sample comprises the 861 business professionals who returned the written survey and were employed at the time.

★ On a nine-point scale where 1 = first-level position and 9 = top executive, we considered responses of 1-3 to represent lower, 4-6 middle, and 7-9 upper-level positions, respectively.

The average age of our business professionals at the time of the survey is 38.4 years. Nearly two-thirds are men, and the vast majority are Caucasians and U.S. citizens.[2] More than 80 percent of the sample are employed in organizations of various sizes, often quite large, and the great majority hold upper- or middle-level positions in those organizations. A sizable minority run their own businesses. Figure Appendix 1.1 provides a snapshot of personal, family, and work background characteristics of the business professionals we studied.

Of course, caution is the watchword when generalizing our findings to the broader population of business professionals. Nevertheless, we believe our sample does represent highly educated men and women who work in middle- and upper-level managerial or professional positions for mid-size or large organizations in various sectors of the economy.

We mailed 4,101 surveys: 3,000 (73%) to alumni of the Wharton School of the University of Pennsylvania and 1,101 (27%) to alumni of the College of Business and Administration of Drexel University in the closing months of 1992. Approximately 60 percent of the surveys were sent to MBA graduates; the rest went to graduates of bachelor's degree programs. The MBA graduating classes of 1969, 1974, 1979, 1984, and 1989 were sampled, as were the bachelor's degree classes of 1964, 1974, and 1984.

To ensure that women would be represented among the respondents, we sent surveys to 100 percent of the women graduates in a given class and only a random sample of men.[3] Of the 4,101 surveys, 2,957 (72%) were sent to men and 1,144 (28%) were sent to women.

Of the surveys we mailed, 33 were returned undelivered, leaving a total of 4,068 surveys we believe reached the alumni. From this group, completed surveys were returned by 927 alumni—a response rate of approximately 23 percent.[4] Women were slightly overrepresented among the respondents: although they received 28 percent of the surveys, women constituted 36 percent of the group that returned completed surveys.

Wharton alumni comprised 71 percent of the respondent group, while Drexel alumni comprised 29 percent. These percentages correspond very closely to the percentages of surveys distributed to alumni of the two institutions.

Finally, of the 927 alumni who returned completed surveys, 861 are employed. This group of 861 constitutes the survey sample we examine throughout the book.

What Did We Ask?

The comprehensive written survey we mailed to the alumni in our main sample is adapted in part from the existing literature; we wrote other sections expressly for this study. We measured data from questions in six categories— the variables described briefly below and in more detail in the sections that follow.[5]

1. *Personal background* includes a variety of demographic characteristics,

life role priorities, and values and beliefs regarding career success and life success.

2. *Career choices and experiences* includes career goals, career involvement, adjustment of work schedule for family and personal reasons, job authority; receipt of key developmental assignments and coaching, participation in networking activities, family supportiveness of employer, and priority of career compared to the priority of the spouse's (or partner's) career.

3. *Career outcomes* includes level of position achieved in the organization, job performance, number of promotions in the current organization, career advancement expectations, probability of attaining career goal, annual income, income relative to peers, job satisfaction, career satisfaction, and organizational commitment.

4. *Family and personal choices and experiences* includes marriage, children, family structure, psychological involvement in family, time devoted to home and childcare, support received from spouse (or partner), and spouse or partner's involvement in career and family.

5. *Family and personal outcomes* includes satisfaction with family, personal life, and overall life, performance as a parent, child's development (emotional, health, and educational), and satisfaction with childcare arrangements.

6. *Role conflicts* includes work interference with family, work interference with leisure, family interference with work, behavioral work interference with family, and tradeoffs between work and family.

Definitions and Measures of Personal Background Variables

Sex (biological sex of the respondent)

One item: 1 = male, 2 = female

Race (racial identity of the respondent)

One item: 1 = African-American, 2 = Asian, 3 = Caucasian, 4 = Hispanic, 5 = Native American, 6 = other.

Age (chronological age of the respondent)

One item: Also recoded into a "decade" variable (from 20's = 1 to 50's = 4)

Educational Aspirations

What is the highest level of education you expect to attain in your life?

1 = bachelor's degree, 2 = bachelor's degree plus professional certificate, 3 = master's degree, 4 = Ph.D. or other advanced degree

Religion

Which of the following best describes your religious beliefs?

1 = Catholic, 2 = Protestant, 3 = Jewish, 4 = Agnostic, 5 = Muslim, 6 = Hindu, 7 = Buddhist, 8 = Other

Life Role Priority (relative priority or focus attached to work role, family role, other life roles)

Based on a combination of responses to three items: (a) a ranking of the two life roles (from career, family, religion, activities aimed at national or international betterment, leisure, and community) that give the respondent the most satisfaction; (b) the rated importance of career on a five-point scale (from measures of Life Success Values described below); and (c) the rated importance of a long-term relationship on a five-point scale (from measures of Life Success Values described below). From the responses to these two items, four life role priorities were identified: career-focused (1), career + family-focused (2), family-focused (3), and self/society-focused (4).

Career Success Values (importance of different factors to respondents' judgment that their career is successful)

Based on a scale developed for this study in which respondents rated (on a five-point scale) the importance of 15 experiences in judging their level of career success. A factor analysis of the 15 items produced five dimensions of career success values:

Status, which consists of the mean of the following four items (alpha = .78):

having social status and prestige
having power and influence
earning a great deal of money
advancing rapidly to high level positions.

Time for self, which consists of the mean of the following three items (alpha = .69):

having flexibility in determining my work hours
having time for myself
having time for my family

Challenge, which consists of the mean of the following three items (alpha = .56):

working on challenging tasks
being creative in my work
enjoying my work

Security, which consists of the mean of the following three items (alpha = .50):

ensuring a comfortable retirement
having secure employment
living in a preferred geographical area

Social, which consists of the mean of the following two items (alpha = .24):

helping other people
being respected by others at work

Life Success Values (importance of different factors to respondents' judgment that their life is successful)

Based on a scale developed for this study in which respondents rated (on a five-point scale) the importance of 12 experiences in judging their level of life success. A factor analysis of the 12 items produced three dimensions of life success values:

Personal Growth, which consists of the mean of the following five items (alpha = .63):

personal growth and development

helping other people
friendships
being politically active
creative activity

Material Wealth, which consists of the mean of the following three items (alpha = .65):

standard of living
career
material wealth

Family, which consists of the mean of the following two items (alpha = .37):

a long-term relationship
parenting

Definitions and Measures of Career Choice and Experiences Variables

Current Employment Status

One closed-ended item coded (1) work in family business, (2) run own business, (3) employed full-time in organization, or (4) employed part-time in organization.[6]

Time Commitment to Work (hours per week devoted to work)

One open-ended item: "In an average week, including weekends, how many hours do you devote to your work responsibilities?"

Psychological Involvement in Career (extent to which the respondent is involved in his or her career and the extent to which the career is a significant part of the respondent's life)[7]

The mean of the following three items (alpha = .79):

A major source of satisfaction in my life is my career.
Most of the important things that happen to me involve my career.
I am very much involved personally in my career.

Career Goal (aspirations for advancement within an organizational hierarchy)

One item: "Assume that you are employed in an organization that has 9 levels of managerial/professional positions, ranging from (1) first level manager/professional to (5) middle level manager/professional to (9) top executive. Please indicate the highest position you would like to achieve."

Recoded to create two additional variables: (a) aspiration to become CEO, coded 9 versus others and (b) aspiration to senior management coded 8 or 9 versus others.

Networking Activities (extent to which the respondent has established contacts or networks)

The mean of the following two items (alpha = .53):

Within the last two years, how often have you
established contacts or networks inside your company?
established contacts or networks outside your company?

Job Authority (extent to which the respondent has authority and decision-making power on the job)

The mean of the following three items[8] (alpha = .85):

I have a great deal of authority in my position.
I have considerable decision-making power on my job.
I have an opportunity to participate in setting company goals and policies.

Developmental Assignments (extent to which the respondent has been given special assignments to provide visibility, exposure, and opportunities to develop new skills)

The mean of the following two items (alpha = .65):

Within the last two years, how often have you
been given highly visible special assignments?
received job assignments that provided you with new skills, experience and exposure?

Coaching (extent to which the respondent has had opportunities to receive coaching, guidance, and training/development)

The mean of the following four items (alpha = .67):

Within the last two years, how often have you
participated in a company-sponsored training, education, or career planning program?
received coaching or counseling from your supervisor?
received coaching or counseling from your peers?
received guidance or assistance from a mentor or sponsor?

Adjustment of Work Schedule for Family and Personal Reasons (extent to which the respondent has adjusted or limited his or her work schedule to meet family or personal needs)

The mean of the following four items (alpha = .70):

Within the last two years, how often have you
adjusted your hours of arrival and departure from work to suit your personal and family activities?
structured your hours at work in order to be home at certain specific times?
limited the time you devoted to work during weekends?
limited the time you devoted to work-related travel?

Employer Support for Family (extent to which the organization supports employees' attempts to balance work and family responsibilities)

The mean of the following five items (alpha = .78):

The level of commitment expected by my organization requires that employees choose between advancing their careers and devoting time to their families. (reverse scored)
My organization is understanding when employees have a hard time juggling work and family responsibilities.
Career advancement is jeopardized if employees do not accept assignments because of their family responsibilities. (reverse scored)
My organization has a satisfactory family leave policy.
My organization allows for flexibility in work scheduling.

Acceptance by Others in Organization (extent to which the respondent experiences mutually positive feelings between him/herself and coworkers)

The mean of the following three items[9] (alpha = .75):

I am accepted in informal business activities with my peers within my organization.

I like the people with whom I work.

I am really a part of my work group.

Career Priority Relative to Partner's Career

(extent to which the respondent sees his or her career as having more or less priority than spouse or partner's career)[10]

One closed-ended item: "Which of the following best describes your current career priority relative to that of your partner?"

My career has a much higher priority than my partner's.

My career has a slightly higher priority than my partner's.

Our careers have equal priority.

My partner's career has a slightly higher priority than mine.

My partner's career has a much higher priority than mine.

Definitions and Measures of Career Outcome Variables

Level of Position in Organization (level of managerial/professional position achieved in current organization)

Single item: "Please indicate the highest position you have achieved in your current organization." A nine-point scale was provided, ranging from (1) first level manager/professional to (5) middle level manager/professional to (9) top executive.

Since level in the organization is an indicator of career success (see Chapter 3), we wanted to develop a measure that was independent of personal background. Therefore, we regressed level on a range of background variables, three of which were related to level: age, organizationally employed versus own/family business, and finance versus other industries. A measure of level was then developed that was adjusted for these three background variables.

Annual Income (personal annual income in dollars)

Single closed-ended item indicating respondent's personal annual income on a scale ranging from (1) $ 0 to $24,999 to (16) $ 500,000 or more.

Since income is an indicator of career success (see Chapter 3), we wanted to develop a measure that was independent of personal background. Therefore, we regressed income on a range of background variables, three of which were related to level: age, organizationally employed versus own/family business, and finance versus other industries. A measure of income was then developed that was adjusted for these three background variables. See note 7 in Chapter 3.

Career Satisfaction (level of satisfaction with the career as a whole)

Single item developed for this study as part of a 12-item measure of different facets of life satisfaction. "Please indicate your current level of satisfaction with your career." A five-point response scale was provided ranging from (1) not satisfied to (5) very satisfied.

Since career satisfaction is an indicator of career success (see Chapter 4), we wanted to develop a measure that was independent of personal background. Therefore, we regressed career satisfaction on a range of background variables, three of which were related to career satisfaction: age, organizationally employed versus own/family business, and finance versus other industries. A measure of career satisfaction was then developed that was adjusted for these three background variables.

Job Performance (self-assessment of job performance during the last year)

Single item which asked respondents "How would you rate your job performance over the last year?" A five-point response option was provided, ranging from (1) deficient and below expectations to (5) far exceeds normal expectations.

Likelihood of Achieving Career Aspirations

Single item: "If you are not currently in the highest position you would like to attain, how likely is it that you will achieve this position?" Five-point response option ranging from (1) not likely to (5) highly likely.

Number of Promotions in Current Organization (number of promotions received since joining the current organization)

Single open-ended item: "How many promotions have you received since joining your current organization?"

Rate of Promotion (frequency of promotion over the total period of employment within the organization)

Computed by dividing the number of promotions received by the number of years the individual has worked in the organization.

Career Advancement Expectations (perceived likelihood of promotion within the next two years)

Single item: "How would you rate your chances for promotion within the next two years?" Five-point response option ranging from (1) poor to (5) excellent.

Income Relative to Peers (income relative to that of peers who graduated from the same college)

Single item which asks respondents to indicate on a five-point scale whether their annual income is (1) much higher than that of fellow graduates from the same college to (5) much lower than that of their peers.

Job Satisfaction (feelings of positive effect toward the job and level of satisfaction with the job)

The mean of the following three items[11] (alpha = .87):

I am satisfied with my present job situation.
My job situation is very frustrating to me. (reverse scored)
I frequently think I would like to change my job situation. (reverse scored)

Organization Commitment (identification with and feelings of loyalty to the organization)

The mean of the following three items[12] (alpha = .87):

I talk up my organization to my friends as a great organization to work for.
I am proud to tell others I am part of the organization
I feel very loyal to my organization.

Definitions and Measures of Family and Personal Choices and Experiences

Marital Status

Based on one closed-ended item: married = 2; not married = 1.

Long-term Relationship (whether the respondent is currently married, living with a partner, or otherwise in a long-term relationship)

Based on one closed-ended item: in a long-term relationship = 2; not in a long-term relationship = 1.

Age Entered Relationship (age at which respondent entered current relationship)

Based on the following open-ended item: "At what age did you enter your current relationship?"

We calculated the length of the relationship by subtracting the age at which the relationship was entered from the respondent's current age.

Parental Status (whether the respondent is currently a parent)

Recoded from the following item: "How many children do you currently have?"

One or more children = 2; no children = 1

Anticipated Parental Status (for those respondents *not* currently a parent, whether they anticipate being a parent at some time)

Based on responses to the following question "Do you have or do you expect to have/adopt any children?" in conjunction with their current parental status.

Anticipate being a parent = 2; do not anticipate = 1

Value on Parenthood (importance of being a parent in the respondent's life)

The mean of the following three items (alpha = .80):

Being a parent gives me the opportunity to do interesting things that I might not otherwise do
Being a parent helps me put my life into better perspective
Being a good parent gives me a good feeling about myself

Number of Children

Based on the response to "How many children do you currently have?"

Anticipated Number of Children (number of children the respondent expects to have)

Based on the response to "How many children in all do you think you will have/adopt?"

Age of Youngest Child

Based on the ages of children listed.

Preschool Children (whether the respondent has any preschool children)

Computed from the age of the youngest child.

Youngest child less than or equal to six = 1; youngest child older than six or no children = 0.

Family Structure (family structure is based on a combination of whether the respondent is in a long-term relationship (LTR), is a parent, has an employed partner, and is a man or a woman)[13]

> If in LTR, is a parent, has an employed partner, and is a man = 1 (dual-earner father)
>
> If in LTR, is a parent, has an employed partner, and is a woman = 2 (dual-earner mother)
>
> If in LTR, is not a parent, has an employed partner, and is a man = 3 (dual-earner man with no children)
>
> If in LTR, is not a parent, has an employed partner, and is a woman = 4 (dual-earner woman with no children)
>
> If in LTR, is a parent, has a non employed partner, and is a man = 5 (single-earner father)
>
> If not in LTR, is not a parent, and is a man = 6 (single man)
>
> If not in LTR, is not a parent, and is a woman = 7 (single woman)

Time Off Following First Child (whether the respondent has taken or expects to take time off from job after the first child) [14]

> "Did you, or do your expect to, take time off from your job with the birth or adoption of each child?" 1 = no, 2 = not sure, 3 = yes.

Amount of Time Off Following First Child (how much time off the respondent has taken or expects to take following the first child)

> "Please indicate your actual or expected time off from work for each child." From none (1) to more than 5 years (10).

Return to Work Full-Time After First Child (whether the respondent has or expects to return to work full time after the first child)

> "Your employment status immediately after your time off." Full-time = 2; part-time = 1.

Part-Time Then Full-Time After First Child (whether the respondent has or expects to return to work part-time initially and then full-time)

> "If you did, or expect to, work part-time initially and then full-time at some later date, please check the box." 2 = checked, 1 = not checked.

Amount of Time Part-Time After First Child (how long the respondent worked or expected to work part-time before returning to work full-time)

> "If you checked a box in question E, indicate how long you worked, or expect to work, part-time before returning to work full-time (in months)."

Primary Childcare Arrangement For First Child

> One closed-ended item that listed 10 possible child care arrangements in addition to an "other" category. The 10 listed arrangements were: own home with parent, own home with a relative, own home with a non-relative, another home with a relative, another home with a non-relative, job-provided daycare center, daycare center funded by self, daycare center funded with job-provided assistance or credit, preschool, school.

Hours a Week in Primary Child Care Arrangement for First Child

"How many hours per week is each child in the primary child care arrangement indicated above?"

Psychological Involvement in Family of Origin (extent to which the respondent is involved in his or her family of origin—parents, siblings, etc.—and the extent to which the family of origin is a significant part of the respondent's life)

The mean of the following three items[15] (alpha = .85):

A major source of satisfaction in my life is my family.
Most of the important things that happen to me involve my family.
I am very much involved personally in my family.

Psychological Involvement in Family of Creation (same definition and measurement as above, except the reference is family of creation—partner, children, etc.).

Alpha = .80

Time Spent on Household (hours a week spent on household activities)

Response to the following open-ended item: "In an average week, including weekends, how many hours do you devote to your household responsibilities (including housework and finances)?"

Time Spent on Childcare (hours a week spent on childcare activities)

Response to the following open-ended item: "In an average week, including weekends, how many hours do you devote to your childcare responsibilities?"

Partner Psychological Involvement in Career (extent to which the partner is involved in his or her career and the extent to which the career is a significant part of the partner's life)

The mean of the following three items (alpha = .89):

A major source of satisfaction in my partner's life is his/her career.
Most of the important things that happen to my partner involve his/her career.
My partner is very much involved personally in his/her career.

Partner Psychological Involvement in Family (extent to which the partner is involved in his or her family and the extent to which the family is a significant part of the partner's life)

The mean of the following three items (alpha = .88):

A major source of satisfaction in my partner's life is our family.
Most of the important things that happen to my partner involve our family.
My partner is very much involved personally in our family.

Partner Personal Support (extent to which partner provides respondent with emotional support regarding primarily personal and family issues)

The mean of the following five items based on the results of a factor analysis (alpha = .86):

My partner . . .
listens to me talk about my personal or family problems
is concerned about my welfare
gives me advice when I have a family or personal problem
praises me for my personal or family accomplishments
respects my personal accomplishments

Partner Career Support (extent to which partner provides respondent with career support)

The mean of the following four items based on the results of a factor analysis (alpha = .60):

My partner . . .
plays an active role in my career
listens to me talk about my job-related problems
gives me advice when I have a work-related problem
praises me for my job-related accomplishments

Partner Time Spent on Household (hours a week partner spends on household activities)

Response to the following open-ended item: "In an average week, including weekends, how many hours does your spouse/partner devote to household responsibilities (including housework and finances)?"

Partner Time Spent on Child Care (hours a week partner spends on childcare activities)

Response to the following open-ended item: "In an average week, including weekends, how many hours does your spouse/partner devote to childcare responsibilities?"

Partner Employment Status

One item recoded to 3 = full-time; 2 = part-time; 1 = not employed

Definitions and Measures of Family and Personal Outcomes

Satisfaction with Family of Origin (extent to which the respondent is satisfied with his or her family of origin)

The mean of the following three items[16] (alpha = .86):

I am satisfied with my present family relationships.
My family relationships are very frustrating to me. (reverse scored)
I frequently think I would like to change my family relationships. (reverse scored)

Satisfaction with Family of Creation (extent to which the respondent is satisfied with his or her family of creation)

The mean of the following three items[17] (alpha = .84):

I am satisfied with my present family relationships.
My family relationships are very frustrating to me. (reverse scored)
I frequently think I would like to change my family relationships. (reverse scored)

Satisfaction with Life (extent to which the respondent is satisfied with a variety of life factors)

Respondents rated their satisfaction (1 = not satisfied to 5 = very satisfied) with each of the following aspects of their lives: standard of living, career, a long-term relationship, parenting, health, material wealth, religious or spiritual development, personal growth and development, helping other people, friendships, being politically involved, and creative activity.

In addition to satisfaction with the individual aspects of life, a measure of *overall life satisfaction* was calculated by averaging the responses to the items listed above.

Child's Behavior Problems (parent's assessment of the behavioral and emotional problems of the child *closest to the age of eight years*)[18]

Respondents rated how true each of the following statements are about their child closest to eight years of age. Ratings were made on a three-point scale from often true to never true that was later collapsed into two levels. The total score was calculated as the mean of the following 23 items (alpha = .88):

Has sudden changes in mood feelings
Feels or complains that no one loves him/her
Is rather high strung, tense, or nervous
Cheats or tells lies
Is too fearful or anxious
Argues too much
Has difficulty concentrating, cannot pay attention for long
Is easily confused, seems to be in a fog
Bullies or is cruel or mean to others
Is disobedient at home
Is disobedient at school
Does not seem to feel sorry after misbehaving
Is not liked by other children
Is restless or overly active, can't sit still
Is sullen, stubborn, or irritable
Has a strong temper and loses it easily
Is unhappy, sad, or depressed
Is withdrawn/doesn't get involved with others
Has a lot of difficulty getting his/her mind off certain thoughts, has obsessions
Feels worthless or inferior
Is impulsive or acts without thinking
Has trouble getting along with teachers
Has trouble getting along with other children

Child's Health (parent's assessment of the health of the child closest to the age of eight years)

"Which of the following best describes this child's general state of health"? 1 = excellent; 2 = very good; 3 = good; 4 = fair; 5 = poor.

Child's School Performance (parent's assessment of the school performance of the child closest to the age of eight years)

"Which of the following best characterizes what kind of student this child is now?" 1 = one of the best; 2 = above the middle; 3 = in the middle; 4 = below the middle; 5 = near the bottom.

Performance in Parental Role (self-assessment of performance as a parent)

Single item which asked respondents to indicate the extent to which they agree with the statement "Overall, I feel that I am a good parent" on a scale from (1) strongly disagree to (5) strongly agree.

Satisfaction with Childcare Arrangement for the First Child

(parent's degree of satisfaction with the child's primary childcare arrangements)[19]

"Please rate your satisfaction with the primary childcare arrangement above by writing in the spaces to the right the appropriate number from 1 to 5, with 1 "Not Satisfied" and 5 "Very Satisfied.""

Definitions and Measures of Role Conflicts[20]

Work Interference with Family (the perception that the demands of the work role interfere with the fulfillment of family role responsibilities)

The mean of the following four items (alpha = .73):

When I spend time with my family, I am bothered by all the things on the job that I should be doing.

Because of my job responsibilities, I have to miss out on home or family activities in which I should participate.

Because of my job responsibilities, the time I spend with my family is less enjoyable and more pressured.

Pursuing a demanding career makes it difficult for me to be an attentive spouse/partner.

Family Interference with Work (perception that family role demands interfere with work role responsibilities)

The mean of the following five items (alpha = .78):

When I spend time on my job, I am bothered by all the things I should be doing with my family.

The demands of family life interfere with achieving success in my career.

Being a parent limits my career success.

Because of my family responsibilities, I have to turn down job activities or opportunities that I should take on.

Because of family responsibilities, the time I spend on my job is less enjoyable and more pressured.

Work Interference with Relaxation (perception that the demands of the work role make it difficult to relax and participate in leisure activities)

The mean of the following two items (alpha = .82):

When I spend time relaxing, I am bothered by all the things at my job I should be doing.

Because of my job responsibilities, any time I spend relaxing is less enjoyable and more pressured.

Behavioral Work Interference with Family: The perception that behavior expected at work conflicts with behavior expected at home.[21]

The mean of the following two items (alpha = .68):

My partner complains that I treat family members as if they are work associates or subordinates.

I find it difficult making the transition from my job to home life.

Tradeoffs Between Work and Family: The belief that one has to trade success in one role to avoid failure in another role.

The mean of the following two items (alpha = .58):

I can "have it all" (a rewarding career, satisfying family relationships, and a fulfilling personal life). (reverse scored)

The conflicting demands of career and family require that I decide which is more important.

Statistical Analyses

The research conclusions we present are based on findings that achieved statistical significance in our study. For example, we present in Chapter 2 our observation that women are more psychologically involved in their families than men. We are drawn to that conclusion because the analysis of our data showed a statistically significant difference in family involvement between men and women. In fact, we established a rule for ourselves in presenting our findings: discussion of a relationship between *any* two variables requires that there be a statistically significant relationship between those variables.[22]

We've tried to keep tables to a minimum within each chapter, using the section at the end of the book, "Additional Tables," to expand on our findings. Most of the tables present our findings in terms of percentages on a particular factor for different segments of the sample—for example, we show the percentage of men and women occupying upper-level positions in their organizations. We present data in this manner to make our findings accessible to the widest possible audience. It should be noted, though, that our analyses to determine whether findings are statistically significant are more complex than the tabular information.

For ease of understanding, the book's tables generally present percentages on variables for different subgroups of the sample. In fact, analyses of covariance, partial correlations, or multiple regression analyses generally served as the basis for our findings. We conducted partial correlations in lieu of multiple regression analyses when the listwise deletion of data, characteristic of multiple regression, would have substantially reduced the sample size in a given analysis.

Analyses statistically controlled for university affiliation (University of Pennsylvania versus Drexel University), and—because on average women are younger than men in our sample—all relationships involving gender controlled for age. To enhance the internal validity of our findings, virtually all analyses also controlled for potentially confounding variables that would have provided rival explanations for the relationship under investigation.

Because of the crucial role of gender in our study, nearly all of the substantive relationships were analyzed separately for men and women. For us to conclude that men and women are different on a variable required that the difference be statistically significant. For us to conclude that the *relationship* between two variables is different for men and women, there had to be a significant interaction between sex and the independent variable and/or a significant difference in the partial correlations or the regression coefficients for men and women. In fact, we required of ourselves the existence of a significant interaction or difference between coefficients to conclude that *any* relationship is different for one segment of the sample compared to another segment.

One final point here. We realize that our cross-sectional methodology—in which all variables are measured at the same time—does not permit us to determine the direction of causality between two factors. So, for example, we can't be sure whether a high level of family involvement causes low career involvement or whether a high level of career involvement causes low family involvement. When we present empirical findings in Chapters 2 through 7, we often infer a causal direction when the data are consistent with a theoretically compelling explanation.

Appendix Two

―――

Personal Life Beyond the Family

Personal life off the job reaches beyond the family to include social, recreational, community, and spiritual activities. Despite the expansive terrain of personal life, our model focuses exclusively on the relationship between work and family. We emphasize family life in the model because it is a major focus of our book, and our measures of family experiences and outcomes are far more extensive than our assessments of other facets of personal life. However, we did measure satisfaction with several other aspects of personal life.

- Personal growth and development (discussed in detail in Chapter 4)
- Helping other people
- Friendships
- Political involvement
- Creative activity
- Spiritual development

These represent a variety of personal life dimensions. Let's revisit our model of work–family relationships. We want to show that resources, involvement, and emotional gratification derived from work and family have important implications for these other aspects of personal life.

Effects of Work and Family Resources

Just as resources emanating from work or family have positive effects on the other role, promoting availability, competence, and emotional gratification, these resources positively affect other aspects of personal life. Authority on the job, key developmental assignments, extensive networking, peer acceptance, and employment by family-supportive organizations translate into satisfaction with virtually all other aspects of personal life we studied. Earning a high income, adjusting work schedules for personal and family reasons, and receiving coaching also have important—though more limited—positive effects on satisfaction with personal life.

We believe the resources provided by these work experiences—flexibility, acceptance, self-esteem, and information—make it possible for people to lead satisfying personal lives. For example, the self-esteem derived from exercising authority on the job, performing developmental tasks, and participating in networking activities enable business professionals to gain competence in other facets of their lives and experience satisfaction with their personal growth and creative development. In a similar vein, the flexibility provided by autonomous jobs and family-supportive employers enables individuals to be more available to other people, both behaviorally and emotionally; this, in turn, produces satisfaction with helping relationships, friendships, and political involvement. Satisfaction with spiritual development is also enhanced by the flexibility and self-esteem provided by supportive employers, as well as by job authority, developmental assignments, and acceptance by peers.

In short, many of the work experiences that promote integration with family life also enhance other aspects of our personal lives. It stands to reason, then, that a shortage of these resources has detrimental effects. Those among us who feel alienated from peers, have little authority on the job, receive infrequent coaching and career-enhancing assignments, and rarely network tend to be dissatisfied with their personal lives. The work experiences of these individuals detract from a satisfying life off the job.

Family resources, too, can enrich the quality of our personal lives. Partner support is particularly significant. Receiving either personal support or career support from a partner results in feelings of satisfaction with personal growth and development, creativity, friendships, and spiritual development.[23] We believe a partner's support provides flexibility, understanding, self-esteem, and information that enable a person to experience personal growth, engage in satisfying interpersonal relationships, and experience a gratifying level of spiritual development. Moreover, performing well as a parent—a rich source of self-esteem and social validation—promotes satisfaction with many aspects of personal life.

Effects of Work and Family Involvement

Whereas an intense involvement in work detracts from a satisfying family life, it does not appear to interfere with other aspects of personal life. In fact, individuals who are highly involved in their work tend to be more satisfied with their personal growth, development, and creativity. These people likely take on many challenges that provide opportunities for personal development and creative expression. So high work involvement has mixed results: while it enables us to feel good about ourselves by meeting our needs for creativity and personal growth, it hampers our participation in—and satisfaction with—our families.

Involvement in family life has interesting effects on personal life that are different for men and women in some respects. For instance, having young children—a sign of a demanding family status—detracts from personal life for both men and women. Parents of preschoolers tend to be dissatisfied with their opportunities to express creativity, their spiritual development, and their level of political involvement. For women, add to this dissatisfaction with personal growth and development. We suspect the time and attention required by young children prevents some parents from attending to other parts of their personal lives, and that women's greater responsibility for the well-being of the kids explains why mothers of young children feel particularly frustrated with their opportunities for personal growth and development.

Although the presence of young children can detract from some aspects of personal life, being psychologically involved in one's family—with or without young children—actually promotes feelings of satisfaction with helping others and spirituality. Therefore, caring deeply about our families, and seeing them as a crucial part of life, enables us to satisfy our altruistic needs—which may further contribute to a sense of spiritual well-being.

Effects of Emotional Gratification from Work and Family

Work satisfaction and family satisfaction, as we've seen, go hand in hand. When we're satisfied with one part of life, our positive emotions spill over and enrich the other sphere. When we are dissatisfied with one role, though, the negative emotions radiate to the other role and produce dissatisfaction in that part of life. How do work satisfaction and family satisfaction affect other parts of our personal lives?

Not surprisingly, people who are satisfied with their jobs or their families are also pleased with all the other aspects of personal lives we studied. Satisfaction with work and family enables people to pursue other aspects of their lives with less stress, distraction, and frustration. In other words, if we're unburdened by dissatisfying work or families, we're in a better position to participate in creative, social, political, or spiritual activities with an energy and optimism that provides satisfying experiences in these spheres of personal life. So, satisfaction with work or family promotes integration with these forms of personal life; dissatisfaction produces conflict.

In short, we see that work and family affect personal life in much the same way as they influence each other. The presence of resources from work and family can enhance the quality of personal life, while their absence can detract from a satisfying life off the job. Moreover, emotional gratification from work and family spill over into one's personal life and determine whether it will be satisfying or frustrating. However, contrary to our model, we find that psychological involvement in work and family seems to promote—rather than detract from—well-being in aspects of personal life other than family.

Additional Tables

TABLE 2a

Profile of the four life role priority groups

		CAREER	FAMILY	CAREER + FAMILY	SELF/ SOCIETY
▶ **HOURS WORKED PER WEEK**	◀	53.2^{ab}	49.7^{b}	53.9^{a}	49.1^{b}
▶ **% WITH HIGH PSYCHOLOGICAL INVOLVEMENT IN CAREER**	◀	$63.5^{a,b}$	18.2^{b}	55.2^{a}	29.5^{b}
▶ **% ASPIRE TO SENIOR MANAGEMENT**	◀	$65.4^{a,b}$	50.8^{b}	75.6^{a}	56.3^{b}
▶ **% ASPIRE TO CEO**	◀	$43.6^{a,b}$	28.7^{b}	44.5^{a}	29.4^{b}
▶ **% BELIEVE THAT CAREER HAS HIGHER PRIORITY THAN CAREER OF PARTNER**	◀	74.6^{a}	52.6^{b}	68.6^{a}	$56.8^{a,b}$
▶ **% MARRIED**	◀	43.0^{b}	88.0^{a}	84.0^{a}	48.0^{b}
▶ **PARENTHOOD**					
% currently parent	◀	30.0^{b}	70.0^{a}	65.0^{a}	31.0^{b}
% expect to become parent	◀	70.0^{b}	95.0^{a}	91.0^{a}	74.0^{b}
# of children expected	◀	1.4^{b}	2.2^{a}	2.0^{a}	1.5^{b}
▶ **% WITH HIGH PSYCHOLOGICAL INVOLVEMENT**					
in family of origin	◀	16.7^{b}	$46.3^{a,d}$	$31.7^{a,c,d}$	$30.0^{b,c}$
in family of creation	◀	46.0^{b}	92.0^{a}	83.0^{c}	65.4^{d}
▶ **CAREER INTERRUPTIONS**					
% took time off after first child	◀	34.9^{b}	63.6^{a}	51.9^{b}	$54.1^{a,b}$
Amount of time taken off (median)	◀	$1d/1wk^{b}$	$6wk/3mo^{a}$	$1d/1wk^{b}$	$6wk/3mo^{a,b}$
% return to work part-time	◀	7.9^{a}	19.2^{a}	8.7^{a}	9.8^{a}
▶ **ADJUST WORK SCHEDULE FOR FAMILY**	◀	7.6^{b}	27.6^{a}	19.5^{c}	21.1^{c}
▶ **HOURS PER WEEK SPENT ON**					
household activities	◀	7.5^{b}	11.8^{a}	9.2^{b}	$9.7^{a,b}$
childcare activities	◀	8.2^{b}	21.7^{a}	15.1^{b}	$13.2^{a,b}$
leisure activities	◀	17.2^{ab}	15.4^{b}	14.5^{b}	19.9^{a}
▶ **AGE**	◀	39.3^{a}	$38.2^{a,b}$	39.3^{a}	36.6^{b}

NOTE: For all group characteristics listed, the differences among the groups are statistically significant ($p < .05$). Groups in the same row with any of the same letters in superscript are not significantly different from each other.

TABLE 2b

Career and life values of the four life role priority groups

		CAREER	FAMILY	CAREER + FAMILY	SELF/ SOCIETY
► **CAREER SUCCESS VALUES**					
% who value status	◄	29.6[b]	20.1[a]	37.2[b]	21.8[a]
% who value time for self	◄	32.4[a]	68.5[b]	48.8[a,b]	67.3[b]
% who value challenge	◄	96.3[b]	82.1[a]	94.7[a]	83.5[a,b]
► **LIFE SUCCESS VALUES**					
% who value growth	◄	33.0[a]	27.1[a]	29.1[a]	45.0[b]
% who value wealth	◄	74.3[b]	44.8[a]	81.5[b]	48.1[a]
% who value family	◄	51.4[a]	91.5[b]	88.2[b]	67.7[a,b]

NOTE: Groups in the same row with any of the same letters in superscript are not significantly different from each other. Respondents who scored 4.0 or higher (out of 5.0) on a value scale are considered to value that outcome.

TABLE 2c

Work experiences of the four life role priority groups

		CAREER	FAMILY	CAREER + FAMILY	SELF/ SOCIETY
► **% WITH HIGH JOB AUTHORITY**	◄	52.8[a,b]	50.7[a]	68.7[b]	45.3[a]
► **% RECEIVING MANY DEVELOPMENTAL ASSIGNMENTS**	◄	35.6[a,b]	42.0[a]	59.5[b]	43.4[a,b]
► **% FEELING ACCEPTED BY OTHERS IN ORGANIZATION**	◄	71.4[a,b]	70.5[a,b]	75.1[b]	61.6[a]
► **% ENGAGING IN EXTENSIVE NETWORKING ACTIVITIES**	◄	52.9[a,b]	46.3[a]	59.8[b]	42.3[a]

NOTE: Groups in the same row with any of the same letters in superscript are not significantly different from each other. Respondents who scored 4.0 or higher (out of 5.0) on a work experience scale are considered to have experienced a high level of that work experience.

TABLE 2d
....
The effect of family structure on career involvement

MEASURE OF CAREER INVOLVEMENT

	Dual-Earner Fathers	Dual-Earner Mothers	Dual-earner Men with No Children	Dual-earner Women with No Children	Single-Earner Fathers	Single Men	Single Women
Hours worked per week	51.1[b]	40.0[a]	56.0[b]	54.0[b]	52.8[b]	51.7[b]	53.5[b]
% with high psychological involvement in career	33.5[a, c]	20.2[a]	34.9[a, b, c]	31.4[a, b, c]	38.9[b, c]	49.0[a, b, c]	62.7[b]
% aspire to senior management	67.0[b, c]	50.6[a, c]	73.7[b]	36.8[a]	77.6[b]	62.2[a, b, c]	35.4[a]
% aspire to CEO	42.9[c, d]	23.5[a, c]	38.4[c, d]	15.8[a]	47.2[b, d]	48.9[c, d]	16.7[a]
% believe career has higher priority than career of partner	78.3[b]	9.8[a]	65.7[b]	22.5[c]	91.1[d]	—	—

....

NOTE: Groups in the same row with any of the same letters in superscripts are not significantly different from each other.

TABLE 3a

Background characteristics and career success

► AGE	% Earning $71,000 or more[♦]	% in Upper Level position	% Highly Satisfied
20s	◄ 31[a]	8[a]	43[a]
30s	◄ 44[a]	31[b]	45[a]
40s+	◄ 71[b]	65[c]	57[b]
► SEX			
Men	◄ 66[a]	54[a]	52
Women	◄ 38[b]	22[b]	46
► RACE			
White	◄ 58	45[a]	51[a]
People of Color	◄ 41	23[b]	39[b]
► EDUCATION			
Bachelor's Degree	◄ 56	42[a, b]	52
Bachelor's and Certification	◄ 64	50[a]	63
Master's Degree	◄ 57	41[b]	48
Doctoral Degree	◄ 52	48[a, b]	49
► LIFE ROLE PRIORITY			
Career	◄ 58[a]	48[a, b]	46[a]
Career + Family	◄ 64[a]	50[a]	64[b]
Family	◄ 58[a]	40[ab]	46[a]
Self/Society	◄ 39[b]	36[b]	35[a]
► TYPE OF EMPLOYMENT			
Self-employed	◄ 63	93[a]	63[a]
Work for an organization	◄ 55	32[b]	46[b]
► CAREER FIELD			
Finance/Banking	◄ 70[a]	43	62[a]
Other Fields	◄ 54[b]	44	49[b]

NOTE: For each comparison, groups in the same column with any of the same letters in superscript are not significantly different from each other.

♦ See Chapter 3, Note 7, for an explanation of these dollar amounts.

TABLE 3b

Effects of family responsibilities on men's and women's work experiences

	MEN	WOMEN
▸ **MARRIED**		
Hours worked per week	◂ 52.3	46.3
▸ **NOT MARRIED**		
Hours worked per week	◂ 53.5	54.2
▸ **PARENT**		
Hours worked per week	◂ 51.8	40.7
▸ **NOT PARENT**		
Hours worked per week	◂ 54.1	53.6
▸ **PARENT**		
% highly involved in careers	◂ 35.7	20.9
▸ **NOT PARENT**		
% highly involved in careers	◂ 30.6	42.6
▸ **PARENT**		
% who adjust work schedule for family	◂ 26.6	42.1
▸ **NOT PARENT**		
% who adjust work schedule for family	◂ 9.5	11.2
▸ **HAVE PRESCHOOL CHILD(REN)**		
% who get extensive developmental assignments	◂ 23.7	17.0
▸ **NO PRESCHOOL CHILD(REN)**		
% who get extensive developmental assignments	◂ 19.9	29.2
▸ **HIGHLY INVOLVED IN FAMILY**		
Hours worked per week	◂ 53.0	46.7
▸ **NOT HIGHLY INVOLVED IN FAMILY**		
Hours worked per week	◂ 52.2	52.5
▸ **EXTENSIVE CHILDCARE ACTIVITIES**		
Hours worked per week	◂ 52.9	37.4
▸ **MODERATE CHILDCARE ACTIVITIES**		
Hours worked per week	◂ 50.6	43.8
▸ **EXTENSIVE CHILDCARE ACTIVITIES**		
% highly involved in careers	◂ 30.0	21.2
▸ **MODERATE CHILDCARE ACTIVITIES**		
% highly involved in careers	◂ 37.4	42.2

NOTE: In all cases, the effects of family responsibilities on work experiences are significantly greater for women than for men.

TABLE 4a

How do personal values affect satisfaction with family?

Percent highly satisfied with family

► IMPORTANCE OF FAMILY IN JUDGING ONE'S LIFE SUCCESS [+]		MEN	WOMEN	TOTAL
Low importance of family	◄	51	68	57
High importance of family	◄	71	79	73

► STATUS VALUE OF CAREER: Material Wealth & Standard of Living [+]				
Low value of status	◄	73	77	75
High value of status	◄	67	78	69

► SOCIAL RELATIONSHIPS VALUE OF CAREER: Helping Others and Friendships [*]				
Low value of social relationships	◄	71	69	70
High value of social relationships	◄	67	81	72

[+] Differences between low and high groups are significant.

[*] The interaction between sex and the social relationships value of career is significant.

TABLE 4b

How do personal values affect satisfaction with personal growth?

Percent highly satisfied with personal growth

► IMPORTANCE OF FAMILY IN JUDGING ONE'S LIFE SUCCESS [+]		MEN	WOMEN	TOTAL
Low importance of family	◄	42	55	47
High importance of family	◄	54	53	54

► IMPORTANCE OF PERSONAL GROWTH IN JUDGING ONE'S LIFE SUCCESS [*]				
Low value of growth	◄	39	41	39
High value of growth	◄	54	56	55

[+] The interaction between sex and the importance of family is significant, but there is no main effect for importance of family.

[*] The main effect of the importance of personal growth and the interaction between sex and the importance of personal growth are significant.

TABLE 4c

How do time allocations affect satisfaction with family?

Percent highly satisfied with family

▸ **WORK HOURS PER WEEK** •

	MEN				WOMEN				TOTAL
	20s	30s	40s+	All	20s	30s	40s+	All	
40 or fewer ◂	—*	53	56	56	88	78	63	79	67
More than 40 ◂	87	71	67	71	93	55	57	76	72

▸ **RELAXATION TIME PER WEEK** •

	MEN				WOMEN				TOTAL
	20s	30s	40s+	All	20s	30s	40s+	All	
10 hours or fewer ◂	75	66	68	69	86	74	54	71	69
More than 10 hours ◂	93	71	63	69	93	83	69	84	73

▸ **TIME OFF FOLLOWING CHILDBIRTH** ▪

	MEN				WOMEN				TOTAL
	20s	30s	40s+	All	20s	30s	40s+	All	
One week or less ◂	94	72	65	70	100	57	56	61	69
More than one week ◂	83	73	73	74	90	82	47	81	79

• The interaction between sex and work hours per week, and the three-way interaction among sex, work hours per week, and age group is significant; there is no significant main effect for work hours per week.

★ There are no men in their twenties who reported working fewer than 40 hours per week.

• The main effect of relaxation time per week and the interaction between sex and relaxation time are significant.

▪ The main effect of time off is significant, as are interactions between time off and sex and the three-way interaction among sex, time off, and age group.

TABLE 4d
....
How do time allocations affect satisfaction with personal growth?
Percent highly satisfied with personal growth

▶ **WORK HOURS PER WEEK** ◆

	MEN				WOMEN				TOTAL
	20s	30s	40s+	All	20s	30s	40s+	All	
55 or fewer ◀	43	45	53	49	68	54	50	55	51
More than 55 ◀	63	39	64	55	45	53	57	53	54

....

▶ **RELAXATION TIME PER WEEK** *

	MEN				WOMEN				TOTAL
	20s	30s	40s+	All	20s	30s	40s+	All	
5 hours or fewer ◀	33	33	63	54	100	40	42	45	50
More than 5 hours ◀	57	44	56	51	55	58	56	57	53

....

◆ The three-way interaction among sex, work hours per week, and age group is significant. There was no significant main effect for work hours.

* The interaction between sex and relaxation time is significant as was the three-way interaction among sex, relaxation time, and age. There is a significant main effect for relaxation time.

TABLE 4e

Work and career factors that influence family satisfaction·

Percent highly satisfied with family

	MEN	WOMEN	TOTAL
▸ **PSYCHOLOGICAL INVOLVEMENT IN CAREER**			
Low involvement	◂ 74	79	76
High involvement	◂ 66	76	69
▸ **ADJUST WORK SCHEDULE FOR FAMILY** *			
Infrequent adjustment	◂ 67	80	70
Frequent adjustment	◂ 73	69	71
▸ **CAREER SATISFACTION**			
Low satisfaction	◂ 72	57	66
High satisfaction	◂ 69	81	72
▸ **JOB SATISFACTION** *			
Low satisfaction	◂ 62	69	64
High satisfaction	◂ 73	84	76
▸ **NETWORK-BUILDING ACTIVITIES**			
Infrequent network-building	◂ 59	70	63
Frequent network-building	◂ 74	83	76
▸ **ACCEPTED BY OTHERS**			
Low acceptance	◂ 65	69	66
High acceptance	◂ 73	86	77
▸ **INCOME COMPARED TO PEERS** *			
Relatively low	◂ 69	76	70
Relatively high	◂ 69	87	74

◆ Main effects for all variables in this table are significant except for adjust work schedule.

★ The interaction between sex and this variable is significant.

TABLE 4f

....

Work and career factors that influence personal growth satisfaction

Percent highly satisfied with personal growth

		MEN	WOMEN	TOTAL
▸ **PSYCHOLOGICAL INVOLVEMENT IN CAREER⁺**				
Low involvement	◂	44	50	46
High involvement	◂	56	56	56
▸ **CAREER SATISFACTION ⁺**				
Low satisfaction	◂	26	30	27
High satisfaction	◂	56	59	57
▸ **ORGANIZATIONAL COMMITMENT⁺**				
Low commitment	◂	35	43	38
High commitment	◂	66	62	65
▸ **AUTHORITY IN JOB ⁺**				
Little authority	◂	41	43	42
Much authority	◂	58	62	59
▸ **RECENT DEVELOPMENTAL ASSIGNMENTS⁺**				
Few developmental assignments	◂	45	37	42
Many developmental assignments	◂	53	62	56
▸ **INCOME COMPARED TO PEERS⁺**				
Relatively low	◂	47	52	49
Relatively high	◂	61	65	62
▸ **LIKELIHOOD OF ACHIEVING ASPIRATIONS FOR HIERARCHICAL ADVANCEMENT⁺**				
Unlikely	◂	43	45	43
Likely	◂	60	63	61
▸ **LIKELIHOOD OF PROMOTION WITHIN NEXT TWO YEARS⁺**				
Unlikely	◂	41	50	44
Likely	◂	59	55	58
▸ **JOB PERFORMANCE***				
Relatively low	◂	37	50	40
Relatively high	◂	56	54	55
▸ **ACHIEVED HIERARCHICAL LEVEL***				
Relatively low level	◂	43	54	48
Relatively high level	◂	56	55	55
▸ **EMPLOYER SUPPORTIVE OF FAMILY NEEDS ***				
Unsupportive	◂	52	48	50
Family-friendly	◂	52	58	54

⁺ Differences between high and low groups are significant.

* The interaction between sex and this variable is significant, and there is no significant main effect for this variable.

TABLE 4g

How do role conflicts affect satisfaction with family?

Percent highly satisfied with family

▸WORK INTERFERENCE WITH FAMILY [*]

	MEN				WOMEN				TOTAL
	20s	30s	40s+	All	20s	30s	40s+	All	
Low interference ◂	88	78	76	78	93	86	53	83	80
High interference ◂	86	60	49	57	100	74	57	72	61

▸WORK INTERFERENCE WITH RELAXATION [★]

	MEN				WOMEN				TOTAL
	20s	30s	40s+	All	20s	30s	40s+	All	
Low interference ◂	100	70	75	76	89	83	44	78	77
High interference ◂	75	67	57	62	100	80	72	80	68
PARENTS									
Low interference ◂	100	79	76	79	100	76	27	66	76
High interference ◂	100	67	55	61	100	84	75	82	82
NOT PARENTS									
Low interference ◂	100	59	69	68	86	87	71	86	77
High interference ◂	70	67	88	68	100	75	67	78	72

▸ BEHAVIORAL WORK INTERFERENCE WITH FAMILY [•]

	MEN				WOMEN				TOTAL
	20s	30s	40s+	All	20s	30s	40s+	All	
Low conflict ◂	80	80	81	82	88	82	54	78	81
High conflict ◂	60	64	52	57	100	58	33	58	57

[*] The main effect of work interference with family and the three-way interaction among sex, work interference with family, and age group is significant.

[★] The main effect of work interference with relaxation, the interaction between sex and work interference with relaxation, and the three-way interaction among sex, work interference with relaxation, and age group is significant. When examined separately for parents and those without children, the main effect is significant for parents only; the interaction with sex is significant for both levels of parental status; and the three-way interaction also is significant for both levels.

[•] The main effect of behavioral work interference with family, the interaction between sex and behavioral work interference, and the three-way interaction among sex, behavioral work interference, and age group are significant.

TABLE 4h

How do role conflicts affect satisfaction with personal growth?

Percent highly satisfied with personal growth

▸**WORK INTERFERENCE WITH FAMILY** [*]

	MEN				WOMEN				TOTAL
	20s	30s	40s+	All	20s	30s	40s+	All	
Low interference ◂	59	50	65	59	50	60	53	58	59
High interference ◂	50	34	49	44	50	42	54	46	44

▸**WORK INTERFERENCE WITH RELAXATION** [*]

	MEN				WOMEN				TOTAL
	20s	30s	40s+	All	20s	30s	40s+	All	
Low interference ◂	57	49	65	59	50	61	52	58	59
High interference ◂	56	39	52	46	64	46	57	51	47

▸**FAMILY INTERFERENCE WITH WORK** [*]

	MEN				WOMEN				TOTAL
	20s	30s	40s+	All	20s	30s	40s+	All	
Low interference ◂	86	50	61	58	48	71	57	64	60
High interference ◂	46	38	56	47	58	39	52	45	46

♦ The main effect of work interference with family and the three-way interaction among sex, work interference with family, and age group are significant.

★ The main effect of work interference with relaxation, the interaction between sex and work interference with relaxation, and the three-way interaction among sex, work interference with relaxation, and age group are significant.

• The main effect of family interference with work, the interaction between sex and family interference with work, and the three-way interaction among sex, family interference with work, and age group are significant.

TABLE 5a

Correlations among parent and child outcomes

	CARE	HEALTH	BEHAVIOR	SCHOOL
▸ **PERFORMANCE AS PARENT** (Poor – Good) ◂	.12	.30[*]	.37[*]	.13[*]
▸ **SATISFACTION WITH CHILDCARE** (Dissatisfied – Satisfied) ◂		.01	.23[*]	.11
▸ **CHILD'S HEALTH** (Poor – Excellent) ◂			.30[*]	.19[*]
▸ **CHILD'S BEHAVIOR PROBLEMS** (Many – Few) ◂				.34[*]
▸ **CHILD'S SCHOOL PERFORMANCE** (Worst – Best) ◂				

[*] Relationship statistically significant at $p < .05$.

TABLE 5b

How personal values and family structure affect performance as parent and satisfaction with childcare

Percent perform well as parent		MEN	WOMEN	TOTAL
▸ **IMPORTANCE OF FAMILY IN JUDGING ONE'S LIFE SUCCESS**[♦]				
Low importance of family	◂	42	33	40
High fmportance of family	◂	71	70	71
▸ **IMPORTANCE OF PERSONAL GROWTH IN JUDGING ONE'S LIFE SUCCESS**[♦]				
Low importance of growth	◂	55	40	53
High importance of growth	◂	72	71	72
▸ **ASPIRATION TO TOP MANAGEMENT**[•]				
Aspired to less than top	◂	79	62	75
Aspired to top management	◂	65	78	67

Percent highly satisfied with childcare		MEN	WOMEN	TOTAL
▸ **IMPORTANCE OF FAMILY IN JUDGING ONE'S LIFE SUCCESS**[★]				
Low importance of family	◂	80	50	66
High importance of family	◂	77	56	70
▸ **IMPORTANCE OF WEALTH IN JUDGING ONE'S LIFE SUCCESS**[•]				
Low importance of wealth	◂	89	52	70
High importance of wealth	◂	75	57	70
▸ **FAMILY STRUCTURE**[■]				
Dual-earner mothers	◂			57[a]
Dual-earner fathers	◂			63[a]
Single-earner fathers	◂			95[b]

[♦] Main effect is significant.

[★] Interaction with sex is significant, but main effect is not.

[•] Main effect and interaction with sex are both significant.

[■] Groups with the any of the same letters in superscript are not significantly different from each other.

TABLE 5c

How personal values affect child outcomes

▶ LIFE ROLE PRIORITY[♦]	% Excellent Health	% Few Behavior Problems	% Above Average in School
Career + Family	◂72	78[a, b]	78[a]
Family	◂77	83[b]	88[b]
Career	◂61	65[a]	70[a]
Self/Society	◂64	83[a, b]	74[a, b]
▶ IMPORTANCE OF FAMILY IN JUDGING ONE'S LIFE SUCCESS[★]			
Low import	◂66	53	60
High import	◂73	82	84
▶ INTRINSIC VALUE OF CAREER: Challenge, Creativity, Enjoyment[●]			
Low value of intrinsic rewards	◂61		
High value of intrinsic rewards	◂80		
▶ VALUE OF CAREER TO SELF AND FAMILY: Flexibility, Time for Myself and My Family[●]			
Low value of self and family	◂		77
High value of self and family	◂		86

♦ Groups with any of the same letters in superscript are not significantly different from each other on child's behavior problems and school performance. There are no significant differences among the four types on child's health.

★ Differences between low and high Importance of family are significant for all three child outcomes; there are no significant interactions with sex.

● Difference between the low and high value of this aspect of career is significant only for the one child outcome for which data are presented in the table.

TABLE 5d

Work and career factors that affect performance as parent

	Percent perform well as parent		
	MEN	WOMEN	TOTAL
▶ INCOME[♦]			
Relatively low	◂ 72	69	71
Relatively high	◂ 57	50	56
▶ JOB PERFORMANCE[♦]			
Poor	◂ 50	66	54
Good	◂ 69	65	68
▶ JOB SATISFACTION[♦]			
Low satisfaction	◂ 62	68	63
High satisfaction	◂ 73	67	72
▶ SUPPORTIVENESS OF EMPLOYER OF FAMILY NEEDS[♦]			
Unsupportive	◂ 61	55	60
Supportive	◂ 70	68	69
▶ EMPLOYED BY SELF OR BY ORGANIZATION[♦]			
By self	◂ 76	75	76
By organization	◂ 66	69	67

♦ Main effect is significant.

TABLE 5e

....

Work and career factors that affect childcare satisfaction

	Percent highly satisfied with childcare		
	MEN	WOMEN	TOTAL
▸ INCOME*			
Relatively low	◄ 74	54	65
Relatively high	◄ 100	100	100
▸ INCOME COMPARED TO PEERS*			
Relatively low	◄ 70	52	63
Relatively high	◄ 89	62	84
▸ AUTHORITY IN WORK ROLE*			
Little authority	◄ 72	38	56
Much authority	◄ 79	64	74
▸ RECENT DEVELOPMENTAL ASSIGNMENTS*			
Few developmental assignments	◄ 85	48	71
Many developmental assignments	◄ 76	50	67
▸ ACCEPTANCE AT WORK: Mutually Positive Feelings About Others*			
Little acceptance	◄ 73	45	64
Much acceptance	◄ 83	64	77
▸ NETWORK-BUILDING ACTIVITIES*			
Infrequent network-building	◄ 78	41	64
Frequent network-building	◄ 80	54	72
▸ ORGANIZATIONAL COMMITMENT*			
Low commitment	◄ 78	44	65
High commitment	◄ 79	64	75

* Main effect is significant.

★ Interaction with sex is significant, but main effect is not.

TABLE 5f

....

Percent use of different childcare arrangements for three types of family structure

	Single-earner Fathers	Dual-earner Fathers	Dual-earner Mothers
▸ AT HOME WITH PARENT	◄ 75.9	35.4	9.6
▸ AT HOME WITH NON-PARENT	◄ 0.8	16.7	28.9
▸ IN ANOTHER HOME	◄ 0.0	8.3	21.7
▸ DAYCARE CENTER	◄ 1.2	5.2	19.3
▸ SCHOOL	◄ 20.5	34.4	20.5

TABLE 5g

Work and career factors that affect children's health

		Percent excellent health	
	MEN	WOMEN	TOTAL
▸ **INCOME** ✦			
Relatively low	◂ 66	73	67
Relatively high	◂ 79	89	80
▸ **AUTHORITY IN JOB** ✦			
Little authority	◂ 59	73	63
Much authority	◂ 77	82	77
▸ **ACHIEVED HIERARCHICAL LEVEL** ✦			
Relatively low level	◂ 64	70	66
Relatively high level	◂ 75	80	75
▸ **NETWORK-BUILDING ACTIVITIES** ★			
Infrequent network-building	◂ 70	60	63
Frequent network-building	◂ 71	92	70
▸ **ADJUSTMENT OF WORK FOR FAMILY** ★			
Infrequent adjustment	◂ 65	75	66
Frequent adjustment	◂ 83	76	82

✦ Main effect is significant.

★ Interaction with sex is significant, but main effect is not.

TABLE 5h

Work and career factors that affect children's behavior problems and performance in school

Percent few behavior problems

	MEN	WOMEN	TOTAL
► **AUTHORITY IN JOB** ⁺			
Little authority	◄ 78	85	80
Much authority	◄ 77	96	79
► **JOB PERFORMANCE** *			
Poor performance	◄ 61	100	70
Good performance	◄ 82	93	84
► **JOB SATISFACTION** *			
Low satisfaction	◄ 72	88	75
High satisfaction	◄ 80	95	83
► **PSYCHOLOGICAL INVOLVEMENT IN CAREER** ⁺			
Low involvement	◄ 81	93	83
High involvement	◄ 75	94	79

Percent above average in school

	MEN	WOMEN	TOTAL
► **ACHIEVED HIERARCHICAL LEVEL** ●			
Relatively low level	◄ 77	78	77
Relatively high level	◄ 82	100	84
► **CAREER SATISFACTION** ⁺			
Low satisfaction	◄ 76	73	75
High satisfaction	◄ 81	97	83
► **NETWORK-BUILDING ACTIVITIES** ⁺			
Infrequent network-building	◄ 84	56	80
Frequent network-building	◄ 81	100	84

⁺ Interaction with sex is significant, but main effect is not.

★ Main effect and interaction with sex are both significant.

● Main effect is significant.

TABLE 5i

Time allocations, performance as parent, and satisfaction with childcare

	Percent perform well as parent		
	MEN	WOMEN	TOTAL
▸ **TIME OFF FOLLOWING BIRTH OF FIRST CHILD?**◆			
No	◂ 64	42	62
Yes	◂ 72	77	73
▸ **AMOUNT OF TIME OFF FOLLOWING BIRTH OF FIRST CHILD**◆			
One week or less	◂ 68	27	66
More than one week	◂ 80	79	79
▸ **PART- OR FULL-TIME RETURN TO WORK FOLLOWING BIRTH**★			
Part-time	◂ 0	94	80
Full-time	◂ 75	57	73
▸ **RELAXATION TIME PER WEEK**★			
5 or fewer hours	◂ 66	47	62
More than 5 hours	◂ 69	81	71

	Percent highly satisfied with childcare		
	MEN	WOMEN	TOTAL
▸ **AMOUNT OF TIME OFF FOLLOWING BIRTH OF FIRST CHILD**★			
One week or less	◂ 79	33	75
More than one week	◂ 62	58	59
▸ **RELAXATION TIME PER WEEK**◆			
5 or fewer hours	◂ 85	30	57
More than 5 hours	◂ 76	74	75
▸ **HOUSEHOLD TIME PER WEEK**★ ◆			
Less than 10 hours	◂ 74	42	66
10 or more hours	◂ 80	60	72

◆ Main effect and interaction with sex are both significant.

★ Interaction with sex is significant, but main effect is not.

TABLE 5j

Time allocations, children's behavior problems, and performance in school

	Percent few behavior problems		
	MEN	WOMEN	TOTAL
▸ **RELAXATION TIME PER WEEK**★			
5 or fewer hours	◂ 82	83	82
More than 5 hours	◂ 78	97	80

	Percent above average in school		
	MEN	WOMEN	TOTAL
▸ **HOUSEHOLD TIME PER WEEK**★			
15 or fewer hours	◂ 84	100	86
16 or more hours	◂ 77	86	79

★ Interaction with sex is significant, but main effect is not.

TABLE 5k

....

Role conflicts, performance as parent, and satisfaction with childcare

	Percent perform well as parent		
	MEN	WOMEN	TOTAL
▸ **WORK INTERFERENCE WITH FAMILY** ✦			
Low interference	◂ 79	87	80
High interference	◂ 52	50	51
▸ **BEHAVIORAL WORK INTERFERENCE WITH FAMILY** ★			
Low interference	◂ 80	67	77
High interference	◂ 54	64	55
▸ **WORK INTERFERENCE WITH RELAXATION** ✦			
Low interference	◂ 79	85	79
High interference	◂ 60	59	60
▸ **FAMILY INTERFERENCE WITH WORK** ✦			
Low interference	◂ 78	71	77
High interference	◂ 61	69	63

	Percent highly satisfied with childcare		
	MEN	WOMEN	TOTAL
▸ **WORK INTERFERENCE WITH FAMILY** ★			
Low interference	◂ 78	64	74
High interference	◂ 75	41	62
▸ **BEHAVIORAL WORK INTERFERENCE WITH FAMILY** ●			
Low interference	◂ 80	69	76
High interference	◂ 78	31	68
▸ **FAMILY INTERFERENCE WITH WORK** ★			
Low interference	◂ 84	82	83
High interference	◂ 72	51	63

✦ Main effect is significant.

★ Main effect and interaction with sex are both significant.

● Interaction with sex is significant, but main effect is not.

TABLE 5I
....
Role conflicts and children's behavior problems

	Percent few behavior problems		
	MEN	WOMEN	TOTAL
▸ **WORK INTERFERENCE WITH FAMILY** [✦]			
Low interference	◂ 85	95	86
High interference	◂ 66	95	72
▸ **WORK INTERFERENCE WITH RELAXATION** [✦]			
Low interference	◂ 84	90	85
High interference	◂ 72	96	76
▸ **BEHAVIORAL WORK INTERFERENCE WITH FAMILY** [★]			
Low interference	◂ 84	95	86
High interference	◂ 66	89	68

✦ Main effect and interaction with sex are both significant.

★ Main effect is significant.

TABLE 6a
....
The effects of partner support on work–family conflict

TYPE OF SUPPORT   Percent who experience extensive conflict

	FAMILY INTERFERENCE WITH WORK	WORK INTERFERENCE WITH FAMILY	WORK INTERFERENCE WITH LEISURE	BEHAVIORAL WORK INTERFERENCE WITH FAMILY
▸ **HELP WITH HOUSEHOLD**				
Low	◂ 5.5	6.6	16.1	5.5
High	◂ 6.0	8.4	18.8	5.1
▸ **HELP WITH CHILDREN**				
Low	◂ 8.1	7.1	21.9	7.2
High	◂ 7.4	9.5	12.7	5.9
▸ **PERSONAL SUPPORT**				
Low	◂ 6.0	9.3	18.2	6.8
High	◂ 5.7	6.0	16.9	3.8
▸ **CAREER SUPPORT**				
Low	◂ 4.1	6.2	15.7	4.1
High	◂ 7.1	7.0	17.6	4.7

NOTE: All four types of work–family conflict are significantly higher for the low personal support group than for the high personal support group.

TABLE 6b

The effects of partner support on satisfaction with family and satisfaction with personal growth

TYPE OF SUPPORT	Percent highly satisfied	
	WITH FAMILY	WITH PERSONAL GROWTH
▶ **HELP WITH HOUSEHOLD**		
Low	◄ 73.8	48.6
High	◄ 72.9	54.4
▶ **HELP WITH CHILDREN**		
Low	◄ 68.5	51.7
High	◄ 73.4	52.0
▶ **PERSONAL SUPPORT**		
Low	◄ 60.1	45.1
High	◄ 84.7	58.5
▶ **CAREER SUPPORT**		
Low	◄ 69.2	42.9
High	◄ 76.5	60.3

NOTE: Significant differences in satisfaction with family and satisfaction with personal growth are found for low personal support versus high personal support and for low career support versus high career support.

TABLE 6c

The effects of partner support on the well-being of children

TYPE OF SUPPORT	% of Children Who Experience			% of Parents Who Feel Good About Their	
	Few Behavioral Problems	Excellent Health	Above Avg. School Performance	Children's Childcare Arrangements	Performance as Parent
▶ **HELP WITH HOUSEHOLD**					
Low	◄ 85.6	72.2	89.3	61.4[a]	75.8
High	◄ 77.5	71.0	78.7	78.0[b]	64.7
▶ **HELP WITH CHILDREN**					
Low	◄ 78.5[a]	70.3	84.7	60.2	66.9
High	◄ 81.1[b]	73.1	79.5	76.2	70.7
▶ **PERSONAL SUPPORT**					
Low	◄ 73.9[a]	69.8[a]	83.0	68.0	66.5[a]
High	◄ 88.4[b]	77.0[b]	82.6	71.8	69.7[b]
▶ **CAREER SUPPORT**					
Low	◄ 79.5	70.6	85.1	72.2	70.2
High	◄ 80.5	73.2	82.2	67.2	67.7

NOTE: For each of the four types of support, numbers in the same column with any of the same letters in superscript are not significantly different from each other.

TABLE 6d

The effects of partner support on career success

TYPE OF SUPPORT

		% EARNING $71,000 *	% IN UPPER-LEVEL POSITION	% HIGHLY SATISFIED WITH CAREER
▸ **HELP WITH HOUSEHOLD**				
Low	◂	52.7	34.2	48.6
High	◂	68.0	58.5	53.5
▸ **HELP WITH CHILDREN**				
Low	◂	64.6[a]	56.7	52.5
High	◂	69.0[b]	51.0	52.0
▸ **PERSONAL SUPPORT**				
Low	◂	61.6	47.3	44.2[a]
High	◂	58.3	45.4	57.8[b]
▸ **CAREER SUPPORT**				
Low	◂	56.9	43.5	45.0[a]
High	◂	60.9	44.8	56.0[b]

NOTE: For each comparison, numbers in the same column with any of the same letters in superscript are not significantly different from each other. The difference in upper-level position is not significant for the sample as a whole, but it is when we look at men only.

TABLE 7a

The impact of employer support for family needs on work and career*

Percent in the most family-friendly firms

▸ **VALUE OF CAREER TO SELF AND FAMILY: FLEXIBILITY, TIME FOR MYSELF AND MY FAMILY**

Low value of flexibility and time	◂	8
High value of flexibility and time	◂	22

▸ **ASPIRATIONS TO SENIOR MANAGEMENT**

Relatively low aspirations	◂	7
Aspire to top levels	◂	22

▸ **LIKELIHOOD OF ACHIEVING ASPIRATIONS FOR HIERARCHICAL ADVANCEMENT**

Unlikely	◂	7
Likely	◂	15

▸ **ACHIEVED HIERARCHICAL LEVEL**

Relatively low level	◂	8
Relatively high level	◂	21

▸ **ORGANIZATIONAL COMMITMENT**

Low commitment	◂	7
High commitment	◂	23

▸ **AUTHORITY IN JOB**

Little authority	◂	6
Much authority	◂	23

▸ **ADJUST WORK FOR FAMILY**

Infrequent adjustment	◂	9
Frequent adjustment	◂	29

▸ **JOB SATISFACTION**

Low satisfaction	◂	9
High satisfaction	◂	22

▸ **CAREER SATISFACTION**

Low satisfaction	◂	9
High satisfaction	◂	17

* All differences are statistically significant.

TABLE 7b

The impact of employer support for family needs on role conflicts, partner support, and personal life *

Percent in the most family-friendly firms

▸ **WORK INTERFERENCE WITH FAMILY**

    Low interference   ◂ 21

    High interference   ◂ 9

▸ **BEHAVIORAL WORK INTERFERENCE WITH FAMILY**

    Low conflict   ◂ 25

    High conflict   ◂ 12

▸ **FAMILY INTERFERENCE WITH WORK**

    Low interference   ◂ 20

    High interference   ◂ 14

▸ **WORK INTERFERENCE WITH RELAXATION**

    Low interference   ◂ 21

    High interference   ◂ 12

▸ **PERSONAL SUPPORT FROM PARTNER**

    Limited support   ◂ 11

    Extensive support   ◂ 22

▸ **PARENT**

    No children   ◂ 13

    Parent   ◂ 18

▸ **PART- OR FULL-TIME RETURN TO WORK FOLLOWING BIRTH**

    Part-time   ◂ 22

    Full-time   ◂ 15

★ All differences are statistically significant.

TABLE 8a

Work, family, and personal life outcomes for the four life role priority groups

Outcomes (in percentages)

	CAREER	FAMILY	CAREER + FAMILY	SELF/ SOCIETY
▸ INCOME OF $71,000 OR MORE	58[a]	64[a]	58[a]	39[b]
▸ IN UPPER-LEVEL POSITIONS	48[a,b]	50[a]	40[a,b]	36[b]
▸ VERY SATISFIED WITH CAREER	46[a]	64[b]	46[a]	35[a]
▸ VERY SATISFIED WITH PERSONAL GROWTH AND DEVELOPMENT	48[a,b]	57[a]	54[a,b]	44[b]
▸ VERY SATISFIED WITH FAMILY	44[c]	74[a]	78[a]	57[b]
▸ VERY SATISFIED WITH LIFE	16[b]	34[a]	26[a]	12[b]
▸ HEALTHY CHILDREN	61	72	77	64
▸ CHILDREN WITH FEW BEHAVIORAL PROBLEMS	65[a]	78[a,b]	83[b]	83[a,b]
▸ CHILDREN ABOVE AVERAGE IN SCHOOL	70[a]	78[a,b]	88[b]	74[a,b]

NOTE: Groups in the same row with any of the same letters in superscript are not significantly different from each other. Respondents who scored 4.0 or higher (out of 5.0) are considered very satisfied.

Notes

Notes to Chapter 1

1. The time requirements most business professionals face in today's competitive marketplace leave less and less time for other activities, as Juliet B. Schor demonstrated so convincingly in her aptly titled book *The Overworked American*. See Schor (1991).

2. For an overview, see Parasuraman & Greenhaus (1993).

3. See Gallos (1989). Why might women be better adapted for the new careers? Gallos writes: "Women also seem to be saying that career is not as distinct an entity for them as it is for men. A career is not something you do for eight plus hours every day until retirement. The boundaries between professional work and everything else in life are more permeable, allowing women to see relationships and family as critical work and reasons to pace their lives differently from men. Career for women means expressing their professional selves over a lifetime with commitment to accomplishment and desires for fair treatment and rewards for their efforts—something very different from needing an ongoing organizational affiliation or making life choices that put occupational progress first" (p. 126). As we describe later in this chapter, this sort of approach to careers is better suited to the demands of careers of the future.

4. Adams, King, & King (1996). Based on their research results, the authors characterized the relationship between work and family as simultaneously both conflict and support.

5. For instructive reviews, see Powell (1993); Gerson (1993); Levine & Pittinsky (1997); and Kimmel (1993).

6. An important argument to this effect was made in Rodgers & Rodgers (1989).

7. Whyte (1959); Papanek (1973).

8. See, for example, Bartolome & Evans (1979).

9. According to the U.S. Bureau of Labor Statistics (BLS), the rate of participation in the workforce of adult U.S. women has doubled since 1948, when the BLS began keeping track. The 1948 rate was 30 percent; in 1999, the rate stands at 60 percent.

10. Wohl (1997).

11. Levine & Pittinsky (1997).

12. Levine & Pittinsky (1997). Their observations also help us understand the social and cultural forces that make it difficult for men to express their interests in taking care of family needs. What they call "DaddyStress" stems in part from the norms and values of most organizations (which themselves reflect larger social mores): that men should not be taking care of families except to earn income for their health and security.

13. Levine and Pittinsky quote our colleague Dana Friedman, who puts the point about gender role inequity quite well: "Women still assume primary responsibility for family life. But the most important conclusion of research comparing men and women is that work–family conflict is related to family roles and responsibilities. When men take more responsibility for their children, they experience the same conflicts as women. To think about work–family conflict as a women's issue is much too narrow a view. This is an issue that goes beyond gender." Levine & Pittinsky (1997), p. 33.

See also Barnett & Rivers (1996). In a large-scale study of dual-earner couples conducted for the National Institutes of Mental Health, Barnett and Rivers found parents (both fathers and mothers) suffer stress-related health problems from worrying about their children. This is consistent with the conclusion Dana Friedman draws. The point, again is that it's the parental role—the responsibility for children's health and welfare—that drains attention and energy away from work and other commitments in life. Traditionally, men have been buffered from these strains and stresses because mothers have taken responsibility for children—and there remains a gender gap in the mental energy committed to the tasks of family and child-rearing, even if this gap is closing.

Elsewhere, Barnett and her colleagues found that "job role quality is significantly negatively associated with psychological distress for women as well as for men and that the magnitude of the effect depends little, if at all, on gender, casting doubt on the widely held view that job experiences more significantly influence men's mental health states than women's." See Barnett, Marshall, Raudenbush, & Brennan (1993).

Conversely, other researchers found that women's boundaries were more permeable. One possible explanation for this disparity is that Barnett et al.'s sample comprised only dual-earner families, where the tasks of parenting are more likely to be shared. See Hall & Richter (1988).

14. Bielby and Bielby observe that "differences between men and women in the roles they play at home and in the workplace largely explain sex differences in family and work identities. Sex differences in work identity are negligible between working husbands and wives with typically 'male' work and family situations. Further, married men who take on the family responsibilities of a typical working wife form family identities not much different than their female counterparts. . . . As individuals become engaged in role behaviors, they develop identities linked to those roles. . . . Job segregation in the workplace and inequality in the household division of labor generate sex differences in commitment. Thus, increased parity between men and women in their workplace and household roles should contribute to

stronger work identity among women and family identity among men." See Bielby & Bielby (1989).

15. The great challenge—indeed, the great hope—is that our society will shift away from traditional gender-based expectations for behavior and instead embrace and encourage a wider range of options for both men and women. See Clinton (1996). In her book, Hillary Rodham Clinton argues forcefully and persuasively for how our culture can, through education and other media of socialization, create this very sort of change.

16. *American Graduate Survey 1998*. The findings listed here are direct quotes from the 1998 report, MBA edition.

17. Covin & Brush (1991).

18. Society plays an active part here, assigning different social roles to men and women in their personal lives. Logically, this would lead one to conclude that men and women would have a different set of values on the personal front, even if similarities were found on the work front. See Chusmir & Parker (1991). These authors found that men and women have similar work values but different personal values, "suggesting that people may have dual hierarchies of values: one for work life and one for home life." Further, they found "different value patterns in women and men managers' work and personal lives, suggesting that the dual hierarchy varies according to gender."

19. Gaylin (1992).

20. Kimmel (1993).

21. Kimmel (1993), p. 56.

22. Kimmel (1993), p. 51.

23. Kimmel (1993), p. 60.

24. Barnett & Rivers (1996); Levine & Pittinsky (1997).

25. For other important insights on the changing nature of men's roles, see Pleck (1987); Gerson (1993); Bernard (1983); and Cohen (1987).

26. According to Kimmel (1993), men may well be increasing time on childcare, but not on housework. He cites Pleck's important review to note that men increasingly need to take advantage of family-friendly employer practices but that they are reluctant to do so because cultural norms, both in and outside of corporations, are antagonistic to such choices. Men will lie about the reasons for their taking time off, because a

childcare demand is just not seen as a legitimate demand on a man's time. "While current economic and social trends are forcing changes on the home front, the source of meaning in men's lives is open to individual interpretation." See Pleck (1993). More recent data from the Families and Work Institute's 1997 study of work indicates that the gender gap in time spent on household chores is narrowing, with men spending somewhat more than they did two decades ago, and women spending less. This study also observed that men are spending more time on child care than they did a generation ago. See Bond, Galinsky, & Swanberg (1998). We take up this subject in more detail in Chapter 5.

27. "What's ahead for working women." *New York Times*, August 31, 1997.

28. *New York Times*, Dec. 16, 1997. The full report is "1997 Catalyst census of women directors of the Fortune 500."

29. Parasuraman & Greenhaus (1993).

30. Parasuraman & Greenhaus (1993) cite several studies: Barnett & Baruch (1985); Baruch & Barnett (1986); Ross, Morowsky, & Huber (1983); and Valdez & Gutek (1986).

31. Parasuraman & Greenhaus (1993) cite Piotrkowski & Katz (1983).

32. Brett, Stroh, & Reilly (1992).

33. Hall (1996).

34. Allred, Snow, & Miles (1996).

35. Schein (1996).

36. Arthur & Rousseau (1996).

37. Bridges (1994a); Bridges (1994b).

38. As Gallos (1989) writes, women and men can be kept from having both fruitful careers and families "only if we continue to foster beliefs that careers require a singular and unwavering devotion to work alone, and that relationships and family are unnecessary diversions from professional accomplishment–interferences with productivity–rather than part of the baggage that *all* workers bring to enrich their contributions to work and organizations." This is consistent with what Lotte Bailyn writes in her critical analysis and call for action in Bailyn (1993).

39. Allred, Snow, & Miles (1996). Edgar H. Schein suggests that "even the way work is defined will change as the boundaries between jobs, between organizations, and between work and family become more fluid

and ambiguous." See Schein (1996).

40. Bailyn articulated this argument early on in Bailyn (1980).

Notes to Chapter 2

1. The clarification of priorities—for individuals and for managers—is the first of three principles for integrating work and personal life described in Friedman, Christensen, & DeGroot (1998).

2. Parasuraman & Greenhaus (1993).

3. For a useful early treatment of the literature on this issue, see Pleck (1985).

4. This effect has been identified for some time now. See Marks (1977); Sieber (1974); Baruch & Barnett (1986).

5. See Lobel (1991). Lobel discusses how utilitarian and social identity theories of role investments yield different conclusions about tradeoffs. In the former, people take the costs and benefits of role investments into account when deciding how much of their time and energy to invest in either work or family. It is assumed, in the utilitarian approach, the more time/energy to one role means less in another and so "the individual who finds both career and family life equally satisfying experiences equivalent pressures to invest in both domains" (p. 509). In the utilitarian approach, "work–family balance, or the stress-free management of work and family roles, would occur only when people's role investments are unequal and correspond to unequal net role rewards." In other words, if you're invested in both work and family equally, you're going to experience some ambivalence and stress. Competition between roles is inevitable—one role gains at the expense of the other. And in this view, tradeoffs *must* occur.

Social identity theory suggests that we have multiple identities in interactions with others in different situations (work, family, etc.). Here, a "favorable cost-benefit ratio is not a necessary condition for identification with a role." Identification depends on perceptions of membership in a group and the values associated with that group. Conflict doesn't necessarily occur when two or more roles are invoked if the identities (values) are similar in the different roles. Balance is achieved, in Lobel's terms, when there is self-consistency across roles.

Managing boundaries, in the social identity perspective, is a matter of ensuring that identities required in different roles are kept "more physically, temporally, and psychologically separate."

6. In Chapter 1 we observe that career involvement has a time component (hours worked per week) and a psychological component. This distinction will prove useful in understanding the career involvement of men and women, as we discuss in subsequent chapters. However, in the present analysis, we formed a composite career involvement score by standardizing and averaging the scores on the number of hours worked per week and psychological involvement in career. This was conducted for ease of presentation, only after determining that the patterns of relationships with family involvement were very similar for the two indicators of career involvement.

7. Greenhaus & Beutell (1985).

8. In describing the characteristics of the four groups, we use words such as high, low, likely, unlikely, not, many, and few in relative rather than absolute terms. We encourage readers to examine the statistical profile of the four life role priority groups, presented in Table 2a in "Additional Tables." The impact of life role priority on career and family involvement is quite similar for men and women. The few gender differences we observed are noted as parenthetical statements in the bulleted items in the text of the chapter describing the life role priority groups.

9. See Barnett & Rivers (1996); Deutsch (1999). These studies also show this with different samples.

10. Lobel (1991) writes of how "men and women cross at mid-life." Men become more cultivating and nurturing of relationships as they begin to see what was missing in their work and career pursuits and women, conversely, are able to express their sense of agency and getting things done in a domain beyond the home once the kids are gone from the home. As Lobel puts it: "Gender differences in process of role investment might reverse direction over the life span."

Lobel suggests that utilitarian approaches have been associated with men's development and choices, whereas social identity explains how women develop and choose. Her analysis is germane to our life role priority variable and findings about differences

across types. It's more likely people who are overinvested in either career or family will experience time/energy shortages. She writes: "an emphasis on personal utilities may be found especially among individuals who have primary orientations to either work or family, in comparison to those who have equally salient work and family roles, which are congruent aspects of self."

Lobel also asserts that "the utilitarian [tradeoff] model may determine short-term behavioral choices, whereas the social identity model may determine long-term general tendencies characterizing role investment." This point is consistent with what we say about how women's choices are more focused on the long term (see our Chapter 4) as compared with the nearer-term emphasis men seem to adopt in making investments of time and energy and psychological attention to either work or family roles.

11. We find that the average age of the children of career-focused parents (mean = 13.6) is significantly greater than the average age of the children of family-focused parents (mean = 8.3).

12. For a classic treatise on changes over the course of adult development, see Levinson et al. (1978).

13. People may become committed to a course of action to which they have devoted substantial time and energy as a way of convincing themselves and others that their initial decision was correct. See Staw & Ross (1987).

14. Kofodimos (1990); Hochschild (1997).

15. See Table 2b in "Additional Tables" for the differences in career and life values for members of the four life role priority groups.

16. We used factor analysis, a statistical technique for determining the underlying dimensions captured in a set of items, to determine these different aspects of career success values and the life success values that follow.

17. See Table 2c in "Additional Tables" for the differences in work experiences for members of the four life role priority groups.

18. This has been indicated in prior research. See Rabinowitz & Hall (1977).

19. Our findings reveal significant intercorrelations among hours worked per week,

psychological involvement in career, aspirations to senior management, and career priority, thereby supporting our view that they are *all* aspects of career involvement. It should be noted, however, that the priority of a career relative to the partner's career might also reflect differences in power and gender-role orientations within the relationship.

20. Our finding that men work more hours a week than women is generally consistent with prior research. A recent survey by the Families and Work Institute revealed a difference of six work hours per week between men (44.8) and women (38.6), although the Institute's sample (unlike ours) includes both managers and nonmanagers and professionals and nonprofessionals. See Galinsky, Bond, & Friedman (1993).

21. See Table 2d in "Additional Tables" for an analysis of the relationship between family structure and career involvement.

22. These findings do not change substantially when age is statistically controlled, indicating that the effect of family structure on hours worked is independent of age.

23. Gallos (1989).

24. See, for example, Campbell (1986). It is also possible that a lack of encouragement and career support from her husband can diminish a woman's career aspirations. See Hiller & Philliber (1982).

25. Morrison, White, & Van Velsor (1987); Thomas (1999).

26. Most studies reveal that women devote more time to home and children than men, although the magnitude of the gender difference varies across studies.

27. Hochschild (1989).

28. Gallos (1989).

29. Piotrkowski, Rapoport, & Rapoport (1987).

30. Pleck (1985); Kimmel (1993); Bond, Galinsky, & Swanberg (1998).

31. Parasuraman & Greenhaus (1993).

32. Parasuraman & Greenhaus (1993), Table 7.2.

33. Random House (1988). *The Random House College Dictionary*, (rev. ed., p. 1392). New York: Random House.

34. Thirty-three percent indicated that such trades were *not* necessary, and 24 percent were neutral on this issue.

35. We do not mean to imply that career-oriented women who remain unmarried

always make a conscious choice not to marry. In some cases, extensive time commitment to work, frequent relocations, and the unavailability of compatible men reduce the likelihood that a career-oriented woman will marry.

36. This is asserted perhaps most powerfully by Schwartz (1989).

37. Devanna (1987); Lewis & Cooper (1988).

38. Greenhaus & Parasuraman (1994).

39. This observation has been made by many researchers. See, for example, Covin & Brush (1991). The authors conclude: "Women appear affected by work–family conflicts to a greater extent than men."

Notes to Chapter 3

1. Respondents indicated how important their careers are in judging their success in life on a five-point scale, where 1 = not important, 3 = moderately important, and 5 = very important. More than four-fifths of the sample (81.7 percent) responded "4" or "5" to this item.

2. Schneer & Reitman (1993).

3. Tharenou, Latimer, & Conroy (1994); Rosin & Korabik (1990).

4. Karambayya & Reilly (1992). Also recall that in the preceding chapter we reported that individuals who are highly involved in their families of creation report lower levels of career involvement than individuals less involved in their families of creation.

5. See, for example, the literature cited by Valdez & Gutek (1986).

6. Much of the research on managers and professionals measures career success in terms of advancement through an organizational hierarchy and/or salary progression.

7. These figures are adjusted to the year 1998 based on increases in income from 1992 to 1996 by age and education, as reported by the U.S. Department of Commerce, Bureau of the Census. The average rate of increase from 1996 to 1998 was estimated based on the average rate of increase from 1992 to 1996. There is a significant difference in the salaries earned by graduates of the two universities sampled in this study. All analyses in this research statistically controlled for university. We thank Dr. Andrew Verzilli of Drexel University for these calculations.

8. Since the men in our sample are slightly older than the women, these analyses statistically controlled for age when examining gender differences in career success.

9. Because the sample contained so few African Americans (26), Asians (26), Hispanics (5), and Native Americans (5) compared to Caucasians (784), race was simply grouped into two categories, Caucasian and non-Caucasian.

10. These findings are consistent with those reported by Greenhaus, Parasuraman, & Wormley (1990).

11. Table 3a in "Additional Tables" shows the relationships between background characteristics and career success.

12. Many studies support this view. See, for example, Howard (1992); Howard & Bray (1988); and Stroh & Brett (1996).

13. Greenhaus & Callanan (1994); McCall (1988).

14. Valdez & Gutek (1986).

15. Kanter (1977).

16. In examining the effects of family life on income, hierarchical level, and career satisfaction, it was necessary to control for selected background factors. Three of the background factors that were most consistently related to the indicators of career success were age, self-employment, and career field (finance/banking versus other fields). Therefore, we conducted regression analyses to create measures of income, hierarchical level, and career satisfaction that controlled for these three factors. These adjusted measures of career success were used in the remaining analyses in this chapter.

17. Put differently, the greater income earned by married men is due in part to the fact that they reach higher organizational levels than unmarried men. In a similar vein, the greater career satisfaction experienced by married men is due in part to the fact that they reach higher levels and earn more money than unmarried men. It is important to note that although married men reach higher organizational levels than unmarried men, the interaction between gender and marriage on organizational level is nonsignificant, indicating that the effect of marriage on level is not significantly stronger for men than women.

18. When we say that authority "explains" the effect of marriage on men's

career success, we mean that when authority was statistically controlled or partialled out, the relationships between marriage and career success were no longer significant. Thus, we can conclude that authority is, at least in part, responsible for the observed relationships between marriage and career success.

19. Although one might posit that married men report more authority than unmarried men simply because the former hold higher-level positions, we found that the partial correlation between marriage and authority remained significant even after controlling for level. We conclude, therefore, that married men do not experience more authority than unmarried men merely because they occupy higher-level positions.

20. Although fathers receive less coaching than men without children, the lack of coaching does not detract from men's career satisfaction.

21. At least one indicator of family commitments was related to each of these aspects of career involvement and career opportunities. In addition, all aspects of involvement and opportunities except for work schedule adjustment contributed to a woman's income or her career satisfaction. We include work schedule adjustment in Figure 3.4 because it may have a long-term effect on women's career success that we cannot detect.

22. Schwartz, with Zimmerman (1992).

23. Table 3b in "Additional Tables" shows the relationships between family responsibilities and career involvement for men and women.

24. More than 80 percent of the single-earner fathers in our sample earn at least $71,000 a year compared to 70 percent of the dual-earner fathers. And 37 percent of the single-earner fathers (compared to only 23 percent of the dual-earner fathers) earn annual incomes of at least $142,000.

25. We cannot rule out the possibility that the wives of dual-earner fathers are employed *because* their husbands make low salaries. This perspective would argue that husbands' incomes determine wives' employment status, rather than the other way around. However, about 70 percent of the dual-earner fathers earn at least $71,000 annually, and 40 percent earn at least $107,000 annually, making it unlikely that

their wives have been forced into the labor market purely out of economic necessity.

26. We say this because after these variables are statistically controlled, single-earner fathers still earn significantly more money than dual-earner fathers.

27. Schneer & Reitman (1993); Stroh & Brett (1996).

28. Schneer & Reitman (1993).

29. We found that single-earner fathers do not perform more effectively on the job than dual-earner fathers.

30. Stroh, L.K. (April 30, 1996). Personal communication.

31. Among our business professionals, we observe that the amount of time dual-earner fathers spend on work is directly proportional to the amount of time their wives spend on household and childcare activities.

32. The importance of authority in explaining these differences was further highlighted when we explored the effects of marriage on achieved organizational level for men in different age categories. We found that the advantages of marriage hold for men in their twenties and thirties but not for men in their forties and fifties. Digging a little deeper, we observed that men in their twenties and thirties who are married report more job authority than those who are unmarried. In contrast, for men in their forties and fifties–where marriage doesn't affect the level they attained–married men report no more authority in their jobs than unmarried men.

33. Schwartz, with Zimmerman (1992).

Notes to Chapter 4

1. As we discussed in Chapter 1, this view has been contested, of course, in Kanter (1977), among many others. There is accumulating evidence that it is no longer valid. See, for example, Barnett, Marshall, & Pleck (1992).

2. Schor (1991).

3. Hochschild (1989). See also South & Spitze (1994).

4. The results shown in Table 4.1 are a comparison of all seven family structures on personal growth. When we look at all seven simultaneously, we find no significant differences. However, when we look at men and women to determine the effect of being a parent on satisfaction with personal growth and development, we do indeed find the sig-

nificant differences reported here in the text.

5. On the experience of fatherhood and personal growth, see Gilbert (1985), pp. 76–90; and Hall (1991). On motherhood and personal growth, see, for example, Spitze (1988).

6. The differences in satisfaction with personal growth are most pronounced among men. When we look at men and women separately, we find that men in the family and career + family groups are more satisfied than the other two types. While the differences among women are not statistically significant among the four types, the pattern is noticeably different from what we observe with men. In particular, women in the career group report the highest level of satisfaction with personal growth and development.

7. Table 4a in "Additional Tables" shows how personal values affect family satisfaction, and Table 4b shows how they affect satisfaction with personal growth.

8. Throughout the tables in this chapter we have simplified the presentation of observed significant relationships between analytic (or continuous) variables and the two satisfaction outcome variables (with family and personal growth) by recoding the analytic variables into dichotomous variables that represent low and high values of these analytic variables. To have concluded that a variable had a significant predictive relationship with a satisfaction outcome variable, we first had to observe significant parameter estimates in multivariate regression equations predicting the satisfaction variable. To have concluded that a significant interaction exists between sex and any given predictor, we had to find that the predictor's parameter estimates for men and women were significantly different from each other. Details of these analyses are available from the authors upon request.

9. Perlow (1997).

10. Table 4c in "Additional Tables" shows how time allocations affect satisfaction with family. It includes not two but three time factors. We discuss the meaning of childbirth-related time allocations, the third factor, later in this chapter.

11. Table 4d in "Additional Tables" shows how work and relaxation time affect satisfaction with personal growth.

12. Table 4e in "Additional Tables" shows the results for the work and career

factors that have a significant influence on the family satisfaction of people in our sample. Table 4f in "Additional Tables" presents the data on the impact of various work and career experiences on satisfaction with personal growth.

13. Kaplan (1991); Kofodimos (1993).

14. See, for example, Bielby & Bielby (1989). Based on the results of a national survey, the authors found that "women balance work and family identities in a way that gives causal priority to identification with the family role. . . . Working wives who identify strongly with the family role avoid identifying strongly with their careers, and, equivalently, women who form weak commitments to the family role in turn tend to identify strongly with their work outside the home. . . . Men make no such tradeoffs in establishing identities toward work and family. Men appear able to form strong (or weak) work identities irrespective of commitments to their families, and vice versa. Thus, it appears that for men, commitment to dual roles is not a zero-sum process. This finding is consistent with a traditional household division of labor. For men, identification with family as a source of meaning and identity is not closely linked to responsibilities and time commitments within the household. Men in traditional families have the freedom to commit or not to commit to family and work roles without confronting the issue of balancing the behavioral and psychic demands of activities in those two spheres. For women, however, balancing identities is not insulated from competing responsibilities in the two realms."

In sum, Bielby and Bielby found that "working women give precedence to family in balancing work and family identities . . . [and that] married men may have the discretion to build identification with work and family roles without trading one off against the other." This shows, they conclude, "how the gender-based structural and cultural context shapes the identity formation process."

15. See Parasuraman & Greenhaus (1993). They cite several studies to show that "women's employment can enhance their self-esteem and emotional well-being, especially if they are employed out of choice and hold jobs that are sufficiently challenging and interesting." These studies include Barnett & Baruch (1985); Baruch & Barnett

(1986); Ross, Morowsky, & Huber (1983); and Valdez & Gutek (1986).

16. See Gallos (1989). She offers a very instructive review of research and theory on women's development and their implications for career theory and for understanding how men and women construe relationships at work differently. One point she makes concerns the importance of differences between men and women in how they think about and create relationships and social attachments. For men, development has "meant increased autonomy and separation from others as a means of strengthening identity, empowering the self, and charting a satisfactory life course." For women, on the other hand, "development is tied to understanding and strengthening the self in relation to others."

Gallos cautions that we must "avoid confusing women's developmental concerns for attachment and relationships with stereotypic conceptions of female dependency and powerlessness—the two are not synonymous. . . . While women may be more dependent on significant others for their identity and self-satisfaction than men, dependency is very much a part of all human development. Independence in male developmental schemes has meant a separation from people, not lack of dependency. Since men have been socialized to achieve their identity primarily through work and professional accomplishments, in that sense, men are heavily dependent on their work. Beliefs in autonomy as the keys to men's development are distorted. . . . It is not that women are dependent and men are not, but that the source of the dependency may be different."

17. For useful discussions on men's capacities for developing intimate social ties, see Levine & Pittinsky (1997); Kimmel (1993); and Gerson (1993).

18. Brass (1985); Ibarra (1992). It is important to note that the more they *participate* in network-building activities, the better both men and women feel about family. See Table 4e in "Additional Tables" for specific findings.

19. Erikson (1980); Levinson et al. (1978).

20. Evidence for the idea that women take greater advantages of social relationships in their careers is seen in women's significantly higher ratings than men on the

value of their career as a means of helping others and developing friendships, as well as on the extent to which they have recently received coaching from others at work. In other words, women not only value social relationships in their careers to a greater degree than men, but they also take greater advantage of coaching from others (or perhaps are provided with more).

21. Tables 4g and 4h in "Additional Tables" show how role conflicts affect family satisfaction and personal growth satisfaction, respectively.

22. See Appendix One for definitions of perceived role conflicts.

23. See Almeida & Kessler (1998). The authors conclude that women are 50 percent more likely to complain of being in a bad mood than are men, and theorize that women typically juggle more roles than men do and thus encounter more opportunities for things to go wrong in their lives. Women also pay more attention to the problems of friends, coworkers, and distant relatives, while men tend to limit their "range of caring" to their spouses and children. The research challenges the idea that women are unhappy more often because they "hold on to bad feelings more," but rather attributes women's bad moods to the fact that "they experience more frequent daily stressors."

24. Thirty-one is the average age at which people in our sample became (or expected to become) a parent. The intensity of childrearing activities are at their peak, therefore, for people in their thirties.

25. See Bailyn (1978). This is perhaps the most important, earliest analysis of the dynamics of boundary management. The author identifies various patterns of accommodation of work to family and describes the costs and benefits associated with each one, as well as the personal and structural factors (at home and at work) that influence whether outcomes are satisfactory.

26. Our observations in Additional Tables 4g and 4h fit with a life cycle development perspective. See Higgins, Duxbury, & Lee (1994).

27. This may be especially true for women. See Hall (1975).

Notes to Chapter 5

1. For summaries, see Menaghan & Par-

cel (1990) and Fuligni, Galinsky, & Poris (1995).

2. There is a growing body of research, however, that directly assesses the impact of work on children. Galinsky (1999) is now the definitive work in this field, in part because of the method by which data were collected from children. Galinsky's powerful and clear arguments rest on a comprehensive analysis of key factors at home and at work. Most of her findings and conclusions are congruent with ours. Considering that we approached this topic using different research methods yet came away with similar conclusions, our confidence in the validity of the main implications of our research is enhanced. A number of observers had earlier discovered important relationships between certain features of parental employment and child outcomes. See, for example, Greenberger & O'Neil (1990); Belsky & Eggebeen (1991); and Hoffman (1989).

Prior to Galinsky (1999), Parcel and Menaghan conducted the most comprehensive study of the impact of parents' work on children. Parcel and her colleagues were the first to focus on the impact of both maternal *and* paternal working conditions, as we do here. See Parcel & Menaghan (1994).

Following Kohn, Parcel and Menaghan demonstrated that there are connections between parents' working conditions and their child-rearing practices. A limitation of their research, though, is their use of occupation as the indicator of job complexity, routinization, and other conditions of employment. Within an occupation, specific jobs can vary considerably. And differences in career values, too, cannot be accounted for without data taken directly from individual respondents. By contrast, our research design allows us to assess directly the detailed effects of work and career experiences of mothers and fathers on their children. Kohn's work in this area is perhaps best represented by Kohn & Schooler (1982).

In one of the few other studies to assess the impact of work on children, Stewart and Barling developed and tested a conceptual model that delineated the processes by which parents' work experiences influenced children's behavior by way of job-related effect and its impact on parenting behavior. In their study, however, only fathers' work experiences were assessed. Their research design had the advantage, however, of teachers' ratings of children's behavior, as opposed to gathering reports of children's behavior from parents, as we did. Both Parcel and Menaghan and Stewart and Barling (1996) found parents' work and career experiences do influence children's behavior and school performance. Galinsky (1999) did, too. Our findings affirm and extend this nascent line of research.

3. The two measures, we acknowledge, are qualitatively and quantitatively different. Indeed, parents in our study are more likely to report satisfaction with their childcare situation than to give themselves high marks as parents. Table 5a in "Additional Tables" shows correlations among the five parent and child outcomes we examine in this chapter. Different types of childcare arrangements, for children under 12, are used according to the following frequency: at home with a parent, 39 percent; school, 26 percent; at home with someone other than parent, 16 percent; at someone else's home, 10 percent; daycare center, 8 percent; other, 1 percent. Note that whether a parent feels satisfied with childcare arrangements does not influence feelings about his or her performance as a parent. See also Table 5f.

4. Previous research in the family and child development literatures indicates it is important to differentiate parental performance from child outcomes. The child outcomes we measure are taken from those used in the National Survey of Children, the National Health Interview Survey, and the National Longitudinal Survey of Youth (see Zill, 1990), conducted under the auspices of the National Institute of Mental Health. These include single-item indicators of general health relative to peers and of school performance relative to peers. The Child Behavior Problems Checklist (a 28-item index of behavior problems included in the National Longitudinal Study of Youth) is used to assess behavior problems. Achenbach developed this instrument, which is now in wide use as a means of gathering parental reports on children's emotional health and development. See Achenbach & Edelbrock (1981).

5. Galinsky's (1999) research provides numerous compelling examples to this point.

6. Bowlby (1982), p. 209.

7. Nippert-Eng (1996), p. 210.

8. Linda Mason, of Bright Horizons Family Solutions, one of the leading providers of corporate onsite childcare, conceives of the childcare center at work from such a community-centered perspective. In this view, the center becomes a locus of opportunities for parents to establish ties with other parents and so to learn and receive support from them. The modern work organization thus takes on a function previously served by the town or village. Mason, L. (1997). Personal communication.

9. In a *New York Times* op-ed piece (Nov. 8, 1996), U.S. Labor Secretary Robert Reich described his decision-making process for his own "family leave act." Reich's rationale—"I had to choose"—was rooted in a win–lose approach to resolving his conflict between career and family. "There's no way of getting work and family into better balance. You're inevitably shortchanging one or the other, or both. You're never able to do enough of what you truly value." In Chapter 9, we argue for alternative ways of addressing these conflicts that might well create a better balance between work and family.

10. Do mothers with different career values respond to their children differently? For one answer to this question, see DeMeis, Hock, & McBride (1986). The authors found that working women who become mothers respond to their young babies in similar ways regardless of whether their career preference is employment outside the home or staying at home. It isn't until about one year after the birth, however, that differences emerge in how the two groups of mothers respond to separation from their children.

11. For an analysis of national labor patterns on this issue, see Waite, Haggstrom, & Kanouse (1986).

12. Table 5b in "Additional Tables" shows how personal values and family structure affect parental performance and satisfaction with childcare for the people in our sample.

13. In our sample, fathers whose spouses work are virtually identical to their female counterparts in how they feel about childcare arrangements. Men whose wives do not work outside the home feel differently—and significantly better—than both the men and women whose spouses earn income. In terms of responsibility for childcare, men in dual-

earner families are likely to have lives more similar to women in dual-earner families than to men in traditional single-earner households, where responsibility for childcare resides in most cases with their spouses. For further discussion of this comparison see, for example, Kimmel (1993). See also Gilbert (1985); Bielby & Bielby (1989).

We did not examine the impact on children's health and school performance of different childcare arrangements, since that would take us too far into a set of "within-domain" questions.

14. Table 5c in "Additional Tables" shows how life role priority and personal values of parents affect child outcomes–health, behavioral problems, and performance in school–for the people in our sample.

15. To check whether the effects of life role priority on these child outcomes are due to the amount of time spent at work by parents classified as career-focused, we conducted additional analyses that included time devoted to work as a statistical control. The results are essentially the same.

16. Table 5d in "Additional Tables" details the work and career factors that affect the parental performance of people in our sample.

17. Table 5e in "Additional Tables" shows the work and career factors that affect the satisfaction with childcare of people in our sample.

18. We looked concurrently at the effects of income and psychological involvement in career on parental performance. Our findings: it is the greater psychological involvement in one's career made by people with very high incomes that results in their relatively low parental performance.

19. See, for example, Thomas & Ganster (1995).

20. There are significant differences among our business professionals in who cares for the children. Fathers are much more likely to have their children at home with mom, whereas mothers rely more on someone other than dad to watch their young children. Fathers spend far fewer hours per week on childcare than do mothers. Table 5f in "Additional Tables" shows the percent use of different childcare arrangements for three types of family structure in our sample.

21. Table 5g in "Additional Tables" presents the work and career factors that affect the health of children of parents in our sample.

22. Table 5h in "Additional Tables" shows the work and career factors of people in our sample that affect the behavior problems and school performance of their children. Note that for psychological involvement in career the conversion to percentages makes it seem equal for women, masking actual mean differences.

23. How fathers are treated on the job affects their parenting, because it affects their self-esteem. Grimm-Thomas and Perry-Jenkins (1994) found that fathers with more autonomy and control over their work have higher self-esteem and are less stringent parents. Grossman, Pollack, & Golding (1988) found that dads with more autonomy and satisfaction on the job play longer and have a better quality of interaction with their kids.

Other research cited by Levine & Pittinsky (1997) shows that fathers have a profound impact on kids' development; in infancy, preschool, and adolescence, a father's involvement is important for a child's social, emotional, and cognitive development.

Galinsky's (1999) treatise shows how the quality of parents' jobs affects their children. Barling, too, has observed the impact of parents' job satisfaction on children's well-being. See Barling (1986); Barling & Van Bart (1984).

24. Greenhaus and Beutell (1985) identify this as "time-based conflict."

25. Table 5i in "Additional Tables" shows how time allocations affect parental performance and satisfaction with childcare among people in our sample. Table 5j in "Additional Tables" shows how time allocations affect children's behavior problems and school performance.

26. That time devoted to work and to children has relatively little impact on parental performance is consistent with previous research. See Williams & Alliger (1994). As the authors conclude from their review of the literature, "the subjective quality of an individual's work and family roles, not employment and family status per se, is the critical determinant of psychological well-being."

This idea is echoed in Stewart and Bar-ling's research on the impact of fathers' work on children. They assert that "employment experiences rather than employment status affect family functioning." See Stewart & Barling (1996). The popular business press has identified this as an area of concern, too. See, for example, Reilly (1990).

Galinsky's (1999) findings, based on her data gathered from children directly, affirm our conclusion: children are less interested in time than in wanting their parents to be less stressed and less tired when they are with them.

27. The relationship behavior problems was in the expected direction, but it fell just short of statistical significance. Time spent on kids, self-reported, is not related to behavior problems, but estimated time spent on kids by partner is.

28. No time off is the modal amount taken by men following the birth of their first child, whereas for women it is in the range of more than six weeks to three months.

29. Alternatively, it is possible that these fathers are especially sensitive to their parental role and are therefore overly critical of their parenting skills, holding themselves to a higher standard.

30. However, we find no connection between how much time is taken off and the three child outcomes in our study—health in general, behavior problems, and school per-formance.

31. Table 5k in "Additional Tables" shows role conflicts and their effect on parental per-formance and satisfaction with childcare among people in our sample. Table 5l in "Additional Tables" shows perceived role con-flicts and their effect on children's behavior.

32. Dix (1991).

33. Galinsky (1999) draws the same con-clusion in her landmark study, using a nationally representative study of parents and their children.

34. Major studies that document this trend, particularly as it relates to parenting, are described in Barnett & Rivers (1996); Bond et al. (1988); and in Deutsch (1999).

Notes to Chapter 6

1. See, for example, Cohen & Wills (1985); Greenhaus & Parasuraman (1994); House (1981); Thoits (1986).

2. Shumaker & Brownell (1984).

3. While support from one's family includes support from children, parents, sib-lings, and other relatives, it is support from one's partner or spouse that is particularly crucial to well-being. Therefore, that sup-port is the focus of our research.

4. The literature often refers to behav-ioral support as "instrumental" support (e.g., House, 1981). We prefer to use the term behavioral support to be consistent with the terminology used in the preceding chapter, where we described parents' availability to their children.

5. The distinction between personal sup-port and career support is based on the results of a factor analysis of the emotional support items included in our survey. The results of the factor analysis are presented in Appendix One under "Partner Personal Sup-port" in the section titled "Definitions and Measures of Family and Personal Choices and Experiences."

6. Cohen & Wills (1985); House (1981); and Shumaker & Brownell (1984).

7. Granrose, Parasuraman, & Greenhaus (1992).

8. There is an apparent inconsistency between the findings reported in Chapter 2, where we saw that dual-earner mothers spend considerably more time with their children than dual-earner fathers, and the findings we report in this chapter where we observe that, as partners, dual-earner moth-ers and fathers spend a similar amount of time with their children. However, the mea-surement of time spent with children is dif-ferent in the two sets of analyses. Chapter 2's results are based on self-reports by men and women of the number of hours they spend with children, whereas here our findings are based on reports of the amount of time *part-ners* spend with the children. We believe it's difficult for people to assess the time spent by partners on childcare since they are not the direct recipients of the attention and may not be physically present when their partners interact with the children. Therefore, we're inclined to put more faith in self-reports of behavioral support, concluding that dual-earner mothers do spend substantially more time with their children than do dual-earner fathers (as reported in Chapter 2).

9. We found that the partners of single-

earner fathers are more psychologically involved in their families than the partners of any other group, and significantly more so than the partners of dual-earner men and women without children.

10. It is not clear why individuals who value personal growth tend to receive *limited* assistance with the household from their partners. One hypothesis, consistent with what we argue in the next section about reciprocity, is that people feel it would be unfair for them to "subsidize" their partner's pursuit of personal growth with the drudgery of additional housework.

11. Long work hours have traditionally been associated more with men than women, as our own findings show. Prior research has found that women place more importance on free or "leisure" time off the job than men. See Manhardt (1972). Although no researchers have found the importance of job security to be more characteristic of women than men, the converse of security—risk taking—*has* been associated with men. See Brenner & Tomkiewicz (1979).

12. Alternatively, it may be that people who are absorbed in their work simply don't think about receiving personal support from their partners.

13. See Shumaker & Brownell (1984) for a discussion of the importance of reciprocity in social support. Other research on dual-earner couples has demonstrated that emotional support—as well as behavioral support—is returned in kind by a partner. See Parasuraman & Greenhaus (1992). We did not study this directly among our business professionals, because we did not have measures of both partners' provision of personal and career support. Our findings, taken together with this prior research, strongly suggests that all types of partner support beget partner support; a virtuous cycle.

14. There are, of course, explanations that may not be about reciprocity. It is possible that partners of people who are highly involved in family life not only believe that support is *needed*, but also is *deserved*. In addition, it is certainly conceivable that family-involved people choose partners who are willing and able to provide emotional support.

15. Recall that the items we used to measure family involvement assess the centrality of the family in the individual's life (e.g.,

"Most of the important things that happen to me involve my family.")

16. Joseph Pleck has observed asymmetrically permeable work–family boundaries for men and women in which society permits men's work to intrude into their family responsibilities and women's family responsibilities to intrude into their work role. See Pleck (1977).

17. See Greenhaus & Parasuraman (1994) for a brief summary of the literature underlying the three functions of social support.

18. The concept of self-efficacy expectations is relevant here. It is possible that receiving social support—especially personal and career support—boosts people's beliefs in their ability to solve problems in the work, family, and personal domains.

19. Table 6a in "Additional Tables" presents the relationships between receiving different types of partner support and work–family conflict.

20. Table 6b in "Additional Tables" presents the relationships between receiving different types of partner support and experiencing satisfaction with family and personal growth.

21. Table 6c in "Additional Tables" presents the relationships between receiving different types of partner support and children's well-being.

22. Marital happiness as it is affected by work experiences has been found to enhance the well-being of children. See Barling, Fullagar, & Marchl-Dingle (1988). When we statistically control for family satisfaction, the negative relationships between personal support and children's behavioral and health problems disappear, suggesting that personal support enhances children's well-being because it has a positive impact on parents' satisfaction with their families.

23. Consistent with this interpretation, when we statistically control for children's behavioral and health problems, there is no longer a positive relationship between personal support and individuals' perception that they are good parents. Alternatively, it could be argued that personal support enables one to become a better parent which, in turn, reduces the incidence of children's behavioral and health problems.

24. This is analogous to an experience that will be familiar to most readers: that

men will steadfastly refuse to ask directions when traveling in the car, whereas women will readily seek assistance. See Tannen (1991).

25. Although we imply in this statement that receiving help with the children *enables* people to work longer hours, we suggested earlier that working long hours encouraged partners to provide extensive assistance with the children. The design of our study does not permit us to determine which is the cause and which is the effect. In fact, there could be a cycle: partners' support with the children makes it possible to work longer hours, which in turn motivates the need for greater support from the partner to take care of the kids.

26. Our analyses reveal that the more money an individual earns, the fewer hours the partner works, and the fewer hours the partner works, the more time the partner spends with the children.

27. We suspected that personal support's beneficial effects on well-being are due to its ability to reduce work–family conflict, which in turn would enhance well-being. And, in fact, this explanation holds for the impact of personal support on children's behavioral problems. However, the positive effects of personal support on satisfaction with family, satisfaction with personal development, career satisfaction, and children's health are *not* due to the decreased level of work–family conflict experienced by individuals who receive extensive personal support.

28. MacEwen & Barling (1988).

29. These conclusions are based on examining relationships between behavioral support and various outcomes when spouses provide high and low levels of emotional support.

30. In terms of the benefits of partner support, we examined 84 relationships of support with work–family conflict, work-related experiences, and well-being. Of these, only six (7.1 percent) are significantly different for men and women. Therefore, we conclude that *in general* men and women receive similar benefits from partner support. In exploring the determinants of support, we examined 68 relationships of providers' and recipients' characteristics with partner support, of which 14 (20.6 percent) are significantly different for men and women. Thus, although there

are some differences in the reasons why men and women receive support, there are more similarities than differences.

Notes to Chapter 7

1. For an excellent example, see the cover story in the May 12, 1997, issue of *U.S. News & World Report* titled "Lies parents tell themselves about why they work."

2. Friedman, Christensen, & DeGroot (1998).

3. Contrast our approach with the typical assessment of employer supportiveness of family needs. Most such assessments measure the number and extent of programs available to employees, in part because data are readily available from human resources departments. So, for example, Osterman measured whether the firms in his sample did or did not have daycare support, referral services, a full-time work/family staff employee, and options for flexible hours. See Osterman (1995).

4. Of course, our assessment of family-friendliness does have some bias, because it comes from only one person: the participant in our study.

5. Friedman & Johnson (1997); Catalyst (1996); and Solomon (1996). See also the cover story in the September 16, 1996, issue of *Business Week* titled "Balancing work and family." This article is based on a study conducted by Brad Googins, of the Boston College Center for Work and Family, that assessed both programs and their utilization.

6. On items 1 and 3, we reversed the scoring so that, on the composite variable, the higher the score the more family-friendly one's organization.

7. This indicator of employer support for family needs, therefore, captures the essence of what others have sought to examine when measuring family-friendliness. See, for example, Galinsky, Friedman, & Hernandez (1991); Morgan & Tucker (1991).

8. For an overview and analysis of the motivations for the adoption of work/family programs, see Osterman (1995). For more general reviews of the emergence of family-friendliness in organizations, see Bailyn (1993); Parasuraman & Greenhaus (1997).

9. Several times in this chapter we compare the experiences of people in firms they consider family-friendly to those in unsup-

portive firms. To make this comparison easier to present, we divide our sample in half at the median score on our composite measure of employer support for family and personal life. As a result, 45 percent of our respondents rate their employers as relatively unsupportive of family and personal life needs (i.e., from one to three, inclusive, on a five-point scale) and 55 percent rate their employers as supportive (greater than three on a five-point scale).

10. The difference between men and women is statistically significant. This gender difference is independent of any differences in perceived family-friendliness that might result from men and women working in different kinds of industries, working for themselves, working in large versus small organizations, or working part- versus full-time. These results are comparable to those observed in large companies (greater than 250 workers) in the Families and Work Institute's 1997 national study of the changing workforce (see Bond, Galinsky, & Swanberg, 1998).

11. Few people in our study are employed on a part-time basis (about 4 percent), and women make up three-quarters of those in this employment category.

12. See Brett's (1997) analysis of the dilemmas both men and women face in modern career structures in her instructive essay. See, also, for example, a *Wall Street Journal* article titled "Hear them roar: More women quit lucrative jobs to start their own businesses" (April, 1997). In another newspaper story, the *Philadelphia Inquirer* (January 7, 1996) writes about women "shifting gears." The article catalogues the changes being made by more and more women in their lifestyles. "These women, usually well-educated, highly paid professionals, are cutting back their hours, turning down assignments with travel or increased responsibilities. . . ."

13. Table 7a in "Additional Tables" shows the impact of employer support for family needs on work and career. Table 7b shows the impact of employer support for family needs on role conflicts, partner support, and personal life.

14. Hochschild (1997). See also Morris's article in the March 17, 1997, issue of *Fortune* magazine titled "Is your family wrecking

your career?" Earlier researchers observed that a high involvement in work can be an escape from discomfort in family roles. See Bartoleme (1983) and Kofodimos (1990).

15. There was no main effect on time spent at work as a result of personal support from partner but there was a significant interaction between personal support and employer support such that the difference in hours spent working between people in supportive versus unsupportive organizations was greater for those people with supportive partners. These analyses were repeated using "acceptance by others" at work instead of "organization support for family needs" and using "family satisfaction" instead of "personal support from partner" as predictors of time spent at work. While personal support from partner by itself had no effect on time worked, we did observe that people who were highly satisfied with their families actually tended to work more than those who were not (one-tailed, p = .10), but neither organization support nor acceptance by others affected this relationship.

16. It may be that we reach a different conclusion than Hochschild because of our method of assessing whether firms are indeed friendly to family and other life interests. Recall that earlier we describe why we opted for a subjective measure–the perception of employees. Hochschild assesses family-friendliness on the basis of whether the employer studied has policies and formal programs that supported family life, regardless of whether these policies are enforced or programs utilized. Also, our sample includes a wide range of organization and industry experiences, and includes primarily highly educated business professionals with considerable access to economic and other resources in society.

17. Kofodimos (1995); Martinez (1997).

18. An alternative explanation for this finding is that fathers with low aspirations have already traded what it takes to pursue high management positions for what it takes to be an available father, and so they do not reap the benefits of organization support to the same degree.

19. This does not explain, however, why employer support was unrelated to career support. It may be that, as we saw in Chapter 6, career support has less pervasive effects

and that it is therefore a less important attribute of a spouse or partner.

20. We did not explore the impact of employer family-friendliness on the buffering function of partner support, having found little evidence of this benefit (see Chapter 6).

21. There is no significant interaction between personal support from partner and employer support with respect to the interference of work on relaxation.

Notes to Chapter 8

1. Our focus in this chapter is on whether experiences in one role enhance (integration) or detract from (conflict) the quality of life in the other role, because of the greater or lesser availability, competence, and emotional gratification in the role. Thus, our definition of work–family conflict is somewhat broader than the one offered by Greenhaus & Beutell (1985), in which work–family conflict is said to exist when participation in one role makes it more difficult to participate in the other role.

2. Appendix Two, "Personal Life Beyond the Family," discusses this model in the context of personal life other than family.

3. Researchers have rarely considered the impact of family-generated resources on work. For discussions of the impact of work-related resources on family life, see Piotrkowski, Rapoport, & Rapoport (1987); Kanter (1977).

4. There is ample documentation of the facilitating effects of self-esteem and self-efficacy—that is, self-perceived competence for a particular task—on task performance. See Bandura (1997); Korman (1976).

5. Crouter referred to the application of skills, attitudes, or perspectives learned in the family to the work setting as educational spillover, a similar concept to Repetti's socialization transfer. Crouter (1984); Repetti (1987).

6. For a discussion of the role of social identity theory in work–family dynamics, see Lobel (1991). Lobel's main contribution in this piece is that social identity theory provides a theoretical foundation for research devoted to viewing work and family as complementary. This supports our construction of work and family as allies, as "integratable." As Lobel writes, "The reframing of role costs

into role rewards, consistent with the social identity approach" opens up the possibility of looking at how transfer of skills from community work to business, for example, makes sense from an economic perspective. Conflict doesn't have to be associated with equally salient identities. Researchers need to shift from an emphasis on role conflict to "how an individual fares in implementing his or her self-concept. . . . The focus on self-consistency, which is part of the social identity definition of work–family balance" leads to a focus on such problems as how to achieve balance by engaging in actions that are consistent in work and family roles (e.g., upholding quality standards at home and work; caring for others at home and work). How organizations can foster self-consistency is another question raised by social identity theory.

7. Hall (1976); Katz and Kahn (1976).

8. See Kanter (1977); Small & Riley (1990). In both cases, the authors discuss the issue of role absorption.

9. For a discussion of role accommodation, see Katz and Kahn (1976); Lambert (1990).

10. See Locke's discussion of the meaning of job satisfaction and Greenhaus et al.'s measure of career satisfaction. Locke (1976); Greenhaus, Parasuraman, & Wormley (1990).

11. Other terms have been used to refer to this concept. See Crouter (1984); Lambert (1990); Repetti (1987); Kanter (1977); and Evans & Bartolome (1980). These authors use "psychological spillover," "spillover," "systemic spillover," "emotional climate," and "negative emotional spillover," respectively.

12. Hall (1976).

13. Of course, there are other nonwork sources of social support—from siblings, parents, extended family, friends, members of the community. We studied only partner support in our research.

14. For a discussion of the impact of social support on the recipient's self-identity and self-esteem, see Shumaker & Brownell (1984).

15. Crouter (1984) discusses the spillover of skills and attitudes learned within the family to the work lives of employees who were members of work teams in a manufacturing

facility. It's likely that such spillover occurs across a broader range of employees, including business professionals.

16. Concerning educational spillover, see Crouter (1984).

17. For example, we find that the more time individuals spend on household activities, the less successful they are in their careers, occupying lower-level jobs, earning lower incomes, and experiencing less career satisfaction. However, the cross-sectional design of our study makes it impossible to determine whether time spent on the household detracts from career success or whether successful individuals simply have less time to spend on home chores. Since the latter explanation is at least as plausible as the former, we believe our findings do not necessarily indicate that time spent on the home is the culprit.

18. The cross-sectional methodology we used in our research precludes an assessment of the causal direction of relationships between variables. A longitudinal design would be required to determine whether satisfaction with work and family mutually reinforce each other over time.

19. The fact that the design of most work–family studies (including our own) is cross-sectional—where all measures are taken at the same time—makes it impossible to determine the direction of causality between a work factor and a family factor. Throughout this book, we've sought to argue for one or another causal direction when we've had a compelling basis for doing so.

20. Table 8a in "Additional Tables" shows the work, family, and personal life outcomes for the four life role priority groups.

21. Recall that of our sample, 42 percent are family-focused, 13 percent career-focused, and 15 percent self/society-focused.

Notes to Chapter 9

1. *Washington Post*, May 22, 1998.

2. IBM & Families and Work Institute (1997), *I Am Your Child* (CD-ROM).

3. For the definitive scholarly treatise on children's needs for parental attachment, see Bowlby (1969). T. Berry Brazelton and Penelope Leach have written extensively on the implications of attachment theory for child-rearing practices. See, for examples, Brazel-

ton (1983); Leach (1994). Galinsky (1999) provides a useful review.

4. Rodgers (1992) discusses the cultural barriers to creating flexibility, and lists critical success factors for implementing flexibility.

5. See Friedman, Christensen, & DeGroot (1998) for a description of these principles as they relate to managerial action. Here we apply them also to individuals, employers, and society.

6. Quoted in "Executives reflect on past choices made for family and jobs." *Wall Street Journal*, December 31, 1997.

7. Friedman and Johnson (1997) makes this point persuasively. The Public Policy Institute at Radcliffe College is making an important contribution to challenging assumptions. The Institute's "New Economic Equation" is a project to create partnerships that bring different domains together in the recognition that "economic well-being = integration of work, family and community." The project's resolves for action are filled with useful ideas for how to create constructive change and new public and private solutions. Of particular interest is the emphasis on gender equity.

8. Greenhaus and Parasuraman (1997) offer a set of "solutions to work–family problems" drawn from the chapters in their edited collection. They conclude, as we do here based on the analysis of our study's findings, that "the most effective solutions must involve partnerships" among various segments of our society—individuals, families, companies, and the public sector.

9. Chira (1998).

10. Levine and Pitinsky (1997) show the way in their highly practical and keenly sensitive book on working fathers.

11. To be fair, though, we must point out that these data were met with some skepticism. In "Superdad needs a reality check," a *New York Times* op-ed piece (April 16, 1998), Carin Rubenstein, a social psychologist and author of *The Sacrificial Mother*, rebutted these numbers, stating that a number of other reliable studies of time allocations have found that mothers spend much more time on childcare than fathers. Hers is a pessimistic conclusion: "Because most of us yearn for a family life that is fair and equitable, we're eager to believe in the results of a

study showing that fathers are spending more time with children. But the reality is, it just isn't so. Mothers will always feel a greater need than fathers to sacrifice for their children. And pretending things have changed won't make a difference."

12. "More executives cite need for family time as reason for quitting." *Wall Street Journal*, March 18, 1998.

13. Baar, K. (1997). "Camps learn to tone down the competition." *New York Times*, August 14.

14. *New York Times*, December 28, 1997.

15. Sue Shellenbarger recently documented a trend in this direction. She observed a "growing number of teenagers are getting a big dose of training in balancing work and family as early as high school." Shellenbarger (1999). Students get lessons in how to manage a well-balanced life." *Wall Street Journal*, February 24.

16. Nippert-Eng (1996).

17. For a resource managers can use, see Friedman, DeGroot, & Christensen (1998). It has 35 learning activities with notes on how to use them. At the publisher's website, an excerpt from the book, "Clarifying Priorities and Building a Network of Support," is available as a sample learning activity. Through the use of self-assessment, peer coaching, intergroup discussion, and brief lectures on the actions required for effective work/life integration, participants can explore their own and others' life and career priorities, learn about the importance of work/life integration skills, and explore ways of strengthening their own support networks. The activity is available at www.jbp.com/wharton.html.

18. For details of this example, see Friedman, Christensen, & DeGroot (1998).

19. Johnson Foundation (1997). Quotes are from conference transcripts.

20. Cooper & Lewis (1994).

21. See Galinsky (1990). This early statement of this belief from one of the leaders in the work–life field still rings true. In the late 1990s there have been many echoes, elaborations, and extensions of this call to action. See, for example, Bankert & Lobel (1997).

22. See Rapoport & Bailyn (1996). This unique major study has gotten wide attention as the major work to date in the area of work redesign for improving both life quality and productivity, and is a good example of challenging assumptions about the nature of work and the "ideal worker."

The authors worked with three large companies, exploring work practices, work structure, and work culture over several years. Their goal was to demonstrate that the true focus of work–life initiatives should be to create a flexible and equitable workplace. They engaged workers in discussions about the specific aspects of work that make it difficult to integrate their work and personal lives. Having established the issues of concern in the workplace, the researchers next linked these issues to business challenges facing the work group. By linking individual work–family needs to business goals and challenging "unchangeable conditions" in the workplace, they were able to achieve solutions with benefits in both the work and family spheres. Focusing both on what workers needed to accomplish on the job and their needs for time and energy outside the workplace, they found win-win solutions that resulted in worker collaboration, more efficient use of time, and legitimization of work–family issues.

23. See, for example, Rodgers & Rodgers (1989). In this seminal article, the authors point to four things a company must do to create an environment where people with dependents can do their best work without sacrificing their families' welfare: develop a corporate policy that is communicated to all employees; train and encourage supervisors to be adaptable and responsible; give supervisors tools and programs with which to work; and hold all managers accountable for the flexibility and supportiveness of their departments. This still holds true a decade later. See also Minnesota Center for Corporate Responsibility (1997). The authors suggest that each company must tailor family-responsiveness to the real demands of its business, and that there is no single model; implementation does not require a massive change process; strategies can be developed and then initiatives introduced one by one; the key is ensuring that those initiatives are connected to the business strategy; and initiatives must be communicated and positive steps rewarded.

24. Some of these suggestions come from the following sources: Barnett & Rivers

(1996); Friedman & Johnson (1997); Cooper & Lewis (1994).

25. Kraut (1992).

26. Kraut (1992).

27. Both Eastman Kodak and Quaker Oats also offer a menu of benefits and give employees credits to buy the benefits in which they're most interested.

28. Googins (1997) persuasively argues that the work and family issues transcend the work and family domains and should, instead, be seen in light of the larger community environment.

29. The *Work and Family Newsbrief* is published by Work & Family Connection, Inc., Minnetonka, Minn. More information is available on the web at http://www.workfamily.com.

30. See, for example, the *Business Week* cover story for September 16, 1996, titled "Balancing work and family." This article, which was the inaugural for *Business Week*'s now-annual survey of family-friendliness, identified important gains for firms. About one of the top ten, First Tennessee National Corp., it said, "Supervisors rated by their subordinates as supportive of work–family balance retained employees twice as long as the bank average and kept 7% more retail customers. Higher retention rates, First Tennessee says, contributed a 55% profit gain over two years, to $106 million." Also, Friedman, Christensen, & DeGroot (1998) identify qualitative evidence from their field research. One of the new important research initiatives investigating the impact of family friendliness, currently under way at the time of this writing, is the National Work/Life Measurement Project, directed by Mindy Fried, at the Center for Work & Family at Boston College.

31. Quoted in Scharlach (1995).

32. Congressional Commission on Family and Medical Leave (1996). In the report's introduction, Commission Chairman Sen. Christopher Dodd noted: "This report is good news for America's families and businesses. The Family and Medical Leave Act is working for millions of workers and their families. The research shows it has clearly become an important tool in the effort to balance the demands of family and work. Fully two-thirds of covered employers have expanded their policies to come into compli-ance with the FMLA. And workers have not been the only ones to benefit. The great majority of companies reported no or only minor new costs, and this in the period in which they had to implement the FMLA. Beyond reporting few problems, some businesses also indicated they have seen a positive benefit from these policies in increased productivity and lower worker turnover."

Then U.S. Secretary of Labor Robert Reich also contributed to the report's introduction: "Fewer workers will have to choose between their jobs and their loved ones if a child or parent should need care. For their part, most businesses find that the new law is easy to administer and costs are small. The majority of leaves are short in duration and most workers return to their jobs. In fact, some businesses have reported reduced employee turnover, enhanced employee productivity and improved morale which they attribute to the FMLA. The Family and Medical Leave Act is good for families and good for business."

33. Scharlach (1995).

34. See Hewlett & West (1998). The authors used both surveys and focus groups to find out what parents need, and observe that "mothers and fathers are desperately worried about the parental time famine. This is the number-one problem in their lives." To remedy this critical problem, they suggest paid parenting leave because low-income parents aren't able to take time off otherwise. They "recommend government-mandated, paid, job-protected parenting leave for twenty-four weeks—thought by many experts to be the minimally adequate period of time for a parent to bond with a new child. This would significantly expand the scope of the Family and Medical Leave Act of 1993."

The authors add that this leave ought to be available for moms and dads, used by one parent or shared between them. Further, it should be allowable for the 120 days to stretch out beyond the twenty-four weeks, if they're staggered. And they suggest—and we would concur—that if "government creates a parenting entitlement that is both generous and available to both sexes, sexual stereo-types may well break down. The Swedish experience is relevant here. In 1974, when parenting leave was first introduced in Swe-den, only 3 percent of fathers took advantage of it. But by 1990, 26 percent of those drawing this benefit were fathers." This, then, is yet another means by which national policy can change social norms about expectations for men and women.

35. Scharlach (1995). The author notes that comparisons between the United States and other nations reveal that "most other countries mandate paid maternity leave, the amount of leave time is much longer than the 12 weeks accorded U.S. mothers, and the leave policies cover all workers rather than just those employed by firms with 50 or more employees. The EEC Social Charter, for example, recently set a minimum standard for parental leave of 14 weeks at a pay rate equivalent to sick time pay."

36. In Sweden, fathers are granted ten days of paid leave on the birth of a child. Designed primarily to allow the father to care for older siblings while the mother recuperates, the policy also permits both parents to be present in the new child's early days. See Cooper & Lewis (1994). These "New Daddy Days" are a good idea for employers in the United States. Lewis (1997) also offers an excellent review of the European Union's perspective on work and family issues. Her thorough and thoughtful summary points to a number of important observations that put the American experience in a new light.

37. In his report on FMLA, Scharlach (1995) makes several public policy recommendations with which we agree: preserve federal mandates for family leave, particularly because voluntary programs result in an inequitable distribution of this resource; promote full implementation of the existing law, since many have failed to comply; reduce resistance by disseminating information about the real costs (which don't appear to be much); eliminate regulatory barriers, such as conflicts with provisions of the Fair Labor Standards Act and the Employee Retirement Income Security Act (ERISA) of 1974, and remove disincentives for employers who offer more generous provisions than those mandated by FMLA; reduce unnecessary administrative burdens, such as tracking eligibility for and utilization of family leave; expand coverage under the FMLA, since the vast majority of American workers are not currently covered; reduce the minimum number of employees to ten;

add tax incentives to reduce undue impacts on small employers; expand FMLA to include employees who work less than full-time; expand the definition of family; and facilitate employee utilization of family leave through public education about its availability and reassurance about fears of job loss.

38. See Williams & Alliger (1994).

39. Galinsky (1999).

40. Quoted in Kelley, T. (1998). "Only disconnect (for a while, anyway)." *New York Times*, June 25.

41. Hochschild (1997).

42. See Perlow (1999). This important article provides a useful review of the time use research and offers a compelling argument for why we need to view work time in systems terms. It is collective time management, Perlow asserts, that ought to be the focus of our analyses and interventions, and not individual time management.

43. Policies and practices for supporting flexible work arrangements are one important means of giving employees greater authority and discretion in how they get their work done. Kossek, Barber, & Winters (1999) show how to remove the barriers to the utilization of flexible work arrangements. Catalyst (1996) is a very useful guide. Early reports from a major research project on the impact of alternative work arrangements, led by Mary Dean Lee and Shelley MacDermid, are very promising. See Lee, MacDermid et al. (1998).

44. Friedman, Christensen, & DeGroot (1998). The authors offer several such examples.

45. Hammonds, K. H. (1997). "Work and family: Business Week's second survey of family-friendly corporate policies." *Business Week*, Sept. 15, 96-104.

46. Not surprisingly, the issue of culture change comes up when flexibility is really on the table. See Perlow (1998). Too often, as Perlow notes, "flexible work options are offered without altering underlying assumptions about how work should be done or what it takes to succeed at work. If one chooses to take advantage of these policies, one risks being seen as 'different,' 'less committed,' and 'less able to perform.' Without deeper cultural change to redefine these actions as acceptable, individuals who pursue

a different path risk negative consequences for not conforming."

47. The accounting and consulting firm Ernst & Young, in a structural innovation, has gone so far as to create an "Office for Retention," which reports directly to the chief executive officer. The firm's goal is "to be the employer of choice among professional services firms for all people, including women." This initiative has gotten deservedly wide attention and is described in *Weaving a Richer Culture: 1998. Office for Retention Annual Report.* New York: Ernst & Young, LLP.

48. McGuire, E. (1998). "Seeking a perfect balance" [Letter to the editor]. *New York Times*, August.

49. Leach (1994).

50. Hewlett & West (1998).

51. In making this last recommendation, Hewlett & West (1998) are following the lead of Ed Zigler, whose model includes all-day care based in the schools for 3- to 5-year-olds, support via home visits for new parents, and training to daycare providers in the school's neighborhood. See Zigler & Frank (1988).

52. U.S. Department of the Treasury (1998).

53. National and local childcare legislation has become a big, important political issue–one influenced, of course, to a great extent by partisan politics. There are many legislative initiatives intended to improve the quality of care. WFD, a leading firm in the provision of services and consulting designed to enhance commitment in organizations, has compiled a very useful summary of the more than fifty pieces of child care legislation currently being developed. The summary is available on the web at http://www.wfd.com/fedcare.htm.

54. Quoted in Seitel (1997).

55. For a comprehensive review of the state of childcare in the United States, see Scarr (1998). The author provides a history of childcare, a labor force perspective, a summary of key research findings, and a policy analysis. She concludes with words we would echo: "I hope the United States will decide that child care is both an essential service for working families and an important service to America's children, especially the poorest among them. Governments have the respon-

sibility to make child care affordable for all working parents and to regulate child care to assure that children are afforded opportunities to develop emotionally, socially, and intellectually. Regardless of who their parents are, children are the next generation for all of us."

56. Hewlett & West (1998) suggest that it is necessary to provide government incentives for employers to become more family-supportive because of the "potential divergence of interest between what is good for the employer and what is good for children." Their recommendations include "carefully tailored tax incentives for companies that offer flexible hours, compressed work weeks, part-time work with benefits, job sharing, career sequencing, extended parenting leave, and home based employment opportunities." While we believe positive market forces will ultimately be shown to result from family-friendly employment policies (through competitive advantages in the labor market and enhanced commitment and productivity), for the time being this set of government-sponsored incentives makes sense. For an informative report on how businesses must collaborate with schools and families in order to support parents' involvement in their children's education, see Casey & Burch (1997).

57. For another example of partnerships, see Kim (1995).

58. Hochschild (1997).

59. Rosemary Jordano and Marie Oates argue forcefully on this point in "Invest in workers for the best child care," *New York Times* (June 21, 1996). Joan Goodman, a professor in the Graduate School of Education at the University of Pennsylvania, created a program intended to change this by training future leaders of the childcare field. She created a joint program with the Wharton School, the University's business school, which offers graduate education in both early childhood *and* business administration.

60. See, for example, Simons, M. (1997). "Child care sacred as France cuts back the welfare state." *New York Times*, December 31.

61. Levine & Pittinsky (1997).

62. Galinsky (1990).

63. Picard (1997).

64. Universum Institutet (1998).

65. *Wall Street Journal*, May 27, 1998.

66. A recent study of high school students' attitudes about career and family issues echoes this theme. The researchers found that students' preferences are for integration of career and family rather than for tradeoffs between them. See Sanders, Lengnick-Hall, Lengnick-Hall, & Steele-Clapp (1998).

Notes to Appendix One

1. There were some significant differences in work and family experiences between the alumni from the two universities, although the pattern of relationships among the variables seemed similar for the two groups. Therefore, the alumni were combined to form one overall sample, and university affiliation was statistically controlled in virtually all analyses through analyses of covariance, partial correlations, or multiple regression analyses.

2. Although entering classes of business students are more sexually and racially diverse than the current sample, our procedure sampled graduating classes that went back as far as 1964. Since we observed that recent graduating classes had higher percentages of women than early classes, all analyses that examined sex statistically controlled for the individual's age.

3. The one exception is the 1984 bachelor's degree class of Drexel University, where 50 percent of the women were surveyed.

4. This response rate is, most likely, an underestimate because we have no assurance that the 4,068 surveys not returned as undelivered actually reached the targeted alumnus or alumna. It is reasonable to assume that some unknown portion of the surveys were lost or discarded by parents or spouses of the potential members of the sample.

5. The survey also included other variables not relevant to the present research which are not described in this appendix.

6. Five other categories were included in this item: volunteer work, full-time homemaker, not currently employed, retired, and full-time student. Respondents who checked any of these categories were not included in our study sample.

7. This scale, adapted from Lodahl and Kejner's measure of job involvement, has been used frequently in the literature. For the most recent use, see Greenhaus, Collins, Singh, & Parasuraman (1997).

8. Nixon (1985).

9. Nixon (1985).

10. This item was used previously by Greenhaus et al. (1989).

11. Hackman & Oldham (1975).

12. Mowday, Porter, & Steers (1982).

13. There was an insufficient number of single-earner women in the sample to form a separate category.

14. Although this variable was calculated for each child, the measure used in this study was only for the first child. We did this because a number of respondents had only one child and we wanted to maximize the number of cases available for analysis. The same holds true for the six variables that immediately follow in this section.

15. These items were identical to the items assessing psychological involvement in career (see earlier note), with "family of origin" substituted for "career."

16. Adapted from Kopelman, Greenhaus, & Connolly (1983).

17. Adapted from Kopelman, Greenhaus, & Connolly (1983).

18. A specific child (closest to eight years of age) was chosen for observation to assure there is no bias by the parent in reporting on their child's problems in terms of the child's birth order or sex. This scale was adapted from National Center for Health Statistics. National health interview survey [Report Series 10, number 173]. The same is true for the two variables that follow in this section. See endnote 4 in Chapter 6 for further information.

19. Although this variable was calculated for each child, the measure used in this study was only for the first child.

20. All the variables in this section were taken or adapted from a variety of studies, including Kopelman, Greenhaus, & Connolly (1983) and Parasuraman, Greenhaus, & Granrose (1992).

21. This definition is consistent with Greenhaus & Beutell (1985).

22. We adopted a two-tail probability level of .10 to determine whether a relationship achieved statistical significance. We selected the .10 level (rather than .05 or .01) to minimize the occurrence of Type II errors,

in which a relationship that exists in a population goes undetected in a particular sample.

Note to Appendix Two

1. Behavioral support in the form of assistance with household and children, however, has minimal effects on satisfaction with personal life.

References

Achenbach, T. S., and C. Edelbrock. 1981. *Behavioral Problems and Competencies Reported by Parents of Normal and Disturbed Children Aged Four Through Sixteen.* Monographs of the Society for Research in Child Development, serial no. 188. Chicago: University of Chicago Press.

Adams, G. A., L. A. King, and D. W. King. 1996. "Relationships of Jobs and Family Involvement, Family Social Support, and Work-Family Conflict with Job and Life Satisfaction." *Journal of Applied Psychology* 91 (4): 411–20.

Allred, B. B., C. C. Snow, and R. E. Miles. 1996. "Characteristics of Managerial Careers in the Twenty-first Century." *Academy of Management Executive* 10 (4): 17–27.

Almeida, D. M., and R. C. Kessler. 1998. "Everyday Stressors and Gender Differences in Daily Distress." *Journal of Personality and Social Psychology* 75 (3): 670–80.

Arthur, M. B., and D. M. Rousseau. 1996. "A Career Lexicon for the 21st Century." *Academy of Management Executive* 10 (4): 28–39.

Bailyn, L. 1978. "Accommodation of Work to Family." In *Working Couples*, ed. R. Rapoport and R. N. Rapoport. New York: Harper & Row.

———. 1980. "The 'Slow Burn' Way to the Top: Some Thoughts on the Early Years in Organizational Careers." In *Work, Family and the Career: New Frontiers in Theory and Research*, ed. C. B. Derr. New York: Praeger.

———. 1993. *Breaking the Mold: Women, Men, and Time in the New Corporate World.* New York: The Free Press.

Bandura, A. 1997. *Self-efficacy: The Exercise of Control.* New York: W. H. Freeman and Company.

Bankert, E. E., and S. A. Lobel. 1997. "Visioning the Future." In *Integrating Work and Family: Challenges and Choices for a Changing World*, ed. S. Parasuraman and J. H. Greenhaus. Westport, Conn.: Quorum Books.

Barling, J. 1986. "Fathers' Work Experiences, the Father-Child Relationship and Children's Behaviour." *Journal of Occupational Behaviour* 7: 61–66.

Barling, J., C. Fullagar, and J. Marchl-Dingle. 1988. "Employment Commitment as a Moderator of the Maternal Employment Status/Child Behavior Relationship." *Journal of Organizational Behavior* 9: 119.

Barling, J., and D. Van Bart. 1984. "Mothers' Subjective Work Experiences and the Behavior of their Preschool Children." *Journal of Occupational Psychology* 54: 49–56.

Barnett, R. C., and G. K. Baruch. 1985. "Women's Involvement in Multiple Roles and Psychological Distress." *Journal of Personality and Social Psychology* 49:135–45.

Barnett, R. C., N. L. Marshall, and J. H. Pleck. 1992. "Men's Multiple Roles and Their Relationship to Men's Psychological Distress." *Journal of Marriage and the Family* 54: 358–67.

Barnett, R. C., N. L. Marshall, S. W. Raudenbush, and R. T. Brennan. 1993. "Gender and the Relationship Between Job Experiences and Psychological Distress: A Study of Dual-Earner Couples." *Journal of Personality and Social Psychology* 64 (5): 794–806.

Barnett, R. C., and C. Rivers. 1996. *She Works/He Works*. San Francisco: HarperSan-Francisco.

Bartolome, F. 1983. "The Work Alibi: When It's Harder to Go Home." *Harvard Business Review* 61 (2): 67–74.

Bartolome, F., and P. Evans. 1979. "Professional Lives Versus Private Lives: Shifting Patterns of Managerial Commitment." *Organizational Dynamics* 7: 3–29.

Baruch, G. K., and R. C. Barnett. 1986. "Role Quality, Multiple Role Involvement, and Psychological Well-Being in Midlife Women." *Journal of Personality and Social Psychology* 51: 578–85.

Belsky, J., and D. Eggebeen. 1991. "Scientific Criticism and the Study of Early and Extensive Maternal Employment." *Journal of Marriage and the Family* 53: 1107–10.

Bernard, J. 1983. "The Good Provider Role: Its Rise and Fall." In *Family in Transition* (third ed.), ed. A. Skolnick and J. Skolnick. Boston: Little, Brown.

Bielby, W. T., and D. D. Bielby, 1989. "Family Ties: Balancing Commitments to Work and Family in Dual Earner Households." *American Sociological Review* 54: 776–89.

Bond, J. T., E. Galinsky, and J. E. Swanberg. 1998. *The 1997 National Study of the Changing Workforce*. New York: Families and Work Institute.

Bowlby, J. 1982. *Attachment and Loss, Volume I: Attachment*. New York: Basic Books.

Brass, D. 1985. "Men's and Women's Networks." *Academy of Management Journal* 28: 327–43.

Brazelton, T. B. 1983. *Infants and Mothers: Differences in Development*. New York: Dell.

Brenner, O. C., and J. Tomkiewicz. 1979. "Job Orientation of Males and Females: Are Sex Differences Declining?" *Personnel Psychology* 32: 741–50.

Brett, J. M. 1997. "Family, Sex, and Career Advancement." In *Integrating Work and Family*, ed. S. Parasuraman and J. H. Greenhaus. Westport, Conn.: Quorum.

Brett, J. M., L. K. Stroh, and A. H. Reilly. 1992. "What Is It Like Being a Dual Career Manager in the 1990s?" In *Work, Families, and Organizations*, ed. S. Zedeck. San Francisco: Jossey-Bass.

Bridges, W. 1994a. "The End of the Job." *Fortune* 19: 62–74.

———. 1994b. *Job Shift: How to Prosper in a Workplace Without Jobs*. Reading, Mass.: Addison-Wesley.

Campbell, B. M. 1986. *Successful Women, Angry Men*. New York: Random House.

Casey, J. C., and P. E. Burch. 1997. *A Catalyst for Educational Change: Promoting the Involvement of Working Parents in Their Children's Education*. Chestnut Hill, Mass.: Boston College Center for Work and Family, Work–Family Policy Paper Series.

Catalyst. 1996. *Making Work Flexible: From Policy to Practice*. New York: Catalyst.

Chira, S. 1998. *A Mother's Place: Taking the Debate About Working Mothers Beyond Guilt and Blame*. New York: HarperCollins.

Chusmir, L. H., and B. Parker. 1991. "Gender and Situational Differences in Managers' Values: A Look at Work and Home Lives." *Journal of Business Research* 23: 325–35.

Clinton, H. R. 1996. *It Takes a Village*. New York: Simon & Schuster.

Cohen, S., and T. A. Wills. 1985. "Stress, Social Support, and the Buffering Hypothesis." *Psychological Bulletin* 98: 310–57.

Cohen, T. F. 1987. "Gender, Work and Family: The Impact and Meaning of Work in Men's Family Roles." *Family Perspective* 22: 292–308.

Congressional Commission on Family and Medical Leave. 1996. *A Workable Balance: Report to Congress on Family and Medical Leave Policies.* Washington, D.C.: United States Senate.

Cooper, C. L., and S. Lewis. 1994. *Managing the New Work Force: The Challenge of Dual-Income Families.* San Diego: Pfeiffer & Company.

Covin, T. J., and C. C. Brush. 1991. "An Examination of Male and Female Attitudes Toward Career and Family Issues." *Sex Roles* 25: 393–415.

Crouter, A. C. 1984. "Spillover from Family to Work: The Neglected Side of the Work–Family Interface." *Human Relations* 37: 425–42.

DeMeis, D. K., D. E. Hock, and S. McBride. 1986. "The Balance of Employment and Motherhood: Longitudinal Study of Mothers' Feelings about Separation from Their First-Born Infants." *Development Psychology* 22 (5): 627–32.

Deutsch, F. M. 1999. *Halving It All.* Cambridge, Mass.: Harvard University Press.

Devanna, M. A. 1987. "Women in Management: Progress and Promise." *Human Resource Management* 26: 469–81.

Dix, T. 1991. "The Affective Organization of Parenting: Adaptive and Maladaptive Processes." *Psychological Bulletin* 110 (1): 3–25.

Erikson, E. 1980. *Identity and the Life Cycle.* New York: W. W. Norton & Company.

Evans, P., and F. Bartolome. 1980. *Must Success Cost So Much?* New York: Basic Books.

Friedman, D. E., and A. A. Johnson. 1997. "Moving from Programs to Culture Change: The Next Stage for the Corporate Work-Family Agenda." In *Integrating Work and Family*, ed. S. Parasuraman and J. H. Greenhaus. Westport, Conn.: Quorum.

Friedman, S. D., P. Christensen, and J. DeGroot. 1998. "Work and Life: The End of the Zero-Sum Game." *Harvard Business Review*, November–December 1998, 119–29.

Friedman, S. D., J. DeGroot, and P. Christensen. 1998. *Integrating Work and Life: The Wharton Resource Guide.* San Francisco: Jossey Bass/Pfeiffer.

Fuligni, A. S., E. Galinsky, and M. Poris. 1995. *The Impact of Parental Employment on Children.* New York: Families and Work Institute.

Galinsky, E. 1990. *Work and Family Policies: The New Strategic Plan.* Washington, D.C.: Conference Board.

———. 1999. *Ask the Children: What America's Children Really Think about Working Parents.* New York: William Morrow and Company.

Galinsky, E., J. T. Bond, and D. E. Friedman. 1993. *The Changing Workforce.* New York: Families and Work Institute.

Galinsky, E., D. E. Friedman, and C. A. Hernandez. 1991. *The Corporate Reference Guide to Work-Family Programs.* New York: Families and Work Institute.

Gallos, J. V. 1989. "Exploring Women's Development: Implications for Career Theory, Practice and Research." In *Handbook of Career Theory*, ed. M. B. Arthur, D. T. Hall, and B. S. Lawrence. Cambridge, England: Cambridge University Press.

Gaylin, W. 1992. *The Male Ego.* New York: Viking Press.

Gerson, K. 1993. *No Man's Land: Men's Changing Commitments to Family and Work.* New York: Basic Books.

Gilbert, L. A. 1985. *Men in Dual-Career Families: Current Realities and Future Prospects.* Hillsdale, N.J.: Lawrence Erlbaum.

Googins, B. K. 1997. "Shared Responsibility for Managing Work and Family Relationships: A Community Perspective." In *Integrating Work and Family: Challenges and Choices for a Changing World*, ed. S. Parasuraman, and J. H. Greenhaus. Westport, Conn.: Quorum Books.

Granrose, C. S., S. Parasuraman, and J. H. Greenhaus. 1992. "A Proposed Model of Support Provided by Two-Earner Couples." *Human Relations* 45: 1367–93.

Greenberger, E., and R. O'Neil. 1990. "Parents' Concerns about Their Child's Development: Implications for Fathers' and Mothers' Well-Being and Attitudes Toward Work." *Journal of Marriage and the Family* 52: 621–35.

Greenhaus, J. H., and N. B. Beutell. 1985. "Sources of Conflict Between Work and Family Roles." *Academy of Management Review* 10: 76–88.

Greenhaus, J. H., and G. A. Callanan. 1994. *Career Management* (second ed.). Fort Worth, Tex.: Dryden.

Greenhaus, J. H., K. M. Collins, R. Singh, and S. Parasuraman. 1997. "Work and Family Influences on Departure from Public Accounting." *Journal of Vocational Behavior* 50: 249–70.

Greenhaus, J. H., and S. Parasuraman. 1994. "Work–Family Conflict, Social Support, and Well-Being." In *Women in Management: Current Research Issues*, ed. M. J. Davidson and R. J. Burke. London: Paul Chapman.

———. 1997. "The Integration of Work and Family Life: Barriers and Solutions." In *Integrating Work and Family: Challenges and Choices for a Changing World*, ed. S. Parasuraman and J. H. Greenhaus. Westport, Conn.: Quorum Books.

Greenhaus, J. H., S. Parasuraman, C. S. Granrose, S. Rabinowitz, and N. J. Beutell. 1989. "Sources of Work–Family Conflict among Two-Career Couples." *Journal of Vocational Behavior* 34: 133–53.

Greenhaus, J. H., S. Parasuraman, and W. M. Wormley. 1990. "Effects of Race on Organizational Experiences, Job Performance Evaluations, and Career Outcomes." *Academy of Management Journal* 33: 64–86.

Grimm-Thomas, K., and M. Perry-Jenkins. 1994. "All in a Day's Work: Job Experiences, Self-Esteem, and Fathering in Working-class Families." *Family Relations* 43 (2): 174–81.

Grossman, F. K., W. S. Pollack, and E. Golding. 1988. "Fathers and Children: Predicting the Quality and Quantity of Fathering." *Developmental Psychology* 24 (1): 82–92.

Hackman, J. R., and G. R. Oldham. 1975. "Development of the Job Diagnostic Survey." *Journal of Applied Psychology* 60: 159–70.

Hall, D. T. 1975. "Pressures from Work, Self, and Home in the Life Stages of Married Women." *Journal of Vocational Behavior* 6: 121–32.

———. 1976. *Careers in Organizations*. Pacific Palisades, Calif.: Goodyear.

———. 1996. "Protean Careers of the Twenty-first Century." *Academy of Management Executive* 10 (4): 8–16.

Hall, D. T., and J. Richter. 1988. "Balancing Work Life and Home Life: What Can Organizations Do to Help?" *Academy of Management Executive* 2: 213–23.

Hall, W. 1991. "The Experience of Fathers in Dual-Earner Families Following the Births of Their First Infants. *Journal of Advanced Nursing* 16: 423–30.

Hammonds, K. H. 1997. "Work and Family: Business Week's Second Survey of Family-Friendly Corporate Policies." *Business Week*, Sept. 15, 96–104.

Hewlett, S. A., and C. West. 1998. *The War Against Parents: What We Can Do for America's Beleaguered Moms and Dads*. Boston: Houghton Mifflin.

Higgins, C., L. Duxbury, and C. Lee. 1994. "Impact of Life-Cycle Stage and Gender on the Ability to Balance Work and Family Responsibilities." *Family Relations* 43: 144–50.

Hiller, D. V., and W. W. Philliber. 1982. "Predicting Marital and Career Success among Dual Worker Couples." *Journal of Marriage and the Family* 44: 53–62.

Hochschild, A. 1989. *The Second Shift*. New York: Viking.

———. 1997. *The Time Bind*. New York: Henry Holt and Company.

Hoffman, L. W. 1989. "Effects of Maternal Employment in the Two-Parent Family." *American Psychologist* 44: 283–92.

House, J. S. 1981. *Work, Stress, and Social Support*. Reading, Mass.: Addison-Wesley.

Howard, A. 1992. "Work and Family Crossroads Spanning the Career." In *Work, Families, and Organizations*, ed. S. Zedeck. San Francisco: Jossey-Bass.

Howard, A., and D. W. Bray. 1988. *Managerial Lives in Transition*. New York: Guilford.

Ibarra, H. 1992. "Homophily and Differential Returns: Sex Differences in Network Structure and Access." *Administrative Science Quarterly* 37: 422–47.

Johnson Foundation, The. 1997. *Families and Work: Developing a Research-Policy Agenda for the Next Decade*. National Research Council/Institute of Medicine. Board on Children, Youth, and Families. Conference held at Wingspread, Racine, Wisconsin, November 3.

Kanter, R. M. 1977. *Men and Women of the Corporation*. New York: Basic Books.

Kaplan, R. 1991. *Beyond Ambition: How Driven Managers Can Lead Better and Live Better*. San Francisco: Jossey-Bass.

Karambayya, R., and A. H. Reilly. 1992. "Dual Earner Couples: Attitudes and Actions in Restructuring Work for Family." *Journal of Organizational Behavior* 13: 585–601.

Katz, D., and R. L. Kahn. 1976. *The Social Psychology of Organizations* (second ed.). New York: Wiley.

Kim, S. C. 1995. "Involving Business in Community Planning Initiatives to Improve Systems of Early Childhood Education and Care." Master's thesis, Graduate School of Education, University of Pennsylvania.

Kimmel, M. S. 1993. "What Do Men Want?" *Harvard Business Review* 71 (6): 50–63.

Kofodimos, J. R. 1990. "Why Executives Lose Their Balance." *Organizational Dynamics* 19 (1): 58–73.

———. 1993. *Balancing Act*. San Francisco: Jossey-Bass.

———. 1995. *Beyond Work–Family Programs: Confronting and Resolving the Underlying Causes of Work-Personal Life Conflict*. Greensboro, N.C.: Center for Creative Leadership.

Kohn, M. L., and C. Schooler. 1982. "Job Conditions and Personality: A Longitudinal Assessment of Their Reciprocal Effects." *American Journal of Sociology* 87: 1257–86.

Kopelman, R. E., J. H. Greenhaus, and T. F. Connolly. 1983. "A Model of Work, Family, and Interrole Conflicts: A Construct Validation Study." *Organizational Behavior and Performance* 32: 198–215.

Korman, A. K. 1976. "A Hypothesis of Work Behavior Revisited and an Extension." *Academy of Management Review* 1: 50–63.

Kossek, E. E., A. E. Barber, and D. Winters. 1999. "Using Flexible Schedules in the Managerial World: The Power of Peers." *Human Resource Management* 38: 33–46.

Kraut. A. 1992. "Organizational Research on Work and Family Issues." In *Work, Families and Organizations*, ed. S. Zedeck. San Francisco: Jossey-Bass.

Lambert, S. J. 1990. "Processes Linking Work and Family: A Critical Review and Research Agenda." *Human Relations* 43: 239–57.

Leach, P. 1989. *Your Baby and Child: From Birth to Age Five*. New York: Knopf.
————. 1994. *Children First: What Our Society Must Do—and Is Not Doing—for Our Children Today*. New York: Knopf.
Lee, M. D., S. M. MacDermid, et al. 1998. *Improvising Careers: Accommodation, Elaboration, Transformation*. West Lafayette, Ind.: The Center for Families at Purdue University.
Levine, J. A., and T. L. Pittinsky. 1997. *Working Fathers: New Strategies for Balancing Work and Family*. Reading, Mass.: Addison-Wesley.
Levinson, D. J., C. N. Darrow, E. B. Klein, M. H. Levinson, and B. McKee. 1978. *Seasons of a Man's Life*. New York: Knopf.
Lewis, S. 1997. *European Perspectives of Work and Family Issues*. Chestnut Hill, Mass.: The Center for Work and Family's Work–Family Policy Paper Series, Boston College.
Lewis, S. N. C., and C. L. Cooper. 1988. "Stress in Dual-Career Families." In *Women and Work: An Annual Review*, ed. B. A. Gutek, A. H. Stromberg, and L. Larwood. Newbury Park, Calif.: Sage.
Lobel, 1991. "Allocation of Investment in Work and Family Roles: Alternative Theories and Implications for Research." *Academy of Management Review* 16: 507–21.
Locke, E. A. 1976. "The Nature and Causes of Job Satisfaction." In *Handbook of Industrial and Organizational Psychology*, ed. M. D. Dunnette. Chicago: Rand-McNally.
MacEwen, K. E., and J. Barling. 1988. "Interrole Conflict, Family Support and Marital Adjustment of Employed Mothers: A Short Term, Longitudinal Study." *Journal of Organizational Behavior* 9: 241–50.
Manhardt, P. J. 1972. "Job Orientation of Male and Female College Graduates in Business." *Personnel Psychology* 25: 361–68.
Marks, S. R. 1977. "Multiple Roles and Role Strains: Some Notes on Human Energy, Time and Commitment." *American Sociological Review* 42: 921–36.
Martinez, M. N. 1997. "The Proof Is in the Profits." *Working Mother*, May, 27–30.
McCall, M. W. 1988. "Developing Executives Through Work Experiences." *Human Resource Planning* 11: 1–11.
Menaghan, E. G., and T. L. Parcel. 1990. "Parental Employment and Family Life: Research in the 1980s." *Journal of Marriage and the Family* 52: 1079–98.
Minnesota Center for Corporate Responsibility. 1997. *Creating High Performance Organizations: The Bottom Line Value of Work/Life Strategies*. Minneapolis: Minnesota Center for Corporate Responsibility.
Morgan, H., and K. Tucker. 1991. *Companies That Care*. New York: Simon & Schuster.
Morrison, A. M., R. P. White, and E. Van Velsor. 1987. *Breaking the Glass Ceiling: Can Women Reach the Top of America's Largest Corporations?* Reading, Mass.: Addison-Wesley.
Mowday, R., L. Porter, and R. Steers. 1982. *Employee-Organization Linkages: Psychology of Commitment, Absenteeism and Turnover*. San Diego, Calif.: Academic Press.
Nippert-Eng, C. E. 1996. *Home and Work*. Chicago: University of Chicago Press.
Nixon, R. 1985. *Perceptions of Job Power Among Black Managers in Corporate America*. Washington, D.C.: National Urban League.
Osterman, P. 1995. "Work/family Programs and the Employment Relationship." *Administrative Science Quarterly* 40: 681–700.
Papanek, H. 1973. "Men, Women and Work: Reflections on the Two-person Career." *American Journal of Sociology* 78: 852–72.
Parasuraman, S., and J. H. Greenhaus. 1992. "Determinants of Support Provided and

Received by Partners in Two-career Relationships." In *The Ties That Bind*, ed. L. A. Heslop. Calgary, Alberta, Canada: Canadian Consortium of Management Schools.

———. 1993. "Personal Portrait: The Life-style of the Woman Manager." In *Women in Management*, Vol. 4, ed. E. A. Fagenson. Newbury Park, Calif.: Sage.

———, eds. 1997. *Integrating Work and Family*. Westport, Conn.: Quorum.

Parasuraman, S., J. H. Greenhaus, and C. S. Granrose. "Role Stressors, Social Support, and Well-being among Two-career Couples." *Journal of Organizational Behavior* 13. 339–56.

Parcel, T. L., and E. G. Menaghan. "Early Parental Work, Family Social Capital, and Early Childhood Outcomes." *American Journal of Sociology* 99: 972–1009.

Perlow, L. 1998. *Finding Time: How Corporations, Individuals, and Families Can Benefit from New Work Practices*. Ithaca, N.Y.: Cornell University Press.

———. 1999. "The Time Famine: Toward a Sociology of Work Time." *Administrative Science Quarterly* 44: 57–81.

Picard, M. 1997. "No Kids? Get Back to Work!" *Training*, September:33–40.

Piotrkowski, C. S., and M. H. Katz. 1983. "Work experience and Family Relations among Working Class and Lower Middle-class Families." In *Research in the Interweave of Social Roles*, Vol. 3: *Families and Jobs*, ed. H. Z. Lopata and J. H. Pleck. Greenwich, Conn.: JAI Press.

Piotrkowski, C. S., R. N. Rapoport, and R. Rapoport. 1987. "Families and Work." In *Handbook of Marriage and the Family*, ed. M. B. Sussman and S. K. Steinmetz. New York: Plenum Press.

Pleck, J. H. 1977. "The Work–Family Role System." *Social Problems* 24: 417–27.

———. 1985. *Working Wives/Working Husbands*. Newbury Park, Calif.: Sage.

———. 1987. "American Fathering in Historical Perspective." In *Changing Men: New Directions in Research on Men and Masculinity*, ed. M. Kimmel. Newbury Park, Calif.: Sage.

———. 1993. "Are 'Family-supportive' Employer Policies Relevant to Men?" In *Men, Work, and Family*, ed. J. C. Hood. Newbury Park, Calif.: Sage.

Powell, G. N. 1993. *Women and Men in Management* (second ed.). Newbury Park, Calif.: Sage.

Rabinowitz, S., and D. T. Hall. 1977. "Organizational Research on Job Involvement." *Psychological Bulletin* 84: 265–88.

Rapoport, R., and L. Bailyn. 1996. *Relinking Life and Work: Toward a Better Future. A Report to the Ford Foundation Based on a Research Project in Collaboration with Xerox, Tandem Computers, and Corning, Inc.* New York: Ford Foundation.

Reilly, B. O. 1990. "Why Grade 'A' Execs get an 'F' as Parents." *Fortune*, January 1.

Repetti, R. L. 1987. "Linkages Between Work and Family Roles." In *Family Processes and Problems: Social Psychological Aspects*, ed. S. Oskamp. Newbury Park, Calif.: Sage.

Rodgers, C. 1992. "The Flexible Workplace: What Have We Learned?" *Human Resource Management* 31 (3): 183–99.

Rodgers, F. S., and C. Rodgers. 1989. "Business and the Family Facts of Life." *Harvard Business Review*, Nov–Dec.: 121–29.

Rosin, H. M., and K. Korabik. 1990. "Marital and Family Correlates of Women Managers' Attrition from Organizations." *Journal of Vocational Behavior* 37: 104–20.

Ross, C. E., J. Morowsky, and J. Huber. 1983. "Dividing Work, Sharing Work, and In-between: Marriage Patterns and Depression." *American Sociological Review* 48: 809–23.

Sanders, M. M., M. L. Lengnick-Hall, C. A. Lengnick-Hall, and L. Steele-Clapp.

1998. "Love and Work: Career-Family Attitudes of New Entrants into the Labor Force." *Journal of Organizational Behavior* 19: 603–19.

Scarr, S. 1998. "American Child Care Today." *American Psychologist* 53 (2): 95–108.

Scharlach, A. E. 1995. *The Family and Medical Leave Act of 1993: Analysis and Appraisal.* Boston: Center on Work and Family, Boston University.

Schein, E. H. 1996. "Career Anchors Revisited: Implications for Career Development in the Twenty-first Century." *Academy of Management Executive* 10 (4): 80–88.

Schneer, J. A., and Reitman, F. 1993. "Effects of Alternate Family Structures on Managerial Career Paths." *Academy of Management Journal* 36: 830–43.

Schor, J. B. 1991. *The Overworked American.* New York: HarperCollins.

Schwartz, F. N. 1989. "Management Women and the Facts of Life." *Harvard Business Review* 67 (1): 65–76.

Schwartz, F. N., with J. Zimmerman. 1992. *Breaking with Tradition: Women and Work, the New Facts of Life.* New York: Time-Warner.

Seitel, S. 1997. *Work and Family Trend Report.* Minnetonka, Minn.: Work and Family Connection, Inc.

Shumaker, S. A., and A. Brownell. 1984. "Toward a Theory of Social Support: Closing Conceptual Gaps." *Journal of Social Issues* 40: 11–36.

Sieber, S. D. 1974. "Toward a Theory of Role Accumulation." *American Sociological Review* 39: 567–78.

Small, S. A., and D. Riley. 1990. "Toward a Multidimensional Assessment of Work Spillover into Family Life." *Journal of Marriage and the Family* 52: 51–61.

Solomon, C. M. 1996. "Flexibility Comes Out of Flux." *Personal Journal,* June: 34–43.

South, S. J., and G. Spitze. 1994. "Housework in Marital and Nonmarital Households." *American Sociological Review* 59: 327–47.

Spitze, G. 1988. "Women's Employment and Family Relations: A Review." *Journal of Marriage and the Family* 50: 595–618.

Staw, B. M., and J. Ross. 1987. "Knowing When to Pull the Plug." *Harvard Business Review* 65 (2): 68–74.

Stewart, W., and J. Barling. 1996. "Fathers' Work Experiences Affect Children's Behaviors via Job-related Effect and Parenting Behaviors." *Journal of Organizational Behavior* 17: 221–32.

Stroh, L. K., and J. M. Brett. 1996. "The Dual-Earner Dad Penalty in Salary Progression." *Human Resource Management Journal* 35: 181–201.

Tannen, D. 1991. *You Just Don't Understand: Women and Men in Conversation.* New York: Ballantine Books.

Tharenou, P., S. Latimer, and D. Conroy. 1994. "How Do You Make It to the Top? An Examination of Influences on Women's and Men's Managerial Advancement." *Academy of Management Journal* 37: 899–931.

Thoits, P. A. 1986. "Social Support as Coping Assistance." *Journal of Counseling and Clinical Psychology* 54: 416–23.

Thomas, D. A. 1999. *Breaking Through: The Making of Minority Executives in Corporate America.* Boston: Harvard Business School Press.

Thomas, L. T., and D. C. Ganster. 1995. "Impact of Family-supportive Work Variables on Work-Family Conflict and Strain: A Control Perspective." *Journal of Applied Psychology* 80 (1): 6–15.

Universum Institutet. 1998. *American Graduate Survey 1988.* Stockholm, Sweden: Universum Institutet for Undgomsinformation AB.

U.S. Department of the Treasury. 1998. *Investing in Child Care: Challenges Facing*

Working Parents and the Private Sector Response. Washington, D.C.: U.S. Department of the Treasury.

Valdez, R. L., and B. A. Gutek. 1986. "Family Roles: A Help or a Hindrance for Working Women?" In *Women's Career Development*, ed. B. A. Gutek and L. Larwood. Newbury Park, Calif.: Sage.

Waite, L. J., G. Haggstrom, and D. E. Kanouse. 1986. "The Effects of Parenthood on the Career Orientation and Job Characteristics of Young Adults." *Social Forces* 65 (1): 43–73.

Whyte, W. H., Jr. 1959. *The Organization Man*. New York: Simon & Schuster.

Williams, K. J., and G. M. Alliger. 1994. "Role Stressors, Mood Spillover, and Perceptions of Work-Family Conflict in Employed Parents." *Academy of Management Journal* 37: 837–68.

Wohl, F. 1997. "A Panoramic View of Work and Family." In *Integrating Work and Family: Challenges and Choices for a Changing World*, ed. S. Parasuraman and J. H. Greenhaus. Westport, Conn.: Quorum Books.

Zigler, E. F., and Frank, M. 1988. *The Parental Leave Crisis: Toward a National Policy*. New Haven, Conn.: Yale University Press.

Zill, N. 1990. *Behavior Problems Index Based on Parent Report*. Washington, D.C.: Child Trends.

Index

Partners/partner support (continued)
  timing of, 87, 99
  types of, 90
  as unbeneficial, 97–99
  ways of providing, 86
  and well-being, 87, 90, 91, 93–94, 95–98, 100, 115, 118– 19, 120
  and work–family conflict, 93, 94–95, 98, 99–100, 115–16, 117, 120, 138, 154
  and work–family integration, 86, 146
  See also specific topic, especially Support
Personal growth
  and action agenda, 155–56
  and allies–enemies issues, 121, 133, 140, 141, 154–55
  and authority, 61
  and choices, 40, 154–55
  and employers/employer support, 108, 113, 115, 118, 119, 120
  and future career prospects, 61, 62
  and gender, 62, 64–65, 66, 133
  and having a life, 56, 57, 58, 59–60, 61, 62, 64–65, 66
  and involvement, 40, 61
  and life role priorities, 27–28, 58
  and meaning of work, 62
  and partner support, 90, 95, 98, 99–100, 115, 118, 119
  and quality of life, 113
  and resources, 133
  and role conflicts, 64–65
  and satisfaction, 57, 61
  and well-being, 95
  and work–family integration, 144
Picard, Michele, 172
Pittinsky, Todd L., 10–11, 171
Power, 27–28, 31, 43, 96, 131, 133, 155
Priorities
  and action agenda, 149, 150, 151, 152, 166, 172
  and "bonus and penalty" hypothesis, 54
  and children as unseen stakeholders at work, 74–76
  and choices, 40, 150, 151, 152
  diversity in people's, 40
  and employers/employer support, 166
  and gender, 152
  and having a life, 59
  and involvement, 40
  and success, 54
  and work–family integration, 146, 149
  See also Life role priorities
Private sector, public sector partnership with, 169–70
Psychological availability. *See* Availability
Psychological involvement. *See* Involvement
Public sector, 153, 169–71

Quality of Employment Survey (U.S. Department of Labor), 151–52

Quality of life, 3, 20, 38, 67, 113, 119, 122, 131, 132, 134, 138
Quality of work, 69, 77, 139

Race, and career success, 44–45
Radcliffe College Public Policy Institute, 164, 170
Rayman, Paula, 170
Recommendations
  in action agenda, 149–72
  summing up, 172–74
  See also Action agenda; specific recommendation
Relationships
  and allies–enemies issues, 134, 135, 139
  and children as unseen stakeholders at work, 80
  and gender, 32, 63, 64, 65, 134
  and having a life, 63, 64, 65, 68
  and involvement, 135
  and partner support, 90, 91, 92, 94, 97
  and resources, 134
  and social world of work, 63, 64
  and success, 97
  and time, 80
  and time horizons, 65
  and well-being, 97
  and work–family integration, 144, 147
Relaxation time. *See* Leisure time
Relocation, 23, 24, 52, 74, 130, 135, 158
Research, future, 159–60
Resources
  and action agenda, 149, 160
  affects on family and work of, 131–34
  and allies–enemies issues, 5, 100, 124, 125, 126, 128, 130, 131–34, 136, 142, 146, 160
  availability of, 8, 125
  and boundaries between work and family, 67
  and changing dynamics between work and family, 5, 8
  and children, 70, 72–73, 74, 75, 76, 78, 79, 83, 128, 130, 131, 132, 133, 134
  and choices/tradeoffs, 38, 128, 131, 160
  definition of, 8, 124–25
  economic and social, 72–73
  and employers/employer support, 120, 125, 128, 131, 132
  examples of, 124–25
  and gender, 63, 64, 78, 79, 128, 130, 132, 133–34, 136
  and having a life, 63, 64, 67
  impact of, 131–34
  and involvement, 38, 126, 136
  and model of work–family relationship, 124–26, 128, 130
  and partner support, 85–86, 92–93, 100, 120, 125, 130, 132–33
  and quality of life, 131, 132
  social, 72–73
  and social world of work, 63, 64
  and support, 85–86, 128, 130, 132, 133, 134
  types of, 8